LED ZEPPELIN

THIS IS A CARLTON BOOK

Published by Carlton Books Ltd
20 Mortimer Street
London W1T 3JW

Text and design © 2017 Carlton Books Ltd

ISBN 978-1-78097-985-4

Project Editor: Matthew Lowing
Editorial: Malcolm Croft, Caroline Curtis and Chris Parker
Layout Design: James Pople and Gemma Wilson
Production: Emily Noto
Picture Research: Steve Behan

A CIP catalogue for this book is available from the British Library

Printed in Dubai

10 9 8 7 6 5 4 3 2 1

LED ZEPPELIN

THE BIGGEST BAND OF THE 1970s

CHRIS WELCH

CARLTON
BOOKS

CONTENTS

PROLOGUE

In 1968, four boys from England formed a group that would later become the greatest rock and roll band ever known. They had the songs. They had the star power. They had each other. They had the time of their lives.

When Led Zeppelin burst on the scene with their debut album in 1969, the reaction ranged from stunned disbelief to incomprehension. The electrifying excitement of 'Dazed and Confused', the menace of 'How Many More Times' and the frantic exuberance of 'Communication Breakdown' were just some of the performances that instantly set Led Zeppelin apart. Here was an album that would redefine rock music, shaping it for the next 25 years.

Few critics could immediately grasp the band's amazing potential, and this led to frustration within the tightly knit group. However, some quickly recognized the significance of the forces being unleashed by this dynamic new outfit. They realized too that Led Zeppelin were not, as the damning press reported, "the last word in savagery".

Even today, when every last iota of evidence about the Zeppelin years has been chronicled and mulled over, there are still those who wince at the mention of their name. All nonsense, of course. It's true there was a slight risk, during the band's more high-spirited moments, of the unwary being tied up with sticky tape and suspended from a fourth-floor office window. Even so, the creative spirits who comprised Led Zeppelin were never mere caricature monsters of rock.

When Jimmy Page first conceived the idea in 1968, his aim was simply to create the best rock group alive. It was always the music that was the *raison d'être* for Led Zeppelin. Nevertheless, the larger-than-life personalities behind the Zeppelin image were crucial, both to their success and appeal.

When the British group first appeared in America, on Boxing Day 1968, they caused a sensation. Girls screamed, boys cheered and other groups refused to play on the same bill. Jimmy Page, with dark curly hair and satin outfits, seemed like the master of revels as he raised his violin bow to scrape the strings of a guitar that howled with raw and ecstatic pain.

Robert Plant, a mass of golden hair cascading over his shoulders, bare-chested and clad in tight jeans, strutted the stage with a cocky impudence that was irresistible. As he sang from deepest tenor to screaming falsetto his voice was like another instrument, fencing with Page's flashing guitar.

Behind them was the ultimate rhythm machine – John Paul Jones, a warm and melodic bass player, whose forays on to a Hammond organ added an eerie and mysterious tone to many a Zeppelin classic. John Bonham, drum master and *bon viveur*, provided a cataclysmic blast of percussion that galvanized the band and inspired their best-known riffs.

It soon became clear they weren't just a hard-rock riff band. The "heavy metal" tag was always ludicrously inappropriate, but such was the power of their impact that many a critic, put on the defensive, resorted to abuse.

The legacy of eight studio albums they recorded between the years 1968 and 1979 contains a rich variety of songs and performances that few can equal.

The sheer diversity reveals a band clearly searching for new ideas and keen to experiment. The blues and rock and roll were at the core of their work, but the variety of ethnic influences in their songs and ballads shows an intelligent face to the Led Zeppelin of myth and legend. Mysterious musical sounds from Middle Eastern deserts and Indian mountains were among the many exotic influences absorbed by chief composers Plant and Page. Soul, funk, folk, country music, West Coast psychedelia, even hillbilly and reggae were all grist to the Zeppelin mill, given their fascination for all aspects of pop music culture.

These elements were judiciously introduced right from the start. From 'Black Mountain Side' on *Led Zeppelin* (1969) to 'Gallows Pole' on *Led Zeppelin III* (1970), from 'Stairway to Heaven' on their untitled fourth album (1971) to 'Kashmir' on *Physical Graffiti* (1975), the group devised a sort of musical alchemy.

There were few moments when they faltered – compared to most of their contemporaries, their output remained at a consistently high level. Sometimes their delving into traditional blues sources led to accusations of plagiarism, but that's a game that could be played with the entire history of rock and roll. It's perhaps enough to say that before 1968 there wasn't a band that sounded quite like Led Zeppelin.

Led Zeppelin may not have captured the public's affection in the same way as the Beatles or the Rolling Stones, and they may not have been as flashy as the Who or the Jimi Hendrix Experience, but they had a monumental power and strength. They were the record breakers, the biggest concert attraction, the greatest album-sellers, the most talked about band of the 70s. And that's the way Page planned it.

Yes, there had been some marvellous British bands in the years before Zeppelin. Jimmy Page's old buddy Eric Clapton had soared to success in the first supergroup Cream. Jeff Beck, another mate from the Yardbirds, had teamed up with Rod Stewart. But when Jimmy Page, aided by manager Peter Grant, set out to launch his own band, he wasn't concerned so much with getting star names as with finding the best performers. All his own experience, gained over years of touring and session work, would be poured into the new project.

James Patrick Page (born 9 January 1944), from Heston, Middlesex, England, had studied painting in his youth and developed an appreciation of antiques and *objets d'art*. But he had also discovered Elvis Presley and rock and roll and, once he was given his first guitar aged 12, he was hooked on rock and determined to become a professional musician.

PREVIOUS PAGE: Robert Plant performs onstage at the legendary Los Angeles Forum, 4 September 1970.
RIGHT: John Bonham, John Paul Jones, Robert Plant and Jimmy Page take a break in 1969.

His family moved away from the noise of Heathrow Airport to live in Epsom, where Jimmy went to grammar school. He studied Bert Weedon's famous guide *Play in a Day* and had a few guitar lessons. But he largely taught himself by listening to solos on records by his favourite artists, particularly Elvis Presley's 'Baby Let's Play House', and the guitar work of Scotty Moore. James Burton was another favourite and Page appreciated the acoustic work of British folk artist Bert Jansch. In 1958 Jimmy formed a skiffle group that veered towards R&B and began playing at local clubs. He also made an appearance on BBC TV's *All Your Own* hosted by Huw Wheldon. Rare black-and-white footage exists of his interview, which shows a well-spoken, intelligent lad already displaying a sense of independence.

He may have looked like "a little shrimp", as his mate Jeff Beck called him, but there was always a steely strength of purpose about Page. At the age of 15 he left school and plunged into the rock life, quickly moving to London, where he visited all the clubs and sat in with band leader Cyril Davies. His first pro job was with singer Red E Lewis and the Red Caps, then he joined Neil Christian and the Crusaders in 1959. But he found the life on the road, living in a van and bedsits, debilitating, and after a bout of glandular fever, he concentrated more on session work in the studios.

Recommended by engineer Glyn Johns, Jimmy played on his first session, which was 'Diamonds' (1963) by Jet Harris and Tony Meehan, both of whom had recently left the Shadows. It reached Number 1. He also worked with pop group Carter Lewis and the Southerners, and pictures of him at this period show a sharp-looking young Mod with a friendly smile. Between 1963 and 1966 he played on countless sessions, including Van Morrison and Them, the Who, the Kinks, Donovan, Lulu, PJ Proby, Mickie Most, Val Doonican, Burt Bacharach and Cliff Richard.

Sometimes he'd play solos, or simply fill in with rhythm guitar. He would often be called in as "insurance" by producers worried that their star bands couldn't cut it. This often led to friction in the studios, as regular band members resented having this unknown player on their sessions.

For many years Page remained a shadowy figure, well respected within the music business but not nearly as well known as the more flamboyant Eric Clapton and Jeff Beck. Eventually, he wanted to become part of a regular group playing his kind of music. As he recalls: "Working in the studios certainly gave me a sense of discipline. I developed different styles of guitar playing. I was also very keen on finger-style acoustic guitar playing, but towards the end of my session period I was just strumming along, and I got fed up with it. It was time to go and it so happened that's when the Yardbirds opportunity turned up."

Page had been asked to join the band before, when Clapton left, and had refused. But he relented finally and joined the Yardbirds in 1966. Jeff Beck was still the band's lead guitarist, and Jimmy came in on bass guitar. This situation developed because the band's regular bassist, Paul Samwell-Smith, had abruptly quit after a huge row. Recalls Page: "We'd always wanted to play together and suddenly the opportunity was there. I took over the bass for a while, until the rhythm guitarist (Chris Dreja) had learned the bass, and then Jeff and I could play lead guitars."

After rehearsing for two hours, Page went off with the Yardbirds on a full American tour. The pressure of heavy touring led to Beck undergoing fits of rage and depression. Sometimes he wouldn't turn up for a gig, so Jimmy took over. Other times Jeff and Jimmy would work together as a dual front line, creating a deafening wall of stereo sound that threatened to blow away the frail Keith Relf. It was very exciting, but it caused tension. Eventually Jeff decided to quit the band in 1968.

Jimmy became the Yardbirds' last lead guitarist as the band concentrated on working in the States. They were highly influential, and had been very popular in their heyday, but were undergoing a severe decline. Exhausted by heavy touring and a lack of chart success, the band decided to split. They broke up after a gig in Luton, Bedfordshire, in July 1968.

Page was encouraged by the Yardbirds' last manager, Peter Grant, to form his own group and plans were laid to recruit new members. The original plan was to bring in singer Terry Reid and drummer BJ Wilson from Procol Harum to help form what would be known as the New Yardbirds. Chris Dreja was briefly retained from the old group and session pianist Nicky Hopkins was also involved, until session bass player and organist John Paul Jones (real name John Baldwin, born 3 June 1946 in Sidcup, Kent) called Jimmy, having heard he was getting a band together.

Reid and Wilson turned down the project. Terry had just signed a solo recording contract and couldn't come in, but he recommended a young singer from the Midlands instead. His name was Robert Plant.

Plant (born 20 August 1948 in West Bromwich) a.k.a. "The Wild Man of Blues from the Black Country", had been singing with the Delta Blues Band and the Crawling King Snakes. He grew up listening to American blues artists, and through singing in local club bands, developed his own immensely powerful and passionate vocal style. By the time he'd joined his last pre-Zeppelin outfit, the Band of Joy, he'd embraced everything from blues to hillbilly and soul. He'd released a brace of solo singles under his own name for CBS in 1966 and '67, but without any commercial success.

The Band of Joy boasted an unusually loud and aggressive drummer called John Bonham (born 31 May 1948 in West Bromwich), who had previously worked with Robert in the Crawling King Snakes. In 1968 the band, with Plant and Bonham, toured the UK, backing American artist Tim Rose. Clashes of temperament ensured there would always be a lively atmosphere within the band – indeed, there was a full-scale fight among the musicians one night when the drummer suggested a new billing: "The Band of Joy featuring John Bonham".

Jimmy and his manager Peter Grant went to see Robert singing with a group called Hobbstweedle at a gig in Birmingham. Jimmy was blown away by Robert's voice and couldn't believe he hadn't already been spotted. The singer was invited to come to London right away and he agreed, after recommending his old mate "Bonzo" Bonham for the drummer's job.

Jimmy went to see Bonham playing with Tim Rose, and recalls that it took ages to get Bonham to agree to join the new band, because he felt he had a "steady" job with Rose's group. Page persisted: "He was exactly the type of powerhouse drummer I was looking for! Eventually we got the four of us into one room and that was it. We just exploded." The New Yardbirds, as they had to be called for contractual reasons, were complete and ready for a ten-day tour of Scandinavia in September 1968.

Page expected the youthful enthusiasm of his new partners to ignite the band's inner fire. He wasn't disappointed. When the feisty four found themselves playing in a cramped rehearsal room in Soho for the first time, the pent-up energy was unleashed as they tore into 'Train Kept A-Rollin'. "It was powerful stuff!" remembers John Paul Jones.

Soon after these first rehearsals, their debut album was recorded in days rather than weeks. Manager Peter Grant had moved with similar speed to get

the band work. On 15 October they made their UK debut at Surrey University under their new name – Led Zeppelin. Apparently Jimmy Page had considered calling the band the Mad Dogs but, as he later commented, "The name wasn't as important as the music. We could have called ourselves the Vegetables or the Potatoes. I was quite keen about Led Zeppelin, as it seemed to fit the bill."

The name Led Zeppelin had derived from a remark by the Who's John Entwhistle that a possible supergroup containing him and Keith Moon, along with Jimmy Page and Jeff Beck would go down like a "lead zeppelin" – a term Entwistle used to describe a bad gig.

The new band arrived at a perfect time. British rock was in limbo with the demise of many excellent bands, yet there was a growing market not just for live bands, but for albums. Club gigs were being replaced by three-day festivals and PA systems were growing ever larger. The age of the one-hit-wonder pop group was over   at least for a while – and the age of stadium rock was dawning. Led Zeppelin were ready for action.

The new band were strong in all departments and thrustingly confident. Plant had been waiting to show the world just how fiendishly well he could sing. Classically trained Jones desperately needed to express his own talents beyond the studio. Bonham was a one-man powerhouse. And Page was bubbling with brilliant ideas: songs, arrangements, sound effects, production and showmanship.

While the new band launched into their early gigs at colleges and small clubs, Peter Grant, an ex-all-in wrestler and film actor, was using all his strength and ferocious personality to win the band a record contract. Eventually they signed to Atlantic Records in New York City for $200,000. It seemed like a lot of money at the time.

The debut album *Led Zeppelin* was recorded in October 1968 and released in January 1969 in the States, and March in the UK. The group had already made their first American concert appearance in Boston, on 26 December 1968, where they caused a sensation and blew US bands Iron Butterfly and Vanilla Fudge off the stage.

Now the world could hear the recordings that have since become part of the soundtrack of a generation, including 'Dazed and Confused', 'Black Mountain Side' and 'Communication Breakdown'. Today, after 40 years of advances in studio technology, these tracks might not seem as dynamic as they did in 1969. However, in the context of the period, these original recordings were a revelation.

Remastered versions of Zeppelin's classic tracks have since revealed new depths and hidden subtleties. Yet the vinyl album, for all its microscopic flaws, has an intriguing atmosphere that can never be reproduced. It was that sound – and the brash enthusiasm of the bubbling new band – that caught the imagination of the lucky few who heard advance review copies of Led Zeppelin.

"Led Zeppelin was the sort of band everyone dreams about. For me it was an honour to be part of it." JIMMY PAGE

Early in 1969, at *Melody Maker*'s untidy Fleet Street office, a young reporter, Tony Wilson, rushed into the editorial department clutching a 12-inch vinyl album. Its striking cover showed the famous news picture of the *Hindenburg* airship crashing in flames at Lakehurst, New Jersey, in 1937. It was an eerie image: part cataclysm, part phallic symbol. The notion of sex and explosions registered before a note was played. Tony had seen Led Zeppelin at the Marquee and was convinced they would be the biggest band of the next decade: "You gotta hear Robert Plant's voice."

That early Marquee show had attracted only a few hundred people. Most were shocked by the battering volume and were unfamiliar with material that seemed to be the blues, but which was played with a ferocious intensity that was almost indecent to audiences more used to the earnest warblings of John Mayall & His Bluesbreakers.

The indifference of the crowds at early UK shows was disappointing. As Page recalls: "It wasn't until we got to America that the audiences went wild. They didn't know what had hit them." Within a year English fans were also yelling with all the enthusiasm of their American counterparts.

There had been earlier clues about what to expect from this untried band. They had all served as session men on an album by PJ Proby, the Texan pop singer who had moved to London during the 1960s. Proby had caused a sensation with hits like 'Somewhere', but his last album *Three Week Hero* (1969) had passed unnoticed. If anybody had bothered to listen to a track called 'Jim's Blues', they would have heard Robert Plant wailing on harmonica. During the track the Zep men's power threatened to blow Proby out of the studio. It was a dress rehearsal for an album now being previewed at radio stations and in magazine offices around the world.

Led Zeppelin were not just the New Yardbirds. This was a stunning record on which the drums thundered, the organ wailed, the guitar rushed like a tempest and the singer seemed on the verge of exploding. This was the album that would set in motion a career full of drama, excitement and a scale of success unimaginable to young musicians who had been struggling for a living wage, let alone a millionaire's fortune.

When Zeppelin first hit the road at the end of 1968, they were still very much a four-piece rock band in a station wagon with a roadie. Robert Plant was still doing the PA mix from the stage using a tiny old 150-watt amplifier he'd owned in the Band of Joy. Even when they played prestige gigs like the Fillmore, San Francisco their PA sound was pretty primitive. But the sheer power of the newcomers soon overwhelmed competition.

This was something more explosive than the Woodstock Generation had ever experienced. Word spread across the States like wildfire and everyone wanted to see this newest example of the British invasion. Page, Plant, Bonham and Jones became mega rock stars and the endless cycle of tours and recordings continued for a turbulent decade.

There were great events – Bath Festival (1969), Carnegie Hall, New York (1969), Madison Square Garden, New York (1970), Earls Court, London (1975) and Knebworth, England (1979). Their albums and singles dominated the charts, and by the end of their first year together it was said they'd already earned some $5m in sales.

Although singles were discouraged by the band's management at home in England, it didn't stop them having hits in America like 'Whole Lotta Love' (1969), 'Immigrant Song' (1970) and 'Black Dog' (1972). Even 'D'yer Mak'er' (1973), 'Trampled Under Foot' (1975) and their 1980 opus 'Fool in the Rain' made it into the US *Billboard* Top 40. Led Zeppelin rapidly became even bigger than Elvis or the Beatles in terms of sales.

Led Zeppelin II (1969) topped charts around the world and yielded 'Whole Lotta Love' and 'The Lemon Song'. Then came *Led Zeppelin III* (1970), *Four Symbols (Untitled)* (1971), *Houses of the Holy* (1973), *Physical Graffiti* (1975), *Presence* (1976), *The Song Remains the Same* (1976), *In Through the Out Door* (1979) and the final release *Coda* (1982). The band were voted best in the world in the 1970 *Melody Maker* readers' poll and stayed at the top for a decade. As they toured the world they were greeted with riots and uproar. At a single concert at Tampa Stadium, Florida in May 1973, they played to more than 56,000 people and grossed $309,000.

In 1974 the band expanded their business activities, setting up their own label Swan Song and signing their favourite artists like the Pretty Things and ex-Stone the Crows singer Maggie Bell, who was managed by Peter Grant. A party held in Chislehurst Caves to launch the label's releases became a byword for excess and debauchery.

In 1975 the band were at a peak of popularity when they played spectacular three-hour shows for five consecutive nights at London's Earls Court. They used a 70,000-watt PA system and a complex lighting rig. Performances of 'Kashmir' and 'Trampled Under Foot' caused a sensation and it was the same story on their American tour that year. Zeppelin flew around the States on their own chartered jet, *The Starship*, and provoked riots at the box offices as tickets sold out within hours of going on sale.

The group even starred in their own film. *The Song Remains the Same* premiered in New York in October 1976. It showed the band in concert and was interspersed with fantasy sequences. John Bonham raced a drag-strip car, Robert Plant rescued a maiden from a castle, John Paul Jones was a masked night rider and Jimmy Page climbed a Scottish mountain on the shores of Loch Ness in total darkness, in search of a mysterious hermit. Manager Peter Grant later called it "the most expensive home movie ever made", but it was a big success around the world.

As they broke box office records during these years of marathon US tours and platinum albums, the band was increasingly plagued by controversy, mainly fed by lurid stories in the rock press. Certainly they exhibited high spirits. John Bonham was seen riding motorcycles down hotel corridors, while rooms were trashed and redecorated with hamburgers and ketchup. Half-naked groupies were pressed into nightly service amid the shattered piles of broken furniture.

But the real culprits were the road crew and not the band. Bonham may not have been an innocent bystander, but certainly Plant and Page were nowhere near this kind of action. They were far too cool to indulge in such stunts. On the road, the band were often quiet and reserved, worried about the next gig, the flight or simply yearning to get home to their respective families. Robert Plant was usually quietly reading magazines or listening to tapes by Joni Mitchell. Away from the gig or hotel, Jimmy Page went about collecting antiques at local flea markets or studying ethnic music forms. Even John Bonham usually preferred a pint of real ale with his mates.

Speculation about Zeppelin's secret goings-on remained rife, but the true turn of events proved much more dramatic. Mishaps like Robert Plant's car crash on the Greek island of Rhodes in 1975, when he and his wife were seriously injured, certainly cast a shadow over the band's success.

Robert recovered sufficiently from his car crash injuries to take part in recording sessions at Musicland, Munich, for the album *Presence* (Swan Song), which was released in April 1976. Although not up to the standards of *Physical Graffiti*, it yielded one blockbuster, the amazing 'Achilles' Last Stand'. In the same year they released their double-soundtrack album from *The Song Remains the Same*, packed with classics, including live versions of 'Rock and Roll', 'Dazed and Confused' and 'Stairway To Heaven'.

Everything seemed to be going their way when, in April 1977, the band set off on their 11th tour of the US, which would be their biggest ever. On 30 April they played to 76,229 fans at the Pontiac Silverdome, which broke another attendance record. Yet clouds were gathering. There was a riot at Tampa, Florida when a show was cancelled because of a storm. Then backstage at the Oakland Coliseum, a minor dispute sparked off a backstage fight between members of the Zeppelin crew and the promoter's security men. This resulted in arrests and criminal charges for assault.

It was a dark time for the band, but life had to go on. Later that year, with Robert sufficiently recovered from his emotional trauma, brought on by the death of his young son, Karac, Led Zeppelin reconvened. In May, they made music together at Clearwell Castle, in the Forest of Dean. It was the best kind of therapy.

During December 1978, the revitalized band went to Sweden and recorded *In Through the Out Door*. In June the following year they embarked on a new European tour and, on 4 and 11 August 1979, they topped the bill at two sensational shows at Knebworth, England. In September, *In Through the Out Door* was released and topped the US charts, selling more than four million copies in America alone.

During April 1980, the band began rehearsing in London for what would be their last European tour and announced plans to return to North America. On 7 July they played a concert in West Berlin, then met up in September at Jimmy Page's home in Windsor to rehearse. Bonham embarked on a vodka-drinking bout. On Thursday, 25 September John was found dead, having suffocated on his own vomit. His funeral was held on 10 October 1980. To fans, his death was as tragic as the losses of Jimi Hendrix and Keith Moon. Tributes poured in, many from his fellow drummers, who saw Bonham as both an idol and a pioneer of heavy rock.

Bonham's death was a shattering blow that precipitated the breakup of the group. In December the band issued a bleak communiqué: "We wish it to be known that the loss of our dear friend and the deep sense of undivided harmony felt by ourselves and our manager, have led us to decide that we could not continue as we were."

As Jimmy Page confirmed, this meant the band could not continue to work as Led Zeppelin without John Bonham. In the aftermath the remaining members seemed unnerved by all that happened. Their fans were left disappointed and crushed by the loss of the greatest rock band they'd ever known. All they had left from the debris was a 1982 album of Zeppelin relics called *Coda*, which was barely advertised and was relegated to the bargain basement bins within weeks of release.

Robert Plant was the first to recover. He began to rebuild his career with a commendable zeal and a bright new image, releasing a succession of solo albums and touring with his own bands. Jimmy Page, after a period spent in seclusion, recovered his nerve and strength, wrote some film music and performed at charity shows and low-key gigs before taking the plunge and forming the Firm in 1985, with former Free vocalist Paul Rodgers. Page later worked in a touring band that featured John Bonham's son Jason, now an excellent drummer, and the singer John Miles.

Fans yearned for a full-scale Led Zeppelin reunion and there were some historic moments – like Jimmy's moving performance of 'Stairway to Heaven' at London's Royal Albert Hall during the ARMS charity show in 1983. This was also the occasion when Page, Eric Clapton and Jeff Beck joined forces on stage for the first time ever. As the decade wore on, new bands paid their dues to the group that had inspired them in their youth. Zeppelin's music was re-evaluated and, while music critics were still wearing punk-rock attitudes on their sleeves, artists were sampling Led Zeppelin, copying their riffs and covering their numbers in a wave of adulation that reached a peak with the bizarre Dread Zeppelin.

Zeppelin watchers were constantly kept busy. There were several collaborations between Page and Plant, including the Live Aid show at Philadelphia's JFK Stadium on 13 July 1985, with Phil Collins on drums, and the Atlantic Records 40th birthday celebrations at New York's Madison Square Garden, in May 1988, when Robert sang 'Stairway to Heaven' and 'Whole Lotta Love', backed by Jason Bonham.

In June 1988 Jimmy released his first solo album *Outrider* and toured with Jason and John Miles. Then came a brief liaison with Whitesnake singer David Coverdale, for the album *Coverdale/Page* (1993), which resulted in just one tour of Japan. It seemed a strange choice to work with Coverdale, who had been criticized by Robert Plant for being a Robert Plant clone. Was this a ploy by Jimmy to encourage Plant to return to the fold where he belonged? If this was so, it certainly worked. The long-awaited reunion finally took place in 1995, when the pair recorded the sensational *Unledded* MTV show followed by a hugely successful Plant-Page world tour.

In the years that followed and well into the New Millennium, Plant, Page and John Paul Jones kept up their musical output. Plant kept his distance from any further Zeppelin activity after the Plant-Page odyssey and then enjoyed his greatest personal success in 2007 with his million-selling album *Raising Sand*, recorded with American singer Alison Krauss.

Jimmy Page played with the Black Crowes and worked on producing several Led Zeppelin "Best of" CDs and oversaw the release of the long-awaited *Led Zeppelin* (2003) 2-DVD set, including breathtaking 1970s "live" footage of performances from the London's Royal Albert Hall and Madison Square Garden.

All of this fuelled a worldwide demand to see Zeppelin live in action, one more time. The ultimate reunion concert, so long denied, was finally delivered with a unique show at London's 02 Arena on 10 December 2007. Once again fans thrilled to the sounds of 'Whole Lotta Love', 'Kashmir' and 'Stairway to Heaven' as Jimmy Page, Robert Plant, John Paul Jones and John Bonham's son, Jason, entertained an ecstatic audience, some of whom had travelled from the other side of the world to be there.

Their devotion arose from exposure to an extraordinary legacy of recordings made during Led Zeppelin's heyday. But where did it all come from, that mysterious outpouring of sounds and ideas captured on those classic albums? What were the influences, the people and the events that sparked Zeppelin's creative flame?

Well, this is how it all began ...

Led Zeppelin exploded on the music scene in 1969 and their legendary sound would redefine rock music forever.
This series of four photographs are multiple exposure solo portraits of the band taken by the American photographer Jim Cummins.

IN THE BEGINNING

Before the fame, before the glory and before the excesses of incredible success, Led Zeppelin were just a twinkle in a young Jimmy Page's eye. He had the vision, all he needed was three other visionaries ...

1968-1970
THE EARLY YEARS

Jimmy Page had already had his vision of a rock supergroup. But this was an era when a plethora of dynamic groups had already been established. How would it be possible to take on the Who, Cream and the Jimi Hendrix Experience? Page, aged only 21, was well placed to try. His session background meant that he knew how studios worked and, having already toured North America with the Yardbirds, he could see the potential audience for ever more powerful rock bands.

During 1967 rifts had begun to open out within the Yardbirds. Original members Keith Relf and Jim McCarty wanted to pursue a style influenced by folk and classical music; Jimmy Page, at a time when the psychedelic blues-rock of Cream and the Jimi Hendrix Experience was massively popular, wanted to go for a "heavier" sound. By March 1968 Relf and McCarty had decided to leave, but were persuaded to stay on for one more US tour. As far as the music was concerned, Page began to get his own way, and during the tour the kind of new rock sound he had in mind gradually came to the fore. The Yardbirds returned to England in the summer of 1968. After one final appearance at Luton Technical College in July, it was all over. The band split.

Page was keen to carry on, and, as the Yardbirds had a contracted tour in Scandinavia still outstanding, he invited rhythm guitarist-turned-bass player Chris Dreja to form part of the new outfit. But after six years on the road Dreja opted instead for a new life. He had recently become interested in photography and decided to try it professionally.

Jimmy Page, thinking back to his earlier notion of a "supergroup", set about creating a new band. He first approached John Paul Jones, an arranger and organist as well as a bass player with whom he'd worked on Donovan's 'Hurdy Gurdy Man'. Page explained there were Yardbirds dates unfilled and he planned to call his replacement outfit "the New Yardbirds". Terry Reid, a solo singer signed to producer Mickie Most, was approached to front the band. Uninterested, he suggested a promising blues vocalist he'd spotted in the Midlands.

The 18-year-old Robert Plant had been with Band of Joy and had just begun fronting the curiously named Hobbstweedle. Page and Grant went to see him singing at a teacher training college gig in Birmingham and were immediately impressed; Page invited him to his home in Pangbourne, Berkshire, and they quickly realized they had very similar musical tastes. The group now had a vocalist, lead guitarist and a bass player and keyboardist. All they needed now was a solid drummer.

Page had been thinking about asking BJ Wilson, now playing with Procol Harum, but Plant suggested that he try out his old colleague from Band of Joy, one John Henry Bonham. At that time he was enjoying regular income backing visiting American singer Tim Rose, but Plant persuaded "Bonzo" to come aboard with promises of fame and fortune. Even if Bonham didn't quite believe him, he liked the music that was on offer.

The group met in September in Soho for its first rehearsal. Page later commented: "The four of us got together in this room and started playing. Then we knew it would work and started laughing. Maybe it was from relief, or maybe from knowledge we could groove together."

In October Jimmy Page visited the *Melody Maker* office in Fleet Street. The resulting interview was headlined "Only Jimmy Left to Form New Yardbirds". By the time it appeared "The New Yardbirds'" had already played their first dates, fulfilling their tour obligations in Scandinavia.

It was clear now that the band could easily be accused of operating under false pretences since nobody in the group had any connection whatsoever with the Yardbirds' classic hits. They agreed a new name was needed. One account of what happened next is that Keith Moon and John Entwistle had previously remarked that a possible supergroup containing themselves, Jimmy Page and Jeff Beck would go down like a "lead zeppelin". The group were purported to have deliberately dropped the "a" from "Lead" at the suggestion of their manager, ex-wrestler and showbiz tough guy, Peter Grant, to prevent "thick Americans" from pronouncing it "Leed".

PREVIOUS PAGES: Led Zeppelin soundcheck onstage at Oude Rai in Amsterdam, the Netherlands, 27 May 1972.

ABOVE: Bill Graham's Fillmore Auditorium venue was at the heart of the Underground Scene when the Yardbirds with Page and Beck played there in October 1966.

OPPOSITE: Robert Plant and Jimmy Page's vocal and guitar "chemistry" instantly transferred from rehearsal room to stage once Zeppelin hit the road from 1968 onwards.

Page himself wasn't that bothered: "The name wasn't really as important as whether or not the music was going to be accepted … but I was quite keen on Led Zeppelin."

The group began recording a debut album at Olympic Studios in Barnes, London, while Grant set about booking gigs in the UK. They made their debut billed as "Led Zeppelin" at Surrey University on 15 October 1968. Three days later they played the Marquee in London to a good crowd. Larger venues followed, including Liverpool University on 19 October and the Roundhouse in London on 11 November. After more university dates in Manchester and Sheffield they returned to the Marquee on 10 December.

The British media, however, were still mostly ignoring the new band. Impatient with the UK's response, manager Peter Grant decided to take his "boys" to America. On Boxing Day 1968, Led Zeppelin made their American debut at Denver Coliseum, supporting Vanilla Fudge and the MC5. They were an immediate hit. Staying on in the US, they opened for another popular American rock group, Iron Butterfly, who were so astounded by the reaction that they refused to go on.

The decision to hit America was an easy one for Led Zeppelin, as Page explained: "I knew you could sit around as a new group for months in England and have no notice taken of you at all. In the States a group can get so much more exposure."

The first Led Zeppelin tour ended in February at Bill Graham's Fillmore East in New York, then a premier rock showcase. More important was the extensive radio play and promotion by Atlantic Records. Entering the *Billboard* Top 40 in February, the band's debut was in the Top 20 by March.

Released in the UK on 28 March, it received more rave reviews. "Jimmy Page triumphs – Led Zeppelin is a gas!" exulted *Melody Maker*. The group flew home for more promotion, fitted in a swift trip to Scandinavia and popped up on BBC2's *How Late It Is,* performing 'Communication Breakdown'.

That month they appeared in the UK film *Supershow,* a pioneering attempt at capturing rock and jazz acts on film. The sessions took place at a studio in Staines and also featured Eric Clapton, Stephen Stills, Buddy Miles, the Modern Jazz Quartet, Roland Kirk, Buddy Guy and Colosseum.

On 24 April the second US tour began, opening at the Fillmore West, San Francisco, alongside Brian Auger and Julie Driscoll. The first full UK tour started at Birmingham Town Hall on 13 June, a Midlands homecoming for Plant and Bonham. At the Bath Festival on 28 June, 12,000 fans flocked to see them. The following night they performed at London's Royal Albert Hall for the "Pop Proms", supported by Blodwyn Pig and Liverpool Scene.

Although they were expected to continue work on the album *Led Zeppelin II*, the call of America proved too strong and a third US tour began on 5 July. More than 20 dates included jazz festivals in Newport, Baltimore and Philadelphia. They missed the Woodstock Festival but, given the conditions, it was probably just as well, avoiding direct competition with Jimi Hendrix and Alvin Lee's Ten Years After. The third tour ended in August at the Texas International Pop Festival in Lewisville.

LEFT: Tight jeans, a big rock star's blouse and cascading golden hair was young Robert Plant's iconic and magnetic look from Zeppelin's earliest days.

OPPOSITE: Zeppelin causing a sensation at the historic Bath Festival at Shepton Mallet, Somerset on 28 June 1970. From left to right – Plant, Page, Jones and Bonham.

Page noted: "At most of the places we play we seem to get mass hysteria. In Boston all the boys in the front row were beating heads in time. When we started the group, we only had enough material for 50 minutes but now this has extended to two hours. The American reaction is more than we ever dreamed could happen."

Some critics had not fully understood the "headbanging" heavy rock revolution Led Zeppelin was fomenting. Asked if they would turn down the volume, Page replied: "No – we're getting louder. Our drummer's amazingly loud. I come off stage with my ears singing."

By now the band was earning $30,000 a night. It was time for a holiday; Page went to Morocco, where he was exposed to what became known as "world music". Back in Britain the band finished off *Led Zeppelin II* at Olympic Studios and played a triumphant concert at the Lyceum Ballroom in the Strand on 12 October – the 54th anniversary of a real Zeppelin raid, when the Lyceum was bombed. When a relative of Count Zeppelin complained about the use of the name by a group of '"shrieking monkeys", Jimmy briefly considered renaming the band to placate her, but by now "Led Zeppelin" was as famous as any airship.

Days later it was back to New York for two concerts at Carnegie Hall – one of the first rock concerts at the venue that was much better known for classical and jazz events. It was especially important for Bonham, as his idols Gene Krupa and Buddy Rich had played on the same stage. Young New Yorkers' exuberance was in contrast to the more reserved attitude among British fans. There was also none of the cynicism they encountered at home. As Plant observed: "A lot of people in Britain have been against us for some reason … they say we're a made-up manufactured group because we were successful right away, but we just got together in the same way all groups get together. We had to prove ourselves on stage. From then on it just grew." By October all the focus was on the release of *Led Zeppelin II*. At Atlantic's Manhattan offices the staff excitedly blew up rubber Led Zeppelin balloons and shouted to anyone who would listen: "Led Zeppelin and the Who are the two biggest acts in America. It's like the Monkees never existed!"

The album was released on 22 October in America and had advance orders of 400,000. Within a couple of weeks it was Number 2. The stand-out track, 'Whole Lotta Love', would become not only the band's anthem

but the signature tune for BBC TV's *Top of the Pops*. Ironically, the band refused to allow it to be put out as a single in the UK, although an edited version was sent to US radio stations; a single version shot to Number 4 in the *Billboard* chart by December. Grant was still against releasing singles, despite Atlantic's demands; if anybody wanted a particular song, they'd have to buy the album. Zeppelin didn't want to be regarded as a "pop singles" band. They were certainly taken seriously by the UK government, as they were high earners and tax-payers. On 11 December, at London's Savoy Hotel, Gwyneth Dunwoody, Parliamentary Secretary to the Board of Trade, presented them with one gold and two platinum albums in recognition of their American sales.

When Page turned up to buy a brand-new Rolls-Royce at a showroom in Berkeley Square his long hair and flamboyant clothes might have startled the salesmen, but they soon realized he meant business – as did Bonham when he walked into a Birmingham showroom with £10,000 and bought a Maserati. The new rock royalty had finally arrived.

Album and ticket sales soared and overnight Plant, Page, Bonham and Jones were millionaires, a far cry from playing in pubs for a few pounds a night. Page resided in a boathouse by the Thames at Pangbourne, bought while with the Yardbirds, and drove a Bentley. Plant and his wife invested in a farm in Worcestershire. Bonham drove his brand-new Maserati to his large house in Stourbridge, more spacious than the caravan he had previously shared with wife Pat and baby Jason.

The year 1970 began with a British trek that included a sold-out concert at the Royal Albert Hall on 9 January. A week later, driving his Jaguar home from seeing visiting American group Spirit, Plant was in a crash, suffered head and facial injuries, and a show in Edinburgh had to be cancelled. He later appeared on stage in a wheelchair.

By now *Led Zeppelin II* was Number 1 on both sides of the Atlantic. 'Whole Lotta Love' was played constantly on radio and was at Number 4 in the *Billboard* chart, yet despite many invitations the band avoided TV appearances. In the age before MTV and promo videos, TV sound was poor and black-and-white images grainy. However, they did allow their Royal Albert Hall concert to be filmed for posterity.

During February Page began working up material for the third album. As well as editing tapes, he practised guitar three hours a day and even took time out to deny the band was to split: "There's no reason to split up. There is nothing inherent musically in Led Zeppelin to harm or destroy. There is variety, great freedom and no restrictions on the players whatsoever. In our band everybody respects each other. Everybody plays something to knock each other out. I can't see any split coming. People say to us, 'Now you're established, when are you going to break up?' That's a terrible attitude. We'll carry on and stick together like the Beatles and the Stones."

When everyone was fit and ready the band flew to Copenhagen, where they actually billed themselves as the Nobs to allay complaints from the Zeppelin family. The European tour ended at the Montreux Jazz Festival on 13 March. On 21 March they started their fifth North American tour in Vancouver with 27 dates on the schedule.

It was not always a happy outing. There was frequent violence among

adolescents hyped up on their perceived heavy metal image. They were greeted with hostility by police and middle-aged Americans who resented their wealth, long hair and flamboyant clothes. In Texas one redneck shouted abuse and pulled a gun. The Vietnam War was polarizing society and tensions were high. Eventually their manager had to hire a posse of bodyguards.

There were brighter moments. In April they were made honorary citizens of Memphis, Tennessee, and fans began lighting candles, matches and cigarette lighters during concerts to greet their more mellow songs. The tour finished in Phoenix, Arizona, at which point Plant collapsed. If the band was to finish its third album, they would have to take some time off.

Page and Plant headed for a secluded cottage in Snowdonia, where Robert had enjoyed many childhood holidays. It was called Bron-Yr-Aur, "golden breast" in Welsh (although some wags have suggested it actually meant "shut the gate.")

After spending the early part of May in Wales, Plant and Page rejoined the rest of the group to begin recording at Headley Grange, a mansion in Hampshire, and there were more sessions at Olympic during June. In an unusual move, they played two dates in the Icelandic capital Reykjavik, on 20 and 21 June, a warm-up for the Bath Festival. It was their second time there and they had reportedly turned down offers of US dates worth $200,000 so they could play at the biggest UK event of the year apart from the Isle of Wight Festival.

Bath turned out to be one of their most memorable concerts. Plant noted: "We went on and knew the next three hours were going to be the ones, as far as holding our heads high. We weren't into it until the acoustic number when we all had a chance to sit down and take a look around. Then it went like clockwork."

There were 200,000 fans packed into the festival site at Shepton Mallet on Sunday, 28 June. Robert told them: "We've been away in America and thought it might be a bit dodgy coming back. It's great to be home!" Zeppelin played for over three hours, climaxing with a marathon solo from Bonham. *Melody Maker* reported: "The crowd went wild demanding encore after encore … a total of five!" The mood wasn't quite so ecstatic backstage. Grant discovered some unauthorized filming and recording, and threw a bucket of water over the equipment.

The following month they embarked on a tour of Germany, where they played to crowds of 11,000 in Dusseldorf, Essen, Frankfurt and Berlin. Some fans smashed windows demanding "free music" and the band broke attendance records for concerts in the country. In August they began their sixth US tour, in Cincinnati. Page managed to finish mixing their third album in Memphis and Zeppelin played its final concerts of 1970 at Madison Square Garden on 19 September.

Back in London the group was feted by readers of *Melody Maker*, who voted them Group of the Year, ending the Beatles' long reign. On 16 October they were presented with gold discs by Anthony Grant, Parliamentary Secretary of the Board of Trade, in recognition of their contribution to exports.

On 23 October, *Led Zeppelin III* was released, and during the last two months of 1970 the lads took a holiday, interrupted for recording sessions at Island Studios. It was already time to think about the fourth album. Page had in mind an extended piece that would epitomize their ambitions. They were ascending the first rungs on the stairway.

OPPOSITE: John "Bonzo" Bonham leaps on to his tom toms at the climax of Zeppelin's concert at the prestigious Royal Albert Hall, London in January 1970.

SUNDAY JULY 3rd

NORTH PIER

AT **6 & 8** P.M. | BOOKABLE SEATS **7/6** & **9/6**

Telephone: 20980   Box Office open 10 a.m.

AUSTIN NEWMAN presents

The Fabulous

YARDBIRDS

"OVER-UNDER-SIDEWAYS-DOWN"

THOSE WILD THINGS

THE TROGGS

BLACKPOOL'S   COMPERE

THE **TRIANGLE** | **JERRY** STEVENS

LIVERPOOL'S No. 1

THE CARROLLS

Sun., 10th July—THE SPENCER DAVIS GROUP

Hastings Printing Company, Drury Lane, St. Leonards-on-Sea, Sussex. Telephone Hastings 2450

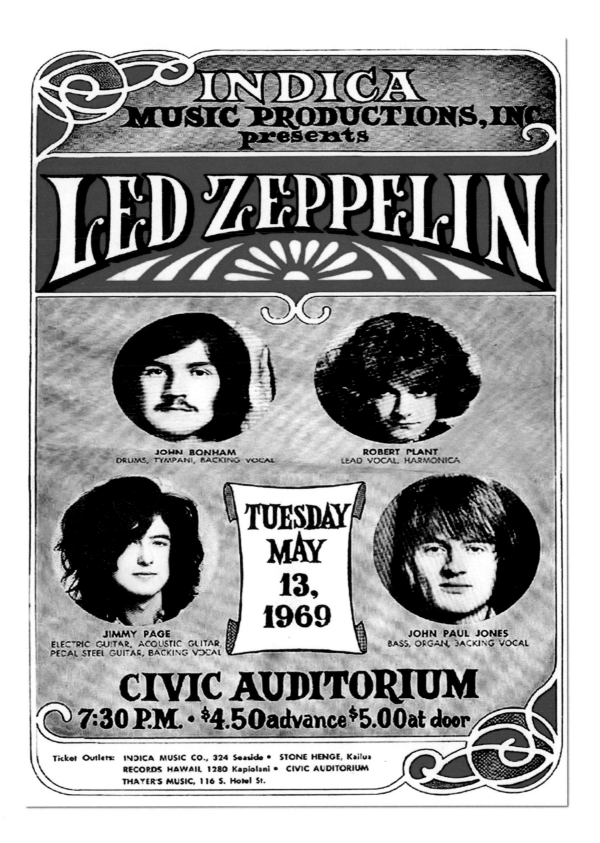

OPPOSITE: A classic concert poster from 1966 for North Pier, Blackpool. Jimmy Page and Jeff Beck were part of the band at that point and the year saw the Yardbirds on an extensive touring circuit.

ABOVE: A Led Zeppelin concert poster from 13 May 1969. The *Honolulu Advertiser* journalist who attended the Civic Auditorium, Hawaii, gig wrote in his review, "The showmanship exceeded any rock performance here to date."

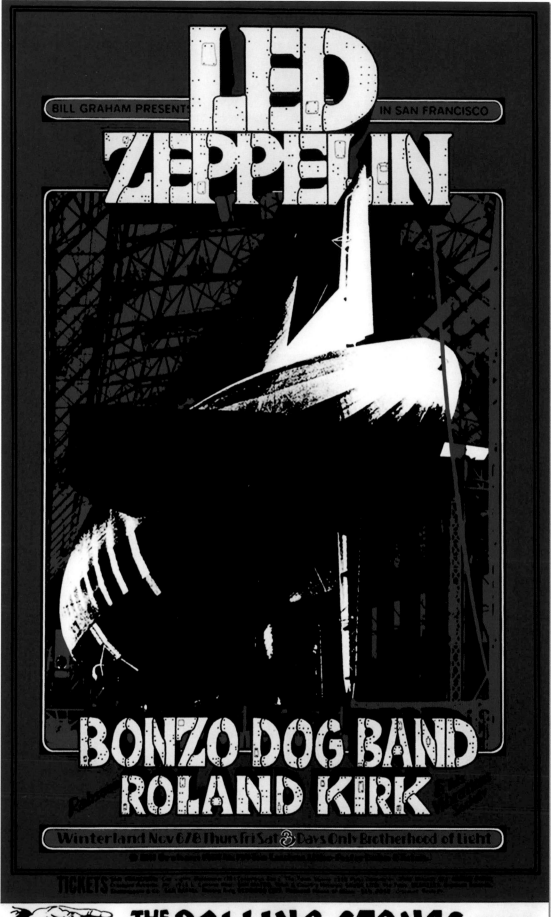

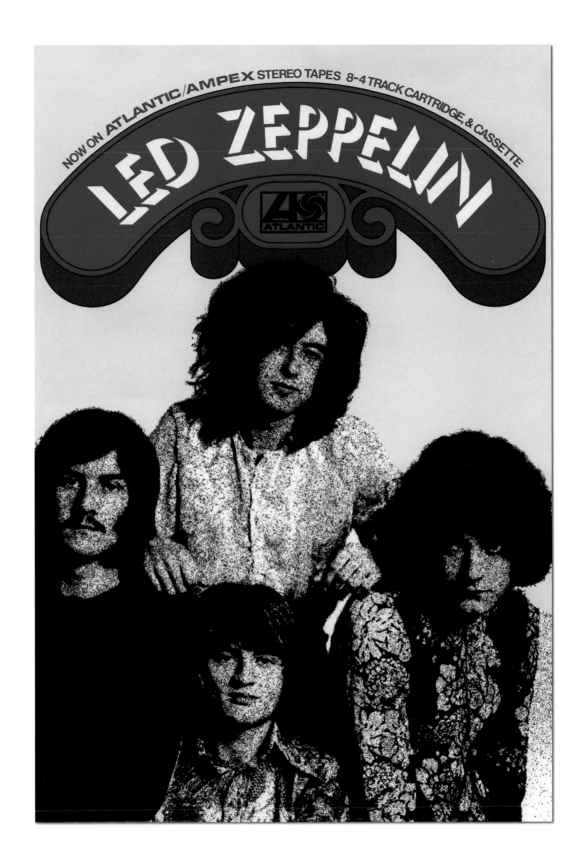

OPPOSITE: Led Zeppelin performed at the Winterland, San Francisco, on 6 November 1969. They were supported by jazz legend Rahsaan Roland Kirk. This is the poster from the event.

ABOVE: A poster promoting the band's debut release, *Led Zeppelin I*. Despite initially receiving negative reviews, the album was commercially successful and critics have come to view it as one of the greatest LPs of all time. The album was released through Atlantic Records.

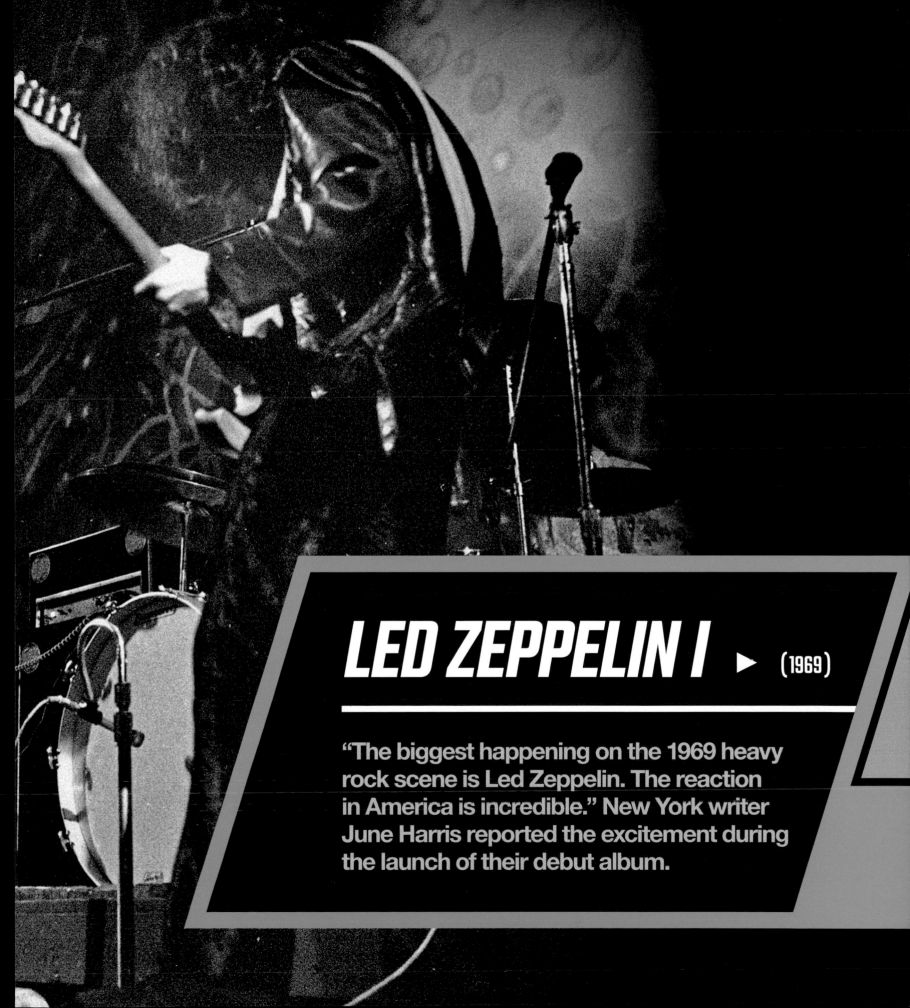

LED ZEPPELIN I ▶ (1969)

"The biggest happening on the 1969 heavy rock scene is Led Zeppelin. The reaction in America is incredible." New York writer June Harris reported the excitement during the launch of their debut album.

LED ZEPPELIN I

When early review copies of *Led Zeppelin I* arrived at music magazines and radio stations from London to New York, they were seized upon with the same eager expectation albums by the Beatles had been accorded in previous years.

The media buzz was matched by fans' growing fervour as word spread about the impending assault. They were not disappointed. When the arms of record players began descending on to the black vinyl for the first time, pounding guitar riffs from Page and screaming vocals from Plant signalled the birth of a new era.

The album had been recorded at Olympic Studios during a nine-day period in October 1968. Engineer Glyn Johns recalled the band spent only 30 hours in the studio at a cost of £1,782. However, between band and producer they managed to capture the essence of their rapidly evolving style. As Glyn explains: "It was a very exciting record to cut."

Led Zeppelin had been together only two-and-a-half weeks when they began recording, but at least they had worked out and practised the material at rehearsals and gigs. An urgency and excitement permeated the nine tracks that would make history and assure the future of the band.

They also had very clear aims and, unlike many young musicians, were not intimidated by the studio environment. Said Page: "We were deliberately aiming at putting down what we could already reproduce on stage. I wanted to use a lot of contrast and get an ambient sound, and I wanted light and shade and dramatic tension."

The penetrating, often eerie sound was partly the result of using backwards tape echo. This complemented the mood and progression of songs that seemed to grow organically. Each track had its own life and identity and was akin to classical music in structure.

The opening salvo, 'Good Times Bad Times', quickly established the stylistic strands that set Zeppelin apart. Whereas the average rock outfit would charge through a 12-bar blues with little thought for dynamics, Zeppelin utilized interplay between vocals and guitar, interspersed solos with breaks and sometimes stopped altogether, allowing a pregnant silence to create additional tension.

"In the days of my youth I was told what it means to be a man!" was Plant's opening statement, matched by an ongoing commentary from Bonham, Page and Jones whose improvisational skills were born out of jazz and blues.

'Babe I'm Gonna Leave You', a song by Anne Bredon found on a Joan Baez album, had intrigued Page since his session days; it was one of the tunes he suggested they might cover at initial meetings with Plant. The Zeppelin version evolves into a clever arrangement full of twists and turns, lulls and crescendos with both electric and acoustic guitars brought into play.

'You Shook Me', a Willie Dixon tune previously recorded by Muddy Waters, features thunderous sping-tingling guitar, with fine harmonica-playing from Plant, and vocal glissando. John Paul Jones' organ underpins the piece, climaxed by a sensational guitar break from Page.

'Dazed and Confused' creeps up on listeners with its ominous walking bass line, played with zest by John Paul Zones. As an arrangement, it turns into a remarkable *tour de force* for the group.

'Your Time is Gonna Come' is launched with Jones' church organ providing an ethereal sound before Robert launches into his protest about a girl who goes "Lying, cheating, hurting … that's all you ever seem to do …" Jimmy used a Fender pedal steel guitar also employed on 'Babe I'm Gonna Leave You'.

Even more atmospheric is 'Black Mountain Side' , a two-minute guitar instrumental that fades in during the closing seconds of the previous track. Page's repeated riff is complemented by tabla from Indian musician Viram Jasani. This hypnotic piece has its roots in Bert Jansch's 'Black Water Side' and the Page composition was often performed during the quieter acoustic medley squeezed into a live show.

PREVIOUS PAGES: The Fillmore East, New York, came complete with a light show that mesmerized hippie fans when it hosted Zeppelin's performance on 2 February 1969.

LEFT: A rich haul of gold albums for the lads, posing for the press in 1969. An inflatable promo Zeppelin can be seen in the background.

OPPOSITE: The boys sported macho beards when they performed at the Civic Auditorium, Florida, 31 August 1971, during their seventh US tour.

In complete contrast comes the joyful explosion of 'Communication Breakdown'. The image of "Golden God" Plant strutting the stage and screaming "Communication breakdown, baby!" came to symbolize Zeppelin in full-on rock and roll mode. Played at breakneck speed, it became the band's anthem, until supplanted by 'Whole Lotta Love' from their next album. Recalls Page: "The idea of 'Communication Breakdown' was to have a really raw, hard-hitting number. It was so exciting and electrifying and always so good to play, so staccato and a knock-out to do."

Taking a deep breath, the band dropped into a slower tempo for 'I Can't Quit You Baby', which became a favourite among all serious fans and those who most appreciated their grasp of the blues. Page's almost neurotic, desultory guitar notes soon give way to a beautifully constructed guitar solo – the kind of lines he would soon become famous for.

'How Many More Times' has more walking bass that urges the group into a series of experimental passages which are more psychedelia than R&B. It includes a trademark exchange of ideas between Bonham and Page before Plant exclaims, "Oh Rosie, steal away now" over a marching rhythm.

This combination of fresh ideas and vibrant performances left most listeners stunned. Reviews were mostly positive, although it still took a while for the media to catch up. While the band went on a tour of the UK, album sales began to mount and by April 1969 Led Zeppelin was in the Top Ten, entering at Number 6 and staying there for 22 weeks.

With their debut album complete, and with each track having a life and purpose of its own, but blended together in a way that seemed to create what is known in classical terms as "programmatic music", *Led Zeppelin I* was a complete and unique sonic experience that served as a warning shot as to how the band intended to go on.

RIGHT: According to Jones, the most pivotal show of their lives, Led Zeppelin's 23 January 1969 performance at Boston Tea Party, Massachusetts.

BELOW: A barefoot Jimmy Page relaxes between shows and enjoys a nice cup of hotel tea during Zeppelin's second US tour in May 1969.

ALBUM TRACKS

Blues, folk and sheer rock and roll was at the heart of the feisty British band's musical direction, unveiled on *Led Zeppelin* – an album whose sound and fury would revitalize the rock revolution.

GOOD TIMES, BAD TIMES

Like a pounding fist clamouring for attention, Page's guitar chords herald the first few seconds of Zeppelin magic on a song that encapsulates the band's style. Here are all the elements that make them special: the interplay between guitar and vocals, the use of breaks to create dynamic tension, and the rumbling aggression of the drums.

Behind Page's opening shots Bonham can be heard building the tension, first with his closed hi-hat, then with tentative tinkles on the cowbell, before the snare drum explodes behind Plant's vocal debut.

"In the days of my youth I was told what it means to be a man!" he howls. "Good times, bad times." Then a split second of pregnant silence is superseded by a shattering burst of notes, like machine-gun fire, from Page's guitar. Bonham's right foot dances on the bass drum pedal with a dexterity that equals the jazz greats he considered his heroes, drummers such as Buddy Rich and Gene Krupa. John Paul Jones' impish bass breaks momentarily hold Plant back from his vocal climax: "I don't care what the neighbours say, I'm gonna love you – each and every day!"

Although ultimately an inconclusive performance, this group composition, with its catchy refrain, was at one time considered worthy of release as a single.

For this opening cut, Page used a Fender Telecaster guitar put through a Leslie Speaker cabinet, normally used with the Hammond organ, which helped attain a distinctive swirling tonal effect. For the rest of the time he used a minuscule amplifier with a 12-inch speaker, which belied the enormous power he seemed to generate throughout the sessions. The tune was played on early gigs but later deleted from the 1970 medley built around 'Communication Breakdown'.

ABOVE: The airship *Hindenburg* crashing in flames at Lakehurst, New Jersey, US in 1937 provided a controversial and striking cover image for *Led Zeppelin I*.

LEFT: The band play loud at the packed Gladsaxe Teen Club, Copenhagen, 7 September 1968.

OPPOSITE: It was a historic night as Zeppelin performed at the Boston Tea Party, Massachusetts, 23 January 1969.

BABE I'M GONNA LEAVE YOU

When Plant first visited Page at his house by the Thames, during the summer of 1968, they sat playing albums by their favourite artists to gauge each other's musical tastes. They listened to everyone from Elvis Presley to Muddy Waters and Joan Baez.

'Babe I'm Gonna Leave You' was a Baez album cut that particularly appealed to Page, who had long been interested in folk music of all kinds. He'd played this behind Marianne Faithfull during his session days and it was one of the first numbers that Page suggested might be worth covering.

Page's arrangement of the piece turned into a dynamic performance that quickly established the band's commitment to using both electric and acoustic modes. The result was certainly a far cry from heavy metal. It turned into a beautifully crafted performance filled with shifting moods and intriguing effects.

Launched by a simple guitar introduction, Plant breathes "Baby, baby, I'm gonna leave you" – a gentle restraint that is suddenly replaced by a voice full of anger and menace, as the band roars behind him to create a dramatic re-enactment of the theme. The mixture of power and control shown here is remarkable. As Plant's voice bids a discreet farewell in the final bars, it is a chastening thought that so little rock music has since attained anything like the standards of sophistication set here.

"It has a very dramatic quality," says Page, who is still very proud of this arrangement. Although the band believed 'Babe I'm Gonna Leave You' was a traditional song (which had also been recorded by Quicksilver Messenger Service), they later discovered that it had been written by composer Anne Bredon, a 60s folk singer, who was later given an appropriate credit on the *Remasters* set of Zeppelin albums.

YOU SHOOK ME

Originally composed by blues man Willie Dixon, this song had also been covered by Jeff Beck on his 1969 album *Truth*. This produced some complaints from the Beck camp in the light of Zeppelin's later success. In the event, 'You Shook Me' was a real Zep blockbuster, on which Plant gives a bravura performance.

The blues was a kind of open house in the UK at the time, when bands like John Mayall's Blues Breakers and Stan Webb's Chicken Shack were all attempting to re-create black American music – with, it has to be said, far less exciting and satisfying results. Zeppelin's confident treatment of the source material ran rings around their competitors.

This track is a real low-down dirty blues in which Plant's harmonica practically spits out his feelings. The use of a glissando in which voice and guitar slide in sexy unison is a masterstroke, and you can hear a burst of

laughter behind Plant's vocals, which shows how much everyone in the studio was obviously enjoying themselves. John Paul Jones excels with double-tracked solos on electric piano and organ which, in the words of Ian Dury, are very funky indeed. Plant's extended harmonica solo is interrupted by an outburst of tom tom fury from the drummer, then Page begins a solo that is illuminated by a heart-stopping guitar break, creating one of the most celebrated moments in Zeppelin lore.

Another great call-and-response sequence follows when the vocalist and guitarist embark on a kind of pitched battle, before Bonham brings everyone safely back down to earth with a few well-chosen claps of bass drum thunder. Heavily featured on their early tours, the number was eventually elbowed aside as more original works dominated the band's live set.

DAZED AND CONFUSED

'Dazed and Confused' was the performance that convinced first-time listeners that here was a band in the throes of making rock history. Most can remember where they were and what they were doing the first time they became conscious of those subtle, doom-laden notes.

Conceived by Page, the basis of this arrangement had first been performed by the Yardbirds. The piece had its origins in an acoustic tune, 'I'm Confused', performed in the 60s by New York folk singer Jake Holmes. Page is believed to have heard him perform it on a visit to New York.

Led Zeppelin's treatment had new lyrics and developed a life and personality of its own. The tune became a staple of live concerts and was frequently extended into a 40-minute showcase, during which Page played his guitar with a violin bow. He later revealed that the idea had come from a fellow musician, during one of his many pre-Zeppelin recording sessions. "I just wanted the guitar to sound different," he explains.

The idea was suggested to him, in fact, by actor David McCallum's father, a session violinist. Page thought it would be difficult because the violin had a specially arched neck while the guitar neck was flat. But in Page's hands the bow became a magical device. He used the technique with the Yardbirds, Led Zeppelin and his 1985 band the Firm.

'Dazed and Confused' is a real mood maker in which the use of eerie silences, the funereal walking bass and spine-tingling notes create an unforgettable atmosphere. Howls greet Plant's angry tale of woe as the band engage in a weird four-way conversation. Bonham impatiently speeds up the tempo, while Page's guitar spatters forth an appropriately confused barrage of notes. Then the return to a slower tempo is both haunting and menacing. This closes the first side of a vinyl album that packs in more brilliant ideas than most bands dream up in their entire lifetime.

YOUR TIME IS GONNA COME

Credited to Page and John Paul Jones, this gave Jones a chance to show off his abilities on the church organ, while Page made use of a Fender pedal steel guitar. Played on the band's early dates in Scandinavia, the song was later dropped from the show.

Jones uses bass pedals on the organ to fill out the sound, until Plant begins to protest at the woeful lack of courtesy shown by the modern girl. "Lying, cheating, hurting, that's all you ever seem to do," he grumbles. But although she drives him insane, one day her time is gonna come and she'll find him gone. The pedal steel that Page uses is slightly out of tune, which adds to the strangely plaintive air that persists until Bonham's sternly bashing drums bring a sense of direction to the final chorus. Part of this song was sometimes used on the band's 'Whole Lotta Love' medley.

BLACK MOUNTAIN SIDE

Although only two minutes long, this little gem epitomizes the tasteful, intelligent approach adopted by Page while wearing his two hats as producer and guitarist. It was considered quite daring to introduce an "instrumental'" into the middle of an album intent on establishing a new band, and to exclude key members, including the highly prized lead vocalist. But why not? The interlude afforded by this showcase for Page's finger-picking acoustic guitar work only makes the subsequent return to all four cylinders the more effective. The piece actually starts well before the end of 'Your Time is Gonna Come', and once again it is one of those little unexpected engineering touches that still delights and intrigues the first-time listener.

Page's repeated figure – played on a Gibson acoustic guitar – sets up a drone matched by the sensuous tabla drums played by Viram Jasani, a respected Indian musician who continues to work and broadcast in Britain. This piece was influenced by the Yardbirds' 'White Summer', which Page recorded with them. Others attribute it to the Bert Jansch tune 'Black Water Side'. Page often played it during Zeppelin tours, as a showpiece in a medley with 'White Summer', when he sat down on a stool and attempted to quieten the audience down to listen. It was partly incorporated in performances with the Firm and his subsequent band.

During the performance on the album he employed what he dubbed a special 'CIA tuning', meaning it contained Celtic, Indian and Arabic influences. This DADGAD tuning would also be employed on 'Kashmir' from *Physical Graffiti* and elements of this tune would later be heard on the Firm's 'Midnight Moonlight'.

OPPOSITE: Head and shoulders above the rest – a vertiginous view of Zeppelin comprising (clockwise from the top) Jimmy Page, Robert Plant, John Paul Jones and John Bonham.

COMMUNICATION BREAKDOWN

"Communication Breakdown, baby!" Plant screams, tossing back his mane of golden hair and kicking his legs with more energy than a thousand Olympic athletes, became an enduring image of the 1970s. "What fun!" as Plant would say.

Hard on the heels of 'Black Mountain Side', this thunderous workout quickly became one of the most popular Zeppelin concert riffs, even though it was, in retrospect, technically the least interesting performance on the album. It was first heard during their early tour dates in Scandinavia during late 1968.

Released as a single in the US in March 1969, coupled with 'Good Times Bad Times', it became something of an anthem, perhaps only rivalled by 'Whole Lotta Love' from *Led Zeppelin II*.

Taken at breakneck speed, this early example of a Plant-Page composition is pure rock and roll, built around a hammering guitar riff, delivered by Page in the spirit of Eddie Cochran. It was hard work to play, but the song remained in the band's set for many years, either as a show opener or as a special encore. There were periods when it was dropped in favour of new material.

Essentially it's a piece of high spirits designed to free audiences from conformity. Plant's lyrics sum up the teenage angst of the tongue-tied and frustrated. "Suck it!" he yells just before a ferocious guitar solo.

I CAN'T QUIT YOU BABY

An outstanding performance, this interpretation of a Willie Dixon tune was one of the highlights of the album, and of many a Zeppelin show. A simple blues, it made most other attempts by British and young American bands to interpret the black idiom sound almost comical.

But it was more than a bash through a 12-bar. It was a loving exploration of a theme, with all its attendant nuances. Page excels as he answers Plant's initial vocal remarks with unpredictable guitar mutterings that leave spaces interspersed with Les Paul-ish blips, splutters and then beautifully constructed phrases.

This contrast between perfection and imperfection is daring and effective. It's the stuff of living music that no machine could emulate, and is what gives these Zeppelin recordings their unique quality. John Bonham's bass drum snaps like a jack hammer, but he plays the merest touch on his Ludwig metal snare drum, showing that he was also capable of restraint and good taste.

HOW MANY MORE TIMES

"How many more times!" yelled fans at Bath Festival when the band played there in 1969. To the uninitiated it seemed as though the audience were complaining. In fact they'd already turned on to Led Zeppelin and were desperate to hear the final explosive item from the album.

It swings into action with another irresistible walking bass line from John Paul Jones that sweeps everything before it, like the roar of a jumbo jet's engines at cruising speed. But beyond the riffs, this piece develops into an extraordinary farrago of freak-outs, in which elements of ideas culled from past Yardbirds and Band of Joy sessions were combined into one devastating arrangement.

The use of a bolero rhythm pushes the piece towards a frantic climax, followed by Bonham's tom toms answering eerie groans from the guitar. Page had produced Jeff Beck's 'Beck's Bolero' earlier, but this idea was only part of a much broader spectrum. Plant's finest vocal moments come when he develops the chant of "Oh Rosie, steal away now" over a New Orleans-style snare drum rhythm, and slots in more vocalist's in-jokes, including a quotation from 'The Hunter'. The engineer uses his knobs to pan the sound for a crash, bang and wallop finale to this spontaneous eight-minute studio extravaganza.

OPPOSITE: Jimmy Page communing with the rock spirits: "Ours is the folk music of the technological age. The group is only as good as its audience."

RIGHT: Multiple exposures of Page, Plant, Bonham and Jones captured their high spirits and joy at success during 1969, the first full year of Zeppelin conquest.

Page and plant performing on stage at the height of their pomp, in the mid-1970s. Photo by Neal Preston.

LED ZEPPELIN II ▶ (1969)

'Whole Lotta Love' was the guitar riff that sparked massive sales for *Led Zeppelin II*. But melodic songs like 'Ramble On' and 'Thank You' took the band in exciting new directions that were to shape their iconic sound and vision forever.

LED ZEPPELIN II

The album sleeve for *Led Zeppelin I* depicted the *Hindenburg* in flames at Lakehurst, New Jersey, in 1937. Designed by George Hardie and based on a photo chosen by Page, it had so striking an impact that elements were retained for the follow-up. For *Led Zeppelin II*, the sleeve was a drab brown, featuring a photograph of a group of pilots that had the band members' heads superimposed.

The tracks had been assembled in odd moments on their 1969 US tours. Recording sessions were set up in Los Angeles, New York and London. Mixing took place at A&R Studios in New York under engineer Eddie Kramer, who had worked on the *Electric Ladyland* album with Jimi Hendrix.

Page would later describe putting the album together as "quite insane"; he and Plant had to write in hotel rooms and backstage. However, when it was released in America on 22 October 1969, even the band's hard-bitten attorney Steve Weiss described it as "a masterpiece". Page confessed he had "lost confidence in it" because he had grown over-familiar with the material amid all the overdubbing in different locations. Whatever the difficulties, their hard rock ethos was firmly established and provided just what their army of fans wanted to hear. Advance orders were phenomenal, including half a million in the US, and during its first week it got to Number 15 in the *Billboard* chart, eventually getting to Number 1 in America and the UK. It sold three million copies in a matter of months.

'What is and What Should Never Be' was a Plant composition recorded at Olympic. He had contributed lyrics to the first album but had not

received a credit due to contractual problems. Here he sings in romantic mood: "And if I say to you tomorrow…". The slow tempo establishes the group's ability to span genres.

'The Lemon Song', recorded at the Mystic studio in Los Angeles, is a traditional blues that allows Plant to indulge in shameless teasing: "Squeeze me, baby, until the juice runs down my leg…" A double-tempo section gives Page a chance to solo with blistering speed before Jones and Bonham slow things down. Plant wraps it up with some final squeals of delight before a high-speed finale.

'Thank You', recorded at Morgan Studios in London and mixed in New York, is much more relaxed and tasteful, from the moment Plant makes his opening remarks: "If the sun refused to shine I would still be loving you …". Jones gets to shine, however, on his Hammond organ, always a subtle but integral part of the early Zeppelin sound.

'Heartbreaker', recorded and mixed at A&R Studios in New York, is a joint composing effort that features one of Page's most explosive guitar breaks. The song was often used as a set-opener on tour, although later relegated to part of a medley.

'Living Loving Maid (She's a Woman)' is surprisingly pop-like, its roots in the Merseybeat era. Page later revealed it was his least favourite track, but it remains a moment of calm amid the album's more violent outpourings.

'Ramble On' is very much a vehicle for Plant, whose lyrics seem inspired by *The Lord of the Rings*. Jones' bass lends sensitive support and the

drummer relinquishes his kit to play with hands on knees. The full band joins in as Robert sings, "I'm gonna ramble on around the world." The piece fades out under the control of engineer Kramer, who recorded it at Juggy Sound Studios in New York.

Bonham's expertise was utilized by Page to power up the band when needed, and he had plenty of energy in reserve. Increasingly long solos became a highlight of the band's every show as Bonham battered his drums with his bare hands until he drew blood. 'Moby Dick' was his showcase; the studio version, however, recorded in Los Angeles, lacked the spontaneity of onstage performances when he would be spurred on by cheering crowds.

'Bring It On Home' celebrates the traditional blues Plant grew to love when he first discovered the early bluesmen. The slow tempo and echoing harmonica reveal the influence of Sonny Boy Williamson, the mood changing abruptly as the rhythm section charges into action. This transforms the piece into a heavy rock interlude before Plant and the harmonica return to wrap up the song and the album.

PREVIOUS PAGES: Recording sessions had to fit in between concerts. Much laughter when Zeppelin finally started work on *Led Zeppelin II* on 23 May 1969 before the band's impending debut UK tour.

OPPOSITE: Jimmy sits in a recording studio during one of the sessions during the making of *Led Zeppelin II,* 29 May 1969.

ABOVE: Even during an acoustic number, Bonham hasn't lost his power. His bass drum is decorated with entwining circles, the symbol of strength that appears on the fourth album inner sleeve artwork.

"I don't think Jonesy's ever worked with anybody like me before, me not knowing any of the rudiments of music or anything like that, and not really desiring to learn them, but still hitting it off ... that's been amazing."

ROBERT PLANT

OPPOSITE: It's December 1968 and the new group poses in front of a temptingly luxurious Jaguar in a London street, for their first record company photo shoot.

ABOVE: Plant and tour manager Richard Cole discuss world domination aboard *The Starship*, 1973.

ALBUM TRACKS

Love permeated the lyrics, the mood of the band and the reaction of their worldwide fans when *Led Zeppelin II* hit the charts in 1969. Hailed as "a masterpiece", this was Zeppelin bringing it on home.

WHOLE LOTTA LOVE

Most bands would kill to have an anthem as strident, confident and effective as Zeppelin's most famous *cri de coeur*. Perhaps it is not so much a cry from the heart as a yell from the pit of the stomach. Certainly it caused a sensation on first hearing and swiftly became the band's most in-demand show buster, remaining a theme instantly associated with their memory.

Page's celebrated opening riff, both menacing and combative, spurred on by the combined forces of Bonham and Jones, gave Plant a platform for his spectacular whoop. Matching Joe Cocker's roar at the end of 'With a Little Help from My Friends', Plant's prolonged outburst of "Woman you need l-o-o-o-v-e" was forceful enough to reach the moon.

'Whole Lotta Love' was recorded at Olympic Studios under the auspices of engineer George Chkiantz and later mixed in New York by Page and Eddie Kramer. The main theme is contrasted by a lengthy improvised section. In edited form it was released as a single in the US, backed with 'Living Loving Maid'. It shot to Number 4 in December 1969 and spent 13 weeks in the *Billboard* chart; the song was also Number 1 in Germany and Belgium.

It seemed destined to be a big hit in Britain too, and no doubt would have been but for one unexpected glitch: Peter Grant didn't want Led Zeppelin to release any singles in the UK. Atlantic Records in London were stunned. When they pressed up copies and tried to put them out, Grant stopped them, believing releasing singles would only harm album sales. In this particular instance, his instincts were proved right.

The object of all this furore opens with a faint laugh and a yell of "Baby I'm not foolin' … I'm gonna give you my love!" Each one of Plant's exultant statements is greeted by a glissando from the guitar and is set against a sonorous jungle rhythm. Page explained later that the descending groan on his guitar was produced by judicious use of a metal slide on the strings and some backwards tape echo.

After some minutes of relentless thunder, the mists of sound part to reveal a new soundscape dominated by an eerie tinkling of temple bells. This is produced by Bonham's prudent use of drum sticks on the centre of his cymbals, while his hi-hat (that foot-operated mechanical device which keeps time) stomps out an insistent echoing beat that is full of foreboding. A spooky interlude develops that is more truly psychedelic than anything to be found on Pink Floyd's albums.

"Love!" gasps Plant as Bonham breaks in with a battering assault on his snare drum. Page snaps back into consciousness, his guitar steaming into a monster riff …

"L-O-O-O-O-V-E!" Boom, crash, pow – the spell is broken.

There never was a real ending to 'Whole Lotta Love' and maybe it should have finished a chorus earlier than the final fade-out. Nevertheless, it is a brilliantly evocative piece of work that is more than just a template for the heavy metal that followed in its wake. The freak-out section was worked up in the studio during a free-form engineering session by Page and Eddie Kramer. Explained Kramer: "It was a combination of Page and myself twiddling every knob known to man."

'Whole Lotta Love' was later recorded by Plant's old mate Alexis Korner (the father of British blues), with his big band outfit known as CCS. It was part of a rock and roll medley and the 'Whole Lotta Love' section was used for many years as the signature tune of BBC TV's *Top of the Pops*. Interestingly CCS also recorded a respectable version of Page's 'Black Dog' on their 1972 album. It seemed like the session men were paying tribute to one of their old studio colleagues.

Years later, it was suggested there were some similarities between this Zeppelin master work and the Willie Dixon composition 'You Need Love'. The band were sued in 1985, when Dixon's daughter noticed a resemblance. Willie said he first heard the Zeppelin tune in 1983, many years after the band's record had been released.

Dixon (born 1 July 1915, in Vicksburg, Mississippi) was the composer of such blues standards as 'Hoochie Coochie Man', 'Wang Dang Doodle', 'My Babe', 'Spoonful', 'You Can't Judge a Book by the Cover' and 'The Red Rooster'. All of these became part of the language of rock and provided the staple diet of many of the revivalist British blues bands of the 1960s, notably the Rolling Stones and, of course, all the groups for which Page and Plant had played. Many of Dixon's songs were originally recorded by Muddy Waters, including 'You Need Love' (1962).

Dixon (who died in 1992) was one of the band's heroes, and after his case with Zeppelin was settled out of court, he used the proceeds to help others. He set up the Blues Heaven Foundation to promote awareness of the blues and buy young musicians instruments at schools in Mississippi.

Although Zeppelin have sometimes been criticized for not always fully crediting their use of America's musical heritage, their records furthered the cause of the blues by introducing blues and traditional themes to new audiences. In so doing they promoted many artists who might otherwise have languished in obscurity. Certainly Zeppelin's productions bore little resemblance to the small band recordings made by the pioneers in the 1940s and 1950s.

'Whole Lotta Love' became an integral part of Zeppelin's set, provided a big finale and was regularly included in their rock and roll medley. It was played at such historic latterday events as their 1979 Knebworth concerts, the Live Aid reunion on 13 July 1985 and at the Atlantic Records' 40th Birthday Concert, New York in 1988.

In 2004, the song was ranked number 75 on *Rolling Stone* magazine's definitive list of the 500 Greatest Songs of All Time. Most recently, in 2014, – proof of the song's undeniable longevity – listeners to BBC Radio 2 voted the track as the greatest guitar riff of all time.

OPPOSITE, TOP: *Led Zeppelin II*, the all-important second album recorded whenever the band could fit in studio time. Jimmy Page: "It took such a long time to make, it was quite insane really."

OPPOSITE, BOTTOM: Jimmy uses his bow on his Gibson, Robert addresses the audience, 1972.

RIGHT: Robert jokes with John Paul Jones backstage at Kezar Stadium, San Francisco on 2 June 1973 when 50,000 fans devoured a two-and-a-half-hour show.

WHAT IS AND WHAT SHOULD NEVER BE

Recorded with George Chkiantz at Olympic Studios, Barnes, and mixed at A&R in New York, this was one of Plant's first compositions to be aired by the band. "And if I sing to you tomorrow" is his opening line as he promises to take a cherished companion for a walk to a castle. Plant's romantic streak and love of myths and legends provided a perfect contrast to the hot-blooded stallion image of the lusty blues shouter. It showed a gentler, more intellectual side to his nature. Even so, the song retains a strong rock section during which Plant returns to a few of his trademark "baby, baby" yelps.

Page plays a solo that owes something to Les Paul, the daddy of electric guitar. Phasing on the vocals, achieved by the art of engineering, gives a shimmering effect, while the guitars pan disturbingly from the left- to right-hand channels. With drums absent from this touching scene, only a shimmering gong reminds us of the brooding presence of Bonham.

The song, taken at a relatively slow and measured pace, was first publicly performed at the Lyceum Ballroom, in the Strand, London on 12 October 1969. The event coincided with the anniversary of a real Zeppelin attack by German air forces who had bombed the building in 1915.

THE LEMON SONG

So should we care about "influences"? The blues is an international language, utilized by countless bands and artists over 50 years of recording and live performance. It would be difficult now to trace who first sang "I woke up this morning" and as for "Squeeze me baby, until the juice runs down my leg" … well similar sentiments can be heard on an Indian pop song complete with sitars, which contains the line "leaky, leaky, down my leg".

And yet Led Zeppelin were constantly being sniped at by nit-pickers and probed by musicologists. The band were careless in crediting their sources of inspiration, but if this album had sold fewer copies, nobody would have noticed references to Howlin' Wolf's 'Killing Floor' during 'The Lemon Song'. Ever the blues enthusiast, Plant sings this line at one point. Although first listed as a band composition, later pressings credited Chester Burnett (Howlin' Wolf) as the true composer after representations by the publishers.

The average record buyer was happy simply to be swept along with the excitement created by this shameless outburst. Recorded at Mystic, Los Angeles, it was notable for the "real" echo the studio produced. There is something of the Yardbirds about the way 'The Lemon Song' revels in guttural guitar lines. When it lunges into a double-tempo section, Page solos at full tilt over three choruses of blistering improvisation. He's still wailing when the band begin to slow down in perfect synchronization; a difficult feat for any band, but expertly done by Bonham and Jones. "Take it down a bit," instructs Plant as he launches into a blues rap.

"The way you squeeze my lemon, I'm gonna fall right off the bed," squeals Plant. To a generation of prudes unused to such sexual innuendo, it all seemed very shocking, and doubtless caused many raised eyebrows in the offices of British radio producers. A spunky dialogue between guitar and vocals follows, then a swift return to frantic tempo.

THANK YOU

One of the most remarkable aspects of Zeppelin's performance on this particular track is not so much what they play, but what they leave out. For a band damned for its supposed excesses, 'Thank You' shows both good taste and the exercise of restraint. It is also one of the best vocal performances by Plant thus far into Zeppelin's recorded career. From his opening statement, "If the sun refused to shine I would still be loving you", this outbreak of deep-rooted sincerity continues to permeate a ballad enhanced by John Paul Jones' mellifluous Hammond-organ tones. Acoustic guitar floats over a wandering bass guitar line and there is a distinct West Coast cool about the vocal harmonies.

With audiences hyped up to expect maximum rock from their favourite band, it took a while for them to accept such soft, romantic material. But for those ready to listen, here was evidence of the band's expanding horizons. "If the mountains crumble to the sea – there would still be you and me," breathes Plant as a church organ provides a delicate pedal figure that fades away … then returns for a brief reprise. Zeppelin could be justly proud of what is virtually an orchestral arrangement which features one of Page's finest acoustic guitar solos.

Dedicated to Plant's wife, 'Thank You' marked the singer's move towards greater involvement in lyric writing. It was recorded at Morgan Studios, London, with engineer Andy Johns, and later mixed in New York by Eddie Kramer. Featured on stage from late 1969 onwards, it was heard during the January 1970 British tour, when it became something of a keyboard showcase for John Paul Jones. Although still popular in the early 1970s, it was eventually dropped from the act.

HEARTBREAKER

Side 2 of the original vinyl album proved rather uneven after the sustained brilliance of the first four tracks. 'Heartbreaker', along with 'Ramble On', was certainly among the highlights. Recorded and mixed at A&R Studios, New York, this featured one of Page's most memorable outbursts. More than just a "guitar break", it was a sonic attack that has stayed sharply defined in the memory of fans. The song begins with a repeated figure that sounds oddly like "Darn, darn, darn, a da-darn" – a savagely intense set-up for Plant's grand entrance. "Hey fellows have you heard the news!" he announces. It's time to head for the hills to avoid one of these dangerous wenches who break the hearts of men and boys with their flirtatious ways.

'Heartbreaker' shows Zeppelin applying great skill to the arrangement. Plant is never drowned out. When it's time for him to sing, apart from a rumbling bass and guitar accompaniment, he is allowed free rein.

The guitar punctuates Plant's vocal lines, then comes one of those nail-biting, cliff-hanging moments when Led Zeppelin stops dead in its tracks. Page sounds an echoing warning blast on his guitar. At live shows, this was invariably the signal for an outburst of expectant cheering from the fans. Harsh, angry, spluttering, furious, the notes cascade from his axe. Drums and bass return as Page solos at full speed. Climax is piled upon climax until another abrupt halt, and Plant returns to continue his diatribe.

"You abused my love a thousand times!" he protests. "So go away Heartbreaker!" The song was sometimes used to open the live set, along with 'Immigrant Song'. Later it was employed as part of a medley of Zeppelin standards. Live, Page expanded the guitar solo and employed bits of other tunes including 'Greensleeves', and Bach's 'Bourée in C minor' which is not nearly as "Bourée" as it sounds.

LIVIN' LOVIN' MAID (SHE'S JUST A WOMAN)

Zeppelin playing a radio-friendly pop song? Well this is the closest they ever got to that during their career. It's got a real 60s feel and might have been designed for the Merseybeats.

Page, asked what were his favourites, once said that it would be easier to cite his least favourite track: 'Living Loving Maid'. Maybe it's the way the band chorus "DOWN!" as Plant sings "You'd better lay your money down!" Either way Page wasn't keen, but it is still a catchy, attractive melody with some fine country guitar work.

Released on the B-side of 'Whole Lotta Love' in the US it later became an A-side in its own right, when it managed to reach Number 65 in the US *Billboard* chart after extensive radio plays. The song about a groupie "with the purple umbrella and the fifty cent hat" was rarely played live. Plant sang the first line after the band had finished playing 'Heartbreaker' at a gig in Hamburg, Germany in March 1970, and later performed it during his own band's Manic Nirvana tour of 1990.

LEFT: The band in a relaxed state of mind, 1971. *"Led Zeppelin II* was very virile," Robert remembers. "That was the album that was going to dictate whether or not we had the staying power and capacity to stimulate."

"Leaves are falling all around – time I was on my way!" More quality writing from Plant emerges on this track, full of phrases like: "I smell the rain and with it pain." A simple enough rhyme, but strangely telling.

Plant's lyrical flowering was inspired by an acquaintance with the works of JRR Tolkien, author of the celebrated trilogy *The Lord of the Rings*, featuring tales of elves, dwarves and magic. Many a pop person came under Tolkien's spell in the early 1970s, including the dear, departed Marc Bolan. Not everyone was enamoured of his writings, however. Tolkien's friend and fellow author CS Lewis was once heard to complain, "Not another fucking elf".

Even so there may well be elvish influences here. Certainly there are magical touches from John Paul Jones' nifty bass guitar, and John Bonham forgoes his trusty Ludwig kit to patter away on his knees with pixie-like pazzazz. When he brings on the drums, he employs the energy that might be expected from one of those Middle Earth creatures, bent on battle with Sauron the Dark Lord.

Bass and guitar engage in a subtle dialogue as Plant embarks on his briskly paced narrative. "I'm gonna ramble on around the world," he insists. Ever the wanderer, Plant once described how a man could take a walk along a street and then turn either left or right and completely change his future life. Tempting. After a multi-track splurge of vocals, there is a very long fade-out, best heard on headphones. Recorded with Eddie Kramer in 1969 at Juggy Sound Studios in New York, 'Ramble On' was never performed live.

"I don't consider that I'm particularly influenced by anyone or anything. But when I started playing, I was influenced by early soul. It was just that feel, that sound."

JOHN BONHAM

MOBY DICK

Led Zeppelin were singularly fortunate in their choice of drummer. John Bonham had gusto and an indomitable spirit. He always wanted to put his own stamp on the drums in a way that matched his no-nonsense personality. However, right from his days with Midlands outfits like the Band of Joy, there were grumbles about his bombastic approach and the sheer volume of his playing. "I got black-listed and barred from all the clubs in Birmingham," he once told me. "I was so keen to play, I'd play for nothing. But I played the way I wanted. 'You're too loud,' they used to say."

Bonham could be a surprisingly shy and modest man. He was always very conscious of his need to deliver the kind of power Zeppelin demanded. His was the most physical role, and yet his drumming was not all about brute strength. He had perfect control of his snare drum, could utilize cymbals and gongs to create different tones and had quite a jazzman's feel for syncopation and big-band-style phrasing.

His foot control over the bass drum pedal was remarkable and he produced a huge sound on a small kit. He was a carpenter and builder by trade, yet admitted: "Drumming was the only thing I was ever good at."

As a teenager he was a bit of a Teddy Boy (Britain's fashion-conscious rockers of the 50s), and his first band, Terry Webb and the Spiders, wore purple jackets and bootlace ties.

Bonham quickly developed his style and, although his influences included Carmine Appice of Vanilla Fudge, Ginger Baker and, to an extent, Buddy Rich, there is absolutely no mistaking his own sound. Bonham's extended concert solos were always a pleasure to behold, so it was a great shame that 'Moby Dick', his showcase on *Led Zeppelin II*, was a let-down.

He needed the adrenaline created by the band to push him into action, and this solo sounds suspiciously as if it was recorded in isolation and then dropped into the otherwise encouraging riff that Page sets up for him. Bonham stops before he really gets started, and launches into a hand drum solo on the snare drum and tom toms. This sort of thing often drew blood on stage and was visually very exciting. In the studio it sounded flat. Even when he switched to sticks, the sound was dead and lacking in ambience.

Recording took place at Mirror Sound, Los Angeles, where Bonham built up a respectable roar with a crescendo of triplets, then relaxed only when Page returned for the final bars. An edited version of his original solo, it should have been entirely re-recorded.

On the road Bonham developed 'Moby Dick' into a 20-minute extravaganza, sometimes utilizing kettle drums. The crowds cheered, the critics made notes and the band disappeared for a quick fag and a sandwich. Plant would re-emerge just as Bonham was taking his bow, and present the exhausted, blood-and-sweat-stained percussionist with a banana.

By the mid-70s Bonham adopted the 'Out on the Tiles' theme to replace his well worn 'Moby Dick'. Plant once observed: "Bonzo always said he was the greatest drummer in the world. When we heard him play, we knew he was!"

BRING IT ON HOME

When Robert Anthony Plant was a teenager, his greatest preoccupations were girls, football and music. Although his parents and teachers rather hoped he'd become a chartered accountant, music began to dominate his life and he became caught up in the great skiffle boom that swept Britain during the late 1950s. Learning to play harmonica, kazoo and the washboard, Plant was soon skipping lessons to form groups.

He was particularly attracted to deep country blues and listened to artists like Memphis Minnie, Bukka White and Skip James, also listening to Willie Dixon, Muddy Waters and Buddy Guy. Plant first heard records by the legendary Robert Johnson when he was 15, and was thrilled by the emotion-packed Johnson style, in which vocal lines are alternated with the guitar. It would leave a lasting impression on the young British singer whose own powerful voice had begun to develop apace.

He gained his first experience singing at the Seven Stars Blues club in Stourbridge, Worcestershire, where he played harmonica with the Delta Blues Band. His father, a civil engineer, used to drop him off at the club where he'd happily roar away on 'Got My Mojo Working' to the local, somewhat earnest, blues enthusiasts. But it was the traditional country blues that Plant re-created on 'Bring It On Home'. The slow drag tempo and echoing harmonica evokes a land much deeper south

than Stourbridge. Plant even adopts a kind of toothless vocal style set to an authentic guitar accompaniment.

This plaintive interlude is rudely interrupted by the full Zeppelin mob bursting in through the studio doors. Together they conspire to produce a great heavy rock riff that is full of mystery and menace. Then, having sated their musical appetite, the band disassembles down to Plant and Page once more. As the harmonica fades to a squeak, you can almost imagine the teenaged Plant rushing to meet his dad for a lift home from the club.

Scholars now claim the piece was influenced by Sonny Boy Williamson's version of 'Bring It On Home'. Although played live quite extensively in the early days of the band, when Page and Bonham indulged in a drums and guitar duel, it was later used as an encore or incorporated into a link between 'Celebration Day' and 'Black Dog'. Whatever the origins, 'Bring It On Home' gave a timely reminder of the inescapable links between rock and the blues.

Sonny Boy Williamson toured with the Yardbirds in the early 60s, long before Jimmy joined the band.

BELOW "We will shortly be landing …" Ignoring all announcements Bonham, Plant and Jones grab some well-deserved sleep on a flight during their second US tour in May 1969.

JOHN PAUL JONES

Mysterious "walking bass" lines on 'Dazed And Confused', funky keyboard riffs on 'Trampled Underfoot' and melodious recorders on 'Stairway to Heaven' are all memorable moments from JPJ's vital contribution to Zeppelin's oeuvre.

JOHN PAUL JONES

The quiet man of the group, John Paul Jones brought a classical grandeur and elegance to their work. Although Plant and Bonham were "new boys" when they joined, "JPJ" knew Jimmy Page well before the group's formation, having played with him on many sessions.

He was born John Baldwin in Sidcup, Kent, on 3 January 1946. Father Joe, a pianist and arranger, had worked with many top British dance bands, and John taught himself piano from the age of six. "I was a choirmaster and organist at our local church at the age of 14," he recalled. "That was how I earned the money to pay for my first bass guitar."

John went to boarding school in Blackheath aged five, because his parents were travelling the world in a musical variety act. He then spent three years at Eltham Green comprehensive school, but didn't do too well in his exams, "mainly because I was out playing in bands at American Air Force bases".

As a teenager John quickly absorbed a wide range of popular music influences. He loved the blues of Big Bill Broonzy as much as Rachmaninoff and was soon immersed in the soul and R&B hits of the Sixties. One of the tracks that inspired him to take up bass guitar was 'You Can't Sit Down' by the Phil Upchurch Combo.

His first regular group, at 15, while still doing his O-levels, was the Deltas, fronted by guitarist Pete Gage, who later worked with Elkie Brooks in Vinegar Joe. Recalled John: "I also played with my dad in a trio at weddings. We did waltzes and quicksteps and a bit of jazz. It was useful experience which I used throughout my session career and ever since. My father was a really good pianist and as I felt I'd never been as good as him, I took up the organ. I liked the way the notes sustained."

He aspired to go to the Royal College of Music, but instead headed for Soho's Archer Street, a gathering-place for musicians seeking work. He met Jet Harris, formerly of the Shadows, and in 1962 joined Jet and Tony, featuring Harris on guitar and Tony Meehan on drums. They'd had a hit with 'Diamonds' and John, now 17, toured with them for 18 months. In 1963 he met Peter Grant, then driving a van for well-known rock and roller Gene Vincent.

After Jet and Tony, John began doing sessions at Decca, thanks to Meehan's help. Between 1964 and 1968 he recorded with artists including Lulu, Cat Stevens, Shirley Bassey, the Rolling Stones, Rod Stewart, Herman's Hermits, Cliff Richard, Paul and Barry Ryan, Kathy Kirby and Dave Berry; in April 1964 he released a single, an instrumental called 'A Foggy Day in Vietnam'. John was a backing musician on BBC radio's Saturday Club and worked with Dusty Springfield, supporting her at London's Talk of the Town and arranging tracks on her album *Definitely Dusty*. As an arranger and bass player he worked on Donovan's 'Sunshine Superman' and came to the attention of producer Mickie Most, eventually becoming his musical director. Most shared an Oxford Street office with Grant, then managing the New Vaudeville Band and the Yardbirds, and he and John met again.

John Baldwin became John Paul Jones at the suggestion of Andrew Loog Oldham, the Stones' manager, who saw it on a film poster. Although he now had a stage name there was little opportunity to appear in public, as he spent so many hours in the studio. He was earning good money, but session work six days a week was burning him out. Then his wife read in *Disc* magazine that Page, whom Jones knew from sessions with Donovan and the Yardbirds, was forming a group, and suggested John give him a call. John asked Grant to put him in touch and before long Jones was rehearsing with the New Yardbirds.

When Jones and Page first got together with Bonham and Plant, there was instant chemistry. "We went to a small room in Lisle Street, Soho. We set the amps up and Jimmy said, 'Do you know "Train Kept A-Rollin'" by the Yardbirds?' I didn't, but was told it was a 12-bar blues with a riff in G. That was the first thing we ever played. It gelled immediately."

Before recording Led Zeppelin the band was called in to provide backing tracks for PJ Proby's album *Three Week Hero*. Jones was booked as arranger and thought it would be a useful source of income for the new group. Proby's album was released in 1969. Jones: "We had Robert on tambourine and that was the first thing we ever did. Then when we recorded Led Zeppelin it was pretty much a recording of our first show. The sound and performance was fantastic. One of the joys of being in the band was you could do anything you liked. It worked and it was so pleasurable. We kept on experimenting and that's why all the Zeppelin albums have a different feel. And it was a really happy band. Everybody thought we were prima donnas, yet there wasn't an ounce of attitude. Page and I had seen it all before and we just didn't want to make any mistakes."

While John was the most laid-back band member ("I'm the boring one," he once remarked), he enjoyed himself on the road just as much. He was described by those working for the band as the wisest and most discreet, but even Jonesy found the tours exhausting and missed his family, to the extent that he considered quitting in 1973. Peter Grant talked him round. Most of the time he loved Led Zeppelin ("You get to the point where you enjoy playing so much you just don't want to come off stage") and he was still cracking wise onstage, and at the eagerly anticipated press conferences, when they re-formed in 2007 for their farewell gig at London's O2 Arena and again in 2012, for the release of that concert's live DVD, *Celebration Day*.

PREVIOUS PAGES: John Paul Jones on stage in Copenhagen, Denmark, in February 1970.
OPPOSITE: Multi-instrumentalist, arranger and John Bonham's partner in rock's greatest rhythm section, John Paul was just as happy plucking a mandolin or bass, as playing a keyboard. Pictured here in 1981.

OPPOSITE: A press advertising poster, featuring the iconic Zeppelin, for a concert in Birmingham Town Hall, 7 January 1970. Dudley-born, and local hero, John Bonham, performed a ten-minute drum solo during "Moby Dick".

ABOVE, CLOCKWISE FROM TOP-LEFT:

A ticket for the New York premiere of *The Song Remains The Same* at Cinema I, 20 October 1976. For the screening, Cinema I was equipped with a quadrophonic sound system hired from Showco in Dallas.

A backstage pass from Led Zeppelin's "Electric Magic" show at Wembley Empire, 20 November, London, 1971. The gigs contained vaudeville circus acts and performing pigs dressed in Policeman's uniforms.

A ticket for for the *The Song Remains the Same* movie. The project's promotional material describes the film as a "personal and private tour of Led Zeppelin" and declares "for the first time the world has a front row seat on Led Zeppelin."

LED ZEPPELIN III ▶ (1970)

"It's all acoustic, folks," Robert announced, before the release of album number three. "It was time to step back, take stock, and not get lost in it all." The inventors of heavy metal, take their foot off the pedal ...

LED ZEPPELIN III

Led Zeppelin III was the first album made with time to sit back and contemplate. Plant had suggested going to Bron-Yr-Aur, a cottage he had visited as a child, to free their minds from the roar of amplifiers and jet engines. They hadn't planned to write, but were prepared to see what came out of musical evenings. Recalled Page: "As the nights wore on, the guitars came out and numbers were being written."

The music was more varied and relaxed than was usual for a band still dubbed "a heavy metal behemoth" by one US critic. Robert described how they wanted to "get more variety into the act. We're not in one particular bag."

Opener 'Immigrant Song', with lyrics by Plant, was a far cry from the supposed calm of Bron-Yr-Aur. "There's a voice at the beginning which somebody thought was a wailing guitar," Page said. "The hiss at the beginning is a tape build-up, and then John Bonham comes in. It's not actually tape hiss, it's more echo feedback." It was laid down at Olympic; and the "Immigrants" were Vikings seeking new lands, redolent of Robert's continuing interest in ancient legends. It was released as a US single in November 1970, backed with 'Hey Hey What Can I Do', and it made Number 16 in the *Billboard* chart.

'Friends' is another Plant composition. Page: "The idea was to get an Indian music effect with strings. The string players weren't Indian, however, and we had to make some on-the-spot changes. John Paul Jones wrote the incredible string arrangement for this and Robert shows off his great range, reaching incredibly high notes. A friend came into the studio during the recording and it was bloody loud and he had to leave." The theme has echoes of 'Mars' from Holst's *The Planets*.

'Celebration Day' consists mainly of Plant extemporizing over a frantically monotonous riff, a 90s rave 20 years ahead of schedule. Perhaps it was appropriate that the master tape nearly self-destructed. Page elucidated: "The tape got crinkled in the studio and wouldn't go through the heads, so the end got ruined, but it worked out all right by bringing the synthesizer down in pitch to the voice."

"Brushes? Nah. Hit 'em as hard as you can."

JOHN BONHAM

A highlight is the slow-paced yet stirring blues 'Since I've Been Loving You', on which the live band emerges from the fog of edits, synthesizers and strings. Originally destined for *Led Zeppelin II*, it was replaced by 'Whole Lotta Love'. Bonham's finely balanced drumbeats nail down the tempo, Jones' organ pedals providing the bass line.

'Loving You' has one of Page's finest solos, one he would reproduce often on stage, but he said modestly: "My guitar solo could have been better, but you know, you're never satisfied with a performance. There are those lucky musicians who can play it perfectly every time."

It was back to rock fury for 'Out on the Tiles', inspired by Bonham. When going out for an evening's entertainment he always chortled a tune that went: "I've had a pint of bitter and now I'm feeling better and I'm out on the tiles." Jimmy turned the theme into a riff and it became one of Zeppelin's more light-hearted pieces.

'Tangerine' commences with a false start, which Page left on as a tempo guide. It's this slightly ramshackle approach that gives the acoustic and the more ethnic tracks on the album their earthy appeal. Page plays pedal steel guitar and Plant supplies both lead vocals and harmonies.

'Bron-Yr-Aur Stomp' shows Zeppelin could be equally powerful in rock or acoustic mode. They sound like a supercharged skiffle group; Bonham clatters on spoons and castanets while Jones adds an acoustic five-string fretless bass. Jimmy claimed they used everything, including a kitchen sink, to get an authentic folk flavour. Written as a tribute to Robert's dog Strider, it had its roots in a piece called 'Jennings Farm Blues'.

The final number was a tribute to Liverpool-born folk legend Roy Harper. Jimmy and Robert first met him at the Bath Festival and selflessly devoted 'Hats Off to (Roy) Harper' to an artist they considered underrated. Roy later toured with the band as one of their opening acts. Jimmy said: "'Hats Off to (Roy) Harper' came about from a jam Robert and I had one night. Robert had been playing harmonica through the amp and then he used it to sing through. It's a sincere hats-off to Roy because he's a really talented bloke."

Led Zeppelin III was packaged with a unique revolving-wheel cover conceived by Page, based on an old gardening catalogue. While some critics thought the album diffuse and weak, Jimmy explained: "It was another side to us, but we'll never stop doing the heavy things because that comes out naturally when we play. The fourth album should be our best ... and if it isn't we should give up and retire with red faces."

PREVIOUS PAGES: Performing live onstage at the K.B. Hallen, Copenhagen, 28 February 1970.

OPPOSITE: The group's second headline billing at the Bath Festival of Blues, 28 June, 1970. The band completed the set, in front of 150,000 fans (ten times more than the previous year's attendance), with a rock medley including 'Long Tall Sally', 'Johnny B Goode', 'Rocky Road Blues', 'Say Mama' and 'That's Alright'.

ALBUM TRACKS

The songs recorded for *Led Zeppelin III* took the band into areas that changed them for ever. "At that time, at that age," Page claimed, "1970 was like the biggest blue sky I ever saw. We were really close to something ..."

IMMIGRANT SONG

One summer's day at Olympic Studios, Barnes, the author was fortunate enough to be in the studio when 'Immigrant Song' was being recorded, and witnessed Page and Bonham laying down the backing tracks. I have this abiding memory of Page slouching around the small, low-ceilinged room clutching his guitar, and Bonham crouched over his kit, hammering with an intensity that would brook no interruption for small talk or chit-chat. Once he got behind the drums, he was gone into another world where he concentrated on generating the heat and the beat to match the sizzling guitar riffs. Page was relaxed and casual as he set up his amp and adjusted the various settings.

I remember noticing how Page and his drummer seemed to be working out the main figure in tandem and how important was Bonham's contribution to shaping the final riff. It turned out to be one of the most powerful in the Zeppelin canon.

The declaiming lyrics reflected Plant's continuing interest in things Celtic and mystical, not to mention those marauding Vikings. Although the backing tracks were recorded earlier in the year, it was the June trip to Iceland that unleashed Plant's interest in "the land of the ice and snow". The piece begins with an attention-grabbing hiss, which stemmed from an echo unit feeding back. "Ah – ah!" yells Plant. "We drive our ships to new lands – Valhalla I am coming!" The shimmering guitar creates a surfing accompaniment that summons – for a brief instant – images of Dick Dale of *Pulp Fiction* fame, before it all comes to an abrupt stop and the Vikings crash out into the sea from whence they came.

Released as a single backed with 'Hey Hey What Can I Do', in November 1970, it got to Number 16 during a 13-week run in the US *Billboard* chart.

ABOVE: *Led Zeppelin III*'s album sleeve was designed by Zacron, an artist whom Page had met in 1963 whilst studying at Kingston College of Art. Page was not overly impressed with the finished product, "I thought it looked very teeny-bopperish," he said.

RIGHT: Robert Plant and Jimmy Page read up on their horoscopes at a Howard Johnson's hotel restaurant called the Barn during the band's second American tour, Boston, May 1969.

FRIENDS

After some mysterious studio conversations, which seemed to include the use of a familiar four-letter word, the players got down to business, bent on creating an intriguing *pot pourri*. Fierce strumming on the acoustic guitar, over a conga drum rhythm, introduces doomy overtones of Gustav Holst's 'Mars' from *The Planets Suite* – a particular Page favourite. It is also interspersed with a touch of Eastern delight and with the use of a droning synthesizer and deep-toned strings. John Paul Jones is clearly responsible for much of this string-laden background. Slashing guitar chords threaten to slice Page's fingers as he bites into the strings, while Plant mumbles and improvises his way into the murk. 'Friends' was also recorded as an exercise by Plant and Page with the Bombay Symphony Orchestra on a trip to India in 1972, but this is a different full-band version. While in Bombay, Page and Plant performed an impromptu gig at a small pub call the Slip Disc, with support from local musicians.

CELEBRATION DAY

The synthesizer is still grumbling as Zeppelin take off on to something completely different. Somewhat overlooked and misunderstood at the time, this is just one of the band's less famous items, which have since become strangely relevant and contemporary.

There is a modern, dance-inclined sound to this 1970 gem with its simple, rough-hewn back beat, clouds of jangling riffs and hypnotic, trance-like mood. 'Celebration Day' was played quite frequently on Zeppelin tours, mainly during 1971 and 1972.

In 2012, when the remaining members, alongside John Bonham's son Jason, reunited to release the concert footage from the O2 Arena show *Celebration Day* was chosen as the appropriate DVD title, but the song itself was not performed during the gig, nor considered at rehearsals.

> "We call ourselves the Nobs when we go to Copenhagen. The first time we played there we invited Eva Von Zeppelin backstage to meet us, to see how we were nice young lads. On leaving the studio, she saw our LP cover of an airship in flames and she exploded! I had to run and hide. She just blew her top." JIMMY PAGE

SINCE I'VE BEEN LOVING YOU

An amazing introduction sets the mood for a piece which stands head and shoulders above everything else on the album. There is a majestic quality about this soulful display. It's very moving on several levels with Page playing some of his most heartfelt solo work. A musician most certainly at the top of his game.

'Since I've Been Loving You' is real and complete. So real, in fact, that you can hear that faint squeak of Bonham's oil-free bass drum pedal. But as John Paul's organ soothes away the tension, the drums swing until Bonham sounds like he's sitting in with the full Count Basie orchestra instead of a four-piece rock group. Even after all these years, it brings a lump to the throat to think of the loss of the man whose drumming is so crucial to this piece's success.

"Working from seven – to eleven," murmurs Plant, beginning a performance that eventually shows the full range of his astounding vocal abilities. There are moments when he sounds not unlike Nina Simone and there are touches of Screaming Jay Hawkins too. But the expression and verbal gymnastics are all Plant's. Page's main solo is full of unremitting power and the ideas flow as he heads towards an inspired but logical conclusion. Great crashing cymbals help to peg the piece in place, while Plant seems to be standing on tiptoe to hit those chattering high notes.

Some have claimed Moby Grape's 'Never' as the inspiration for the tune. This performance was done virtually live in the studio, with John Paul Jones playing the bass pedals of the Hammond organ with his feet. The blues mood seems almost at odds with the rest of the album's folksy material, and that's because it was originally intended to be included on the more raunchy *Led Zeppelin II* but was held over in favour of 'Whole Lotta Love'.

OUT ON THE TILES

Phil Carson, MD at Atlantic Records in London during the 1970s, remembers that John Bonham was the inspiration behind this exuberant performance. "He used to have a little ditty that he would sing when we were going out to play. Rubbers refers to "rub-a-dub-dubs" – clubs of course. Page turned the tune that John sang into a riff, and that's the derivation of 'Out on the Tiles'. It was probably the most fun song Zeppelin ever did!"

Bonham's lyrics were replaced by something more suitable for general consumption, although Plant retains the jaunty air of a reprobate on the prowl. "As I walk down the highway all I do is sing this song," he says, addressing a band frantically engaged in bashing out a singularly violent riff. A rumbling, grumbling guitar is locked in deadly embrace with the drums, which trip over themselves into a brace of accents that sound like a warning cry of "Uh oh, uh oh!"

Whichever club they are heading for, there is obviously bound to be trouble before the night is out. When Plant sings, "I'm so glad I'm leaving you", a ghostly voice can be detected in the mix pleading, "Stay".

GALLOWS POLE

A traditional folk tune, based on a work by Huddie Ledbetter (known as Leadbelly), the celebrated American blues singer, prison convict, 12-string guitarist and folk composer. Leadbelly's version of the song was called 'Gallis Pole' and it has also been called 'Maid Freed from the Gallows' and 'Gallows Line'.

In this version Page plays banjo, six-string and 12-string guitars as well as lead electric. John Paul Jones adds the mandolin. It was one of the first times Page had played the banjo, which he borrowed from Jones. He'd first heard the song played on a record by 12-string-guitar player Fred Gerlach, and devised this arrangement for the band who performed it in Copenhagen on their 1971 European tour.

Plant pleads with the hangman to wait a while as he sees first his friends, then his brother and sister coming to the rescue, bearing gifts of silver and gold. Will his execution be stayed, or will he soon be swinging from the gallows pole? As the singer becomes increasingly desperate, drums and banjo launch into an incongruously jolly rhythm that creates a kind of *danse macabre*.

A strangely exciting climax is reached in which tradition is turned on its head and a full-blooded Zeppelin *tour de force* takes over. This was one of Page's personal favourites from the album, and from time to time Plant made references to the song by tossing a few lines from 'Gallows Pole' into other tunes like 'Trampled Underfoot' from *Physical Graffiti*.

TANGERINE

After a false start, Page sets off on acoustic guitar to deliver a very pretty ballad that had its origins in a tune previously written and recorded by him with the Yardbirds. Page delays his entrance in order to set the right tempo. He plays pedal steel guitar, creating the kind of country ballad that you'd expect to hear on the radio while driving a pick-up truck across the Texas plains.

Plant intones Page's words with tender care. "Think how it used to be," he murmurs, on a song of lost love and a fondly remembered past affair. Although quite sweet and brief, the piece doesn't stop changing tack for more than a few bars at a time, revealing the arranger's craft and skill at sustaining interest. No drum machines or tape loops here. 'Tangerine' was frequently played on the band's acoustic set until the summer of 1972, and was revived for the Earls Court, London shows of 1975.

OPPOSITE: Peter Grant, an imposing, managerial figure, poses with Plant in New York, May 1974 when the band was launching Swan Song Records.

ABOVE: The band return to the Los Angeles Forum, 31 May 1973 Jimmy had a sprained finger, an injury he obtained jumping a fence at San Diego airport.

THAT'S THE WAY

A singularly attractive performance that, above all, shows the difference between perceived ideas about the band's musical aims and ambitions and Zeppelin's own philosophy. Here are fine melodies and lofty sentiments, far removed from the grosser aspects of Zeppelin output. The acoustic guitars swirl and cosset a theme rich in images of velvet clothes, burning incense, golden hair and mountain streams. It's a love song steeped in poetry in which brutish drums and metallic guitars are banished. Only a gentle tambourine keeps up a steady rhythm, while Plant sings, "Yesterday I saw you standing by the river" – one of those intimacies guaranteed to clutch at a young girl's heart. And then he adds: "Yesterday I saw you kiss tiny flowers."

At this point one might have expected Bonham to start demolishing the studio furniture with scornful fury, but he keeps a respectful distance and joins in the folk club spirit. Originally titled 'The Boy Next Door' (one of the lines), it is clearly a product of the writing sessions at Bron-yr-Aur cottage and reflects Plant's desire to escape from the harsh realities of life on the road into a more romantic world of peace and love.

As he later explained: "The great thing about our stay in Snowdonia was there was no motion, just privacy and nature and the beauty of the people there. It was a good experience in every way." During the trip Page and Plant often went for walks around the countryside armed with a tape recorder to make sure that if a good idea came up it wouldn't go to waste. 'That's the Way' came about in this fashion. Page: "This was written in Wales when Robert and I stayed at the cottage. It was one of those days after a long walk and we were setting back . . . we had a guitar with us. It was a tiring walk coming down a ravine, so we stopped and sat down. I played the tune and Robert sang a verse straight off. We had the tape recorder ready and got the tune down."

BRON-YR-AUR STOMP

This particular ditty was written in honour of Plant's pet dog Strider and not, as one might suspect, in honour of one of his early girlfriends. Strider, incidentally, was named after Aragorn's alter-ego in JRR Tolkien's *Lord of the Rings*. As Page launches into some nimble finger-pickin', bluegrass style, Plant tells how he walks down a country lane – "calling your name".

This canine boogie is enlivened by Bonham playing spoons and castanets. John Paul Jones uses an acoustic five-string fretless bass to get an authentic Lonnie Donegan-style skiffle feel. The tune has its origins in a piece called 'Jennings Farm Blues', which the band played at the beginning of these *Led Zeppelin III* sessions. The 'Stomp' was recorded at Headley Grange in 1970, using the Stones' mobile, and finished off at Island, London and Ardent Studios, Memphis, Tennessee. It was played live during Zeppelin's 1972 tours of the UK, US and Japan and at Earls Court in 1975.

> **"'That's the Way' was written in Wales when Robert and I stayed at the cottage. It was one of those days after a long walk and we were setting back . . . we had a guitar with us. I played the tune and Robert sang a verse straight off. We had the tape recorder ready and got the tune down."**
> JIMMY PAGE

HATS OFF TO (ROY) HARPER

Jimmy Page had met the great Liverpool-born folk singer at the Bath Festival and he was an uncompromising, charismatic artist whom both Plant and Page admired. This song was intended as a tribute to Harper, who never managed to attain major success or recognition.

Harper enjoyed the lifestyle and the perks of being behind the scenes with the Zeppelin entourage, which proved to be quite an eye-opener. In later years, Page and Harper would record an album together called *Whatever Happened to Jugula* (1985).

'Hats Off to (Roy) Harper' achieves a remarkably authentic traditional sound and is based on a Bukka White blues called 'Shake 'em on Down'. It features some of Jimmy Page's finest bottleneck guitar work. Plant sings with all the primitive intensity of a 1920s country bluesman, and you can almost imagine him pulling on a jug of whisky, while waiting for the train whistle to blow, the levee to break and the sun to go down.

Supposedly composed by one 'Charles Obscure' and never performed live, 'Hats Off' was greeted with some dismay by hardcore Zeppelin fans on first hearing. It seemed a low-key way to end such a crucial album. However the piece has grown in stature over the years, and curiously enough now seems as authentically ancient as the original blues 78 rpm records did, when viewed from the 1970s.

OPPOSITE: Jimmy pulls up outside Rodney Bingenheimer's English Disco in Los Angeles, pictured here with BP Fallon, the band's PR officer.

RIGHT: John Paul Jones entertains *The Starship*'s frequent flyers and mile-high clubbers, en route to America, 1969.

THE BIGGEST BAND IN THE WORLD

During 1970 Led Zeppelin did six US tours, at one point playing six nights a week for a month. Said Bonham: "I was doing a long drum solo every night on tour and my hands were covered in blisters." The band were tired, but in demand ... and still yet to record their _magnum opus_. That was to come next ...

Time off the road at least offered a chance to work on the fourth album. With less pressure to record in a rush this time they adjourned to Headley Grange, their Hampshire rehearsal studio. During January 1971, they utilized the Rolling Stones' mobile studio to record. Page later flew to Los Angeles to mix the tapes.

By the end of February the new album was complete and once more Led Zeppelin hit the road for a British tour, including a visit to Ireland. The show at the Ulster Hall, Belfast, on 5 March was exciting both because of the hysterical welcome – many fans believing Led Zeppelin were American – and because at the height of the Troubles there was a riot going on just down the road from the venue.

The band were themselves pleased to be reunited; as Plant said after the show, "We're all different personalities but there's a kind of magic when we get together again." He again refuted rumours that they were on the verge of breaking up. Fans were rewarded with an especially dynamic performance that kicked off with 'Immigrant Song'. A typical set at this time included 'Heartbreaker', 'Dazed and Confused' and 'Whole Lotta Love'. Slow blues 'Since I've Been Loving You' was greeted with a storm of applause and 'Black Dog' also got an airing.

The biggest surprise came with an unannounced new ballad featuring a moving vocal performance from Robert and a 12-string guitar interlude from Jimmy. From gentle opening chords to a drum-fuelled climax, the piece progressed through an arrangement that left the audience stunned. Asked to identify the new number, Robert replied: "It's called 'Stairway to Heaven.'" It was the first time audiences had been exposed to what would become one of Led Zeppelin's greatest works, an enduring rock classic and one of the most played tracks on American radio.

An ovation greeted 'Stairway' in both Belfast and at Dublin's Boxing Stadium, where they also performed an unusual version of 'Whole Lotta Love' with Atlantic Records' Phil Carson sitting in on bass. Carson repeated this unscheduled appearance during a trip to Japan when the band quit the stage and left him to twist in the wind, attempting to solo in front of a booing crowd.

During March the band played mostly universities and clubs throughout England, climaxing with a return trip on the 23rd to the Marquee in Soho, where their odyssey had begun back in 1968. The philosophy behind the "small club" tour was explained by Page. "We were losing contact with people. By doing a tour this way we'll re-establish contact with our audience and re-energize ourselves on their reaction."

A full European tour began in May, ending on 5 July with a troubled show at Milan's Vigorelli Stadium. Here 12,000 fans were attacked with tear-gas and beaten with batons by police and soldiers who overreacted when the audience stood to cheer after a few numbers. This sparked a full-scale riot, with youths jumping on the stage and climbing into the backstage area. The band escaped through a tunnel and locked themselves into their band room while their road crew tried to salvage equipment.

July wasn't a good month; it was discovered the new album had not been mixed properly at a studio in California and had to be remixed. In August they started their seventh North American tour in Vancouver after two warm-up dates at the Montreux Festival in Switzerland. They played some 20 dates and reputedly earned another million dollars in the process.

In September the group took a holiday in Hawaii after two final tour dates in Honolulu, and at the end of the month a five-date tour of Japan commencing in Tokyo included a charity show for victims of the Hiroshima atomic bombing. However, apart from this well-intentioned gesture the group also began to earn a reputation for mayhem; they were banned for life from the Tokyo Hilton. The band were now used to travelling on a scale few of their age group could contemplate in the era before gap years and backpacking. Robert and Jimmy went on a trip to Thailand, India and Hong Kong.

> **"We enjoy playing. Every gig is important to us. In this business, it doesn't matter how big you are, you can't afford to become complacent. If you adopt that attitude you're dead. That'll never happen to us."**
>
> JOHN BONHAM

RIGHT: "It was sheer pandomonium" whenever Led Zeppelin took to the stage, remembers the band's tour manager, Richard Cole.

"All our albums are different and in four years we've covered all sorts of ground.."

ROBERT PLANT

On 11 November their second UK tour of the year began at Newcastle City Hall. The following day the album sometimes known as *Led Zeppelin IV* was finally released, without a title or any information on the sleeve. On 20–21 November Zeppelin performed at the Empire Pool, Wembley; all 19,000 tickets sold in an hour, though some fans grumbled at the price [75p]. They were supported by Bronco, Home and Stone the Crows on two five-hour "Electric Magic" shows. The tour ended in Bournemouth on 2 December and Atlantic released a single with 'Black Dog' on the A-side in the US. The group resisted great pressure to release 'Stairway to Heaven' as a single and once again no singles were released in England. The working year ended with a final UK date in Salisbury on 15 December.

The year 1971 had been one of consolidation as well as great progress. It was all part of a whirlwind of activity that left them and their fans breathless.

The year saw the scale of the band's operations grow exponentially, as enormous crowds were attracted to increasingly elaborate shows. Zeppelin won awards, topped polls and embarked on new projects. At the same time, headlines gave the first hints of strange undercurrents.

They began 1973 fulfilling dates on the UK tour begun the year before. It wasn't all smooth sailing. On 2 January the Bentley transporting Plant and Bonham to Sheffield City Hall broke down and they nearly missed the show. Then Plant succumbed to influenza and some shows had to be rescheduled. The tour finished in Preston on 30 January.

The album was delayed by arguments over the sleeve. Eventually released on 26 March, *Houses of the Holy* had an eye-catching gatefold cover depicting naked children crawling over rocks, but minus a band name or title. This scarcely mattered. Within days it was Number 1 in both the UK and US, and went gold in Germany even before release.

Discussing the album, Plant claimed: "All our albums are different and in four years we've covered all sorts of ground. We have a track called 'The Crunge' which is really funny, and we've also written a reggae number, which I'd like to put out as a single." In the event the song, 'D'Yer Mak'er', was released in the States and by December was Number 20 in the *Billboard* chart.

A European tour commenced in Copenhagen on 3 March winding up in Paris on 1–2 April with two nights at the Palais de Sport. During April the band was busy rehearsing a stage show involving lots of special effects. Their ninth US tour opened on 4 May in front of 50,000 at the Atlanta Braves' stadium. An excited city mayor called the show "the biggest thing to hit Atlanta since *Gone with the Wind*." But even this wasn't their biggest audience. The following day they entertained 56,800 ecstatic fans at the Tampa Stadium, Florida, breaking the record for a gig by a single group set by the Beatles at Shea Stadium in 1965.

Grant proudly told the *Financial Times* that Led Zeppelin expected to earn $30 million during 1973; Atlanta earned them $250,000 and Tampa Stadium grossed $309,000. Audiences were transfixed by elaborate stage sets by Showco of Dallas, Texas. Thirty tons of light and sound equipment included strobe lights, spinning mirrors and dry ice machines. The Zeppelin entourage journeyed across the States like a wagon train rolling west, while the band flew in a private Boeing 707, *The Starship*. The tour concluded with another sold-out show at the Los Angeles Forum on 3 June.

It was clear to Grant that Zeppelin would become a major part of rock history and the experience should be filmed for posterity. Work began on a film, to be called *The Song Remains the Same*, the title of the new album's opening track. It was directed by Joe Massott, a friend of Page's girlfriend Charlotte Martin, and filming began on 18 July with a crew covering gigs in Baltimore, Boston and Pittsburgh, plus three nights at Madison Square Garden in New York on 27–29 July, where engineer Eddie Kramer deployed a 24-track mobile recording unit. Massott planned something more than a static "rockumentary", presenting each band member in personality-driven "fantasy" sequences, intercut with concert footage.

Real-life events began to upstage any Zeppelin fantasies. After the second night at Madison Square Garden, tour manager Richard Cole and attorney Steve Weiss put $186,700 of wages money into a safe deposit box at the Drake Hotel in Manhattan. Overnight the money went missing. An after-show party was scheduled where gold discs were presented, but when press and TV asked about the alleged robbery the band refused to discuss it. To make matters worse, Peter Grant was subsequently arrested for hitting a photographer.

OPPOSITE: Jimmy and Robert flash their smiles on stage, 1971.

RIGHT: Madison Square Garden, New York City was the ultimate gig for all UK rock bands. Led Zeppelin owned the stage when they played there on 3 September 1971 during their seventh US tour.

Cole was cleared of any involvement in the theft, but the money was never found. From then on the band attracted unwelcome publicity and suffered more than their share of bad luck. Page had been ill during the tour and strained a finger, affecting his playing. Back in the UK, he announced he just wanted to go to sleep. He thought they would start work on another new album, but yearned for a break. "I can't remember when we weren't working. It's been an incredible tour, but we're all terribly worn out."

In September, Plant was voted Top Male Singer in *Melody Maker's* annual readers' poll. The band started work on the successor to *Houses of the Holy* at Plumpton Place, Jimmy's eighteenth-century residence set in 20 hectares (50 acres), in East Sussex. He also bought Boleskin House near Loch Ness in Scotland, once owned by the occultist Aleister Crowley. As work progressed on *The Song Remains the Same*, a scene was filmed there in December, with Page as a hermit climbing ice-covered rocks in the moonlight. Sequences filmed during October depicted Plant as an Arthurian knight on a quest for a princess and Bonham driving a dragster at Bedfordshire's Santa Pod Raceway. Jones was a masked brigand terrorizing a village before returning to his Sussex family home. Even Grant was roped in, driving a vintage car and posing as Al Capone, with Cole his henchman.

By the end of 1973 thousands of feet of film awaited editing. It would prove a difficult task. The band sometimes felt out of their depth with the project; they were more at home at Headley Grange, where they continued work on the sixth album.

One of the demo tracks was a strange, Eastern-sounding theme Grant privately thought "a dirge". In fact, it was the first rumblings of one of their most celebrated tracks, 'Kashmir'. After an exhausting year, the creative juices were flowing again.

They certainly deserved a break, and enjoyed the novelty of being at home with their wives and girlfriends, but they didn't break with music entirely; one project in particular occupied Jimmy Page and Peter Grant.

The concept of the "artist-owned label" had grown during an era when artists fought to gain control of their music and money. Elton John had Rocket, the Beatles owned Apple and the Rolling Stones their own eponymous label. Now Led Zeppelin entered the fray. Their contract with Atlantic had expired; they wanted to broaden their activities by setting up their own label, Swan Song Records, to be distributed by Atlantic.

In typically oblique fashion, they eschewed flashy offices in a shining tower block in favour of dusty rooms above the British Legion headquarters in London's New King's Road. With cheap furniture and few staff, it gave no hint of the band's immense wealth, perhaps to discourage visiting artists from imagining they too might be in line for a fortune.

The label name had been the subject of heated debate; suggestions included Slag, Eclipse, De Luxe, Stairway and Zeppelin Records. Swan Song was originally intended as the name of an acoustic guitar track, then an album title, until finally applied to the label. The chosen logo depicted two graceful swans, similar to those on the lake at Jimmy's house.

Among its first signings was Scots singer Maggie Bell, formerly of Stone the Crows, who was managed by Grant. Long-established R&B band the Pretty Things were given a contract as was rock and roll producer, artist and writer Dave Edmunds. The most successful, however, proved to be Bad Company, a lusty young group featuring former Free vocalist Paul Rodgers. A second office was set up in Manhattan, where it was hoped major stars would be secured.

That month the group convened to start work on their sixth album, with sessions at Headley Grange. Jones was back on board, having considered quitting due to the strain of touring and becoming choirmaster at Winchester Cathedral. Grant succesfully convinced him to stay.

Although no Zeppelin gigs were scheduled, they had fun turning up at other people's and sitting in; one memorable night Page joined old pal Roy Harper on stage at London's Rainbow Theatre.

On 10 May, Swan Song Records was officially launched with two lavish receptions for the media and music industry. The first, at the Four Seasons restaurant in New York, reputedly cost $10,000. As Atlantic's promotions department couldn't find any swans, they hired a flock of geese; Grant was furious that they thought nobody would notice. When two were chased outside by Bonham and Richard Cole, they were run over by a car.

The second was in Los Angeles, at the Bel Air Hotel. On the flight Grant and his 12-strong party were mocked, berated and sworn at by a drunken fellow passenger who eventually produced a gun, demanding to know how "hippies" could afford to fly first-class. On landing he was arrested by the FBI and the somewhat shaken group continued on their way.

In Hollywood, their party guests included comic legend Groucho Marx, Micky Dolenz of the Monkees and Rolling Stone Bill Wyman. During the visit John Paul Jones was introduced to Elvis Presley, an honour repeated the following year for the rest of the band.

Swan Song got a big boost when Bad Company's debut album topped the US charts and the single 'Can't Get Enough' was a hit on both sides of the Atlantic. The first British release was the Pretty Things' album *Silk Torpedo*. Label managers yearned for a major artist such as John Lennon but the biggest act remained, of course, Led Zeppelin, five of whose albums were on Swan Song.

Grant was offered a chance for the group to headline a one-day festival at Knebworth in July and a date at the Munich Festival on 29 August. He declined; they were too busy concentrating on the label, their new album and a film.

The band had begun losing interest in the film after seeing incomplete rushes, and the project was taken over by Australian director Peter Clifton. He had made films for Australian TV, about Chuck Berry and US soul acts visiting London in the 1960s, which had impressed the band. He took them to Shepperton Studios for more filming.

"I can't remember when we weren't working. It's been an incredible tour, but we're all terribly worn out."

JIMMY PAGE

In July mixing sessions were held at Olympic Studios. As they had quite a few tracks left over from previous albums, it was decided the next should be a double. Release was scheduled for the following year.

The summer saw many Zeppelin sideshows. Jones formed a group with Dave Gilmour of Pink Floyd to back Roy Harper at a free concert in Hyde Park. In September Page jammed with Bad Company during their US tour, and the band went to see Crosby, Stills, Nash and Young at Wembley Stadium.

On 31 October Swan Song held a party at Chislehurst Caves in the south London suburbs to celebrate *Silk Torpedo*'s release. Guests included

Zeppelin, Bad Company and the Pretty Things; booze flowed like water and entertainment was provided by fire-eaters and semi-naked serving wenches. Their inspiration was the notorious Hell Fire Club, which held orgiastic revels in caves at High Wycombe in the eighteenth century. Those attending Led Zeppelin's twentieth-century version remained hungover for days afterwards.

Once recovered, Led Zeppelin announced double album *Physical Graffiti* would be released on 29 November and that a US tour would begin in January. As rehearsals began in earnest at an Ealing theatre, Page commented: "1974 didn't really happen. 1975 will be much better."

ABOVE: "We're all different personalities, but there's a kind of magic when we get together."
Robert Plant, on his bandmates.

ABOVE: A poster from Led Zeppelin's "Electric Magic" shows at the Wembley Empire Pool, London, in November 1971. Nearly 10,000 tickets sell out within an hour and a second date was added.

OPPOSITE:

1. A ticket for Led Zeppelin's concert at Budokan Hall, Tokyo, Japan, 2 October 1972. It was during this Japanese tour that the band dropped their acoustic set, and kept the gig runtime to under two hours.

2. A ticket to see Led Zeppelin perform in Cologne, Germany, on 16 July 1970. This seven-date summer tour saw the band play the Bath festival and visit Germany and Iceland.

3. A rare ticket to see Led Zeppelin in concert with Barclay James Harvest at the Usher Hall, Edinburgh, Scotland, 1970. This rescheduled 17 February 1970 gig had been postponed "due to an accident involving Robert Plant".

4. A ticket for Led Zeppelin's show at the Locarno Ballroom, Sunderland, England, on 12 November 1971. The 14-song concert included performances of "Immigrant Song", "Whole Lotta Love" and "Stairway to Heaven".

1.

2.

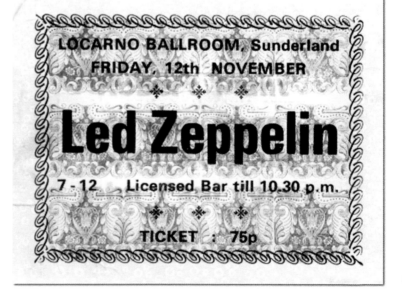

3.

4.

FOUR SYMBOLS ► (1971)

'Rock and Roll' and 'Stairway to Heaven'. What more could Zeppelin fans hope for than a brace of classic new tracks? In 1971 they were rewarded with a fourth album that has become legendary.

FOUR SYMBOLS

Although one of their most productive and well-balanced, the fourth album had a low-key greeting on its release in 1971. A new album was less of a novelty and there was still a residue of disappointment at its predecessor; but the critics waiting to sit in judgement were rewarded with an untitled album that revelled in the concept of art sheltering in anonymity and achievement triumphing over celebrity

Work had started at Island Studios, London, in December 1970, but later the group borrowed the Rolling Stones' mobile studio and moved to Headley Grange, a former Victorian workhouse in Hampshire recommended by Fleetwood Mac, which engineer Andy Johns came to believe was haunted. Plant and Bonham refused to sleep there and decamped to a hotel, but Page liked the atmosphere, especially the acoustics. Among the songs composed at Headley Grange were 'Misty Mountain Hop' and 'The Battle of Evermore', and seated before a blazing log fire (lit because the house was freezing) Plant wrote lyrics to an epic that became known as 'Stairway to Heaven'.

The album was finished in February and the tapes mixed at Sunset Sound studios in Los Angeles. The decision to leave the album untitled was made by Page, reluctant to call it prosaically *Led Zeppelin IV*. It was also decided not to have photos on the cover, as no one could agree who should appear on the front. There were no words either, only an old postcard image of a bearded old countryman bent under the weight of a bundle of rods, contained within a picture frame hung on the wall of a crumbling house. Heavy with yet more symbolism, the inner sleeve was adorned with a charcoal drawing of a hermit holding a lantern, inspired by a tarot card.

Although Grant approved the anonymous cover, the record company men entrusted with promoting the album pronounced it "professional suicide". At a time when the phrase "hype" was in wide circulation among critics, Jimmy explained that they simply wanted to "play down the group's name" and "Led Zeppelin" didn't really mean anything anyway. Only the music mattered.

As the album rocketed to Number 1 the lack of a title certainly caused problems for those publishing the charts, and in the end it was designated either *Untitled* or *Four Symbols*, after the gnomic sigils adorning the label. A feather represented Plant; Bonham was allocated three intertwined rings, signifying strength. Jones' symbol was three leaf shapes linked by a ring and Page's a magical image that looked like "Zoso" indicating his astrological chart, split between Cancer and Capricorn with Scorpio rising.

Having decided that the mixes produced in the States were substandard, the album was remixed in London. The opener, 'Black Dog', one of Zeppelin's heaviest riffs, was inspired by a creature seen wandering around Headley Grange. It was also the name Sir Winston Churchill gave to his fits of depression. Jones devised the theme and an arrangement that included 4/4 and 5/4 time signatures. Page overdubbed four guitar tracks and engineer Johns triple-tracked his rhythm guitars for extra depth.

'Rock and Roll' celebrated their shared musical roots listening to Little Richard in the 1950s. Bonham sets the mood with hi-hat and snare and

Rolling Stones tour manager Ian 'Stu' Stewart, who supervised the mobile studio, adds boogie piano. The piece developed when Plant and Page began improvising to break the tension caused by attempting a more difficult piece. 'Rock and Roll' became a stage favourite.

In complete contrast, 'The Battle of Evermore', featuring additional vocals from Sandy Denny, former member of folk rock group Fairport Convention, is an acoustic ballad inspired by Scottish folklore. The melody was devised by Page, using Jones' mandolin, during a session at Headley Grange. They met Sandy during a trip to Los Angeles and performed with her at the Troubadour Club. She died on 21 April 1978.

The fourth track, 'Stairway to Heaven', arrived virtually unheralded and only began to make an impact as it was introduced into live shows. Page's acoustic guitar introduction became a theme all young guitarists aspired to master. He uses a double-necked six- and 12-string guitar to accompany Plant's airy lyrics and Jones plays wooden recorders, adding a touch of medieval magic. In the midst of the calm Bonham comes crashing in, followed by Page's storming Fender Telecaster solo, recorded at Island. It was to become the band's anthem, though in later years Plant professed he was embarrassed by the lyrics about a "gilded lady" and tried to avoid singing it at reunions. Page played an instrumental version at a charity concert at the Royal Albert Hall in 1982 and later called it "a glittering thing" summing up all they were trying to achieve.

'Misty Mountain Hop', featuring Jones on electric piano, offers light relief after the drama of 'Stairway' and Plant later revealed it was inspired by an illicit 'love-in' he attended.

'Four Sticks', heavily processed and pre-dating electro dance music by 20 years, was intended to be a hypnotic experience inspired by Plant and Page's trip to India. Recorded in one take at Island, it was attempted only once on stage. The title refers to Bonham's use of four drumsticks rather than the usual two.

The awesome back beat of 'When the Levee Breaks' was so powerful it would be sampled by record producers from the 1980s onwards. It was obtained by hanging microphones in Headley Grange's towering stairwell while Bonham played what Plant called "a sex groove". The theme was loosely based on a blues by Memphis Minnie and Page's bottleneck guitar gives it an authentic New Orleans flavour; New Orleans' canal levees really would break in the wake of Hurricane Katrina in 2005.

PREVIOUS PAGES: The opening show of two sell-out nights at Wembley Empire Pool, London, 20 November 1971.

OPPOSITE: Hitting their stride, Led Zeppelin ramblin' on at Wembley Empire Pool, London, 20 November 1971.

ALBUM TRACKS

Untitled, Four Symbols – it really didn't matter what it was called. From the riff-laden 'Black Dog' to the triumphal 'Stairway to Heaven' and cataclysmic 'When the Levee Breaks', this was their finest hour. It has sold 37 million copies.

BLACK DOG

'Black Dog' was one of the heaviest Zeppelin riffs of all time, and one that was beloved of the new breed of heavy rock bands who emerged a decade later. Many wondered if the name was inspired by some strange mythical beast, but there is a more prosaic explanation for this particular apparition: it was named after a friendly mutt seen lurching about the building during the sessions.

A distant guitar warms up, giving some idea of the strange ambience at Headley Grange. Engineer Andy Johns says the band recorded the basic track for this one in what had once been a crypt. Robert Plant's voice, bold, sensuous and oozing sweat and sex, yells to the rooftops: "Hey, hey Mama, said the way you move, gonna make you sweat, gonna make you groove!" Here Led Zeppelin display their complete grasp of the use of dynamics. The entire band answer Plant's lone exclamations in unison. There's no danger of missing a syllable of his vocal statements, as the "call and response" blues routine underpins his vocal attack. This ruse was inspired in part by Fleetwood Mac's 'Oh Well', but it was also a device frequently used in traditional jazz and blues. An unexpected Latin funk groove from Bonham lifts the piece out of the rhythmic rut, while Page's guitar riff is astonishingly basic but entirely self-assured. In fact, the piece chugs over an odd time signature (a mixture of 4/4 set against 5/4) and is full of unpredictable rests, which belie its apparent simplicity. John Paul Jones was responsible for the riff and arrangement, while Page overdubbed no fewer than four guitar tracks using a Gibson Les Paul guitar put through a direct injection box. Andy Johns recalls that they tripled-tracked three rhythm guitars to get a satisfying stereo spread. Page later said that the band always tried to encourage the laid-back John Paul Jones to write more material, and this was undoubtedly one of his most effective and powerful themes. The strange noise at the beginning of the piece was, as Page described it: "The guitar army waking up. Rise and shine!"

'Black Dog' remained a favourite on live shows until it was replaced by material from *Presence* during their 1977 US tour. It was released as a single in the US in December 1971, and got to Number 15 in the *Billboard* chart. Peter Grant used to rage and fulminate against his American record company executives when they insisted on releasing singles against his wishes. In fact he only achieved the co-operation of Phil Carson, who was Atlantic's chief in London on this matter, which was why the 'no singles' policy only really worked in the UK. As Grant constantly explained, Zeppelin tracks would need editing if they were to be released in this fashion, thus spoiling the musical content, and in any case the albums would sell even more copies if they contained the tracks people most wanted to hear.

TOP: The 19th-century painting on the front of the album was purchased from an antique shop by Plant. The painting was then affixed to the wall of a demolished surburban house. The juxtaposition of the city/country was a theme the band wanted to explore further.

ABOVE: Robert Plant salutes fans in Copenhagen, Denmark, on 3 May 1971, while his protective tour manager Richard Cole looks worried they might invade the stage.

OPPOSITE: Jimmy performs on stage at Oude Rai, Amsterdam, the Netherlands, 27 May 1972.

ROCK AND ROLL

Led Zeppelin let their hair down on this celebration of the golden age of innocence. This was the way countless British beat groups interpreted American rock of the 1950s. It was a nostalgic trip in 1971, and still retains its authentic flavour today. The band get the high-stepping beat just right while a boogie piano in the background (courtesy of Ian Stewart) adds a suitable barrage of "plink, plink, plinks" behind Plant's hysterical vocals. "Oh yeah!" is as deep as he gets on this one, but with a suitably crazed guitar solo to top off the madness, this is Zeppelin having fun.

According to Page, the drum intro was inspired by the original recording of Little Richard's 'Keep A-Knockin', which Bonham began playing one afternoon while the tape was still running. They were supposed to be recording another piece, but Bonham's impatience signalled the need for something to break the tension. Page got stuck into a suitable riff which he later confessed, "ground to a halt after 12 bars".

But Plant began improvising a vocal and, says Page: "It was spontaneous combustion. I think we might have been attempting 'Four Sticks' and it wasn't actually happening that day." Bonham just started drumming and, says Page: "I played a riff automatically and that was 'Rock and Roll'. I think we got through the whole of the first 12 bars and said, 'Wait a minute, this is great. Forget "Four Sticks", let's work on this.' That's one we literally did on the spot. I think we did it in three or four takes."

The number was incorporated into the band's touring set and it became a regular encore from 1971 until it was redeployed as an opening number, then put into a medley with 'Whole Lotta Love'. It has been played regularly whenever ex-Zeppelin men get together, notably at Live Aid and Jason Bonham's wedding, and by such bands as Def Leppard and Heart, while John Bonham's sister Debbie sings the number with her own band.

THE BATTLE OF EVERMORE

The late Sandy Denny, at the time a successful solo artist, was called in to share vocal duties with Plant on this moody acoustic piece, inspired by tales of the Scottish wars. The melody was created by Jimmy Page while playing John Paul Jones' mandolin at the manor house. Said Page: "It may have sounded like a dance-around-the-maypole number, but it wasn't purposely like that. I used Jonesy's mandolin. We were living in the house and some would go to bed early and I used to sit up and play quite a bit. I picked up the mandolin and this tune just came out. I'd never played one before."

Plant had read a book about Scottish history before going to Headley Grange and described 'The Battle of Evermore' as: "More of a playlet than a song. After I wrote the lyrics, I realized I needed another completely different voice to give the song its full impact." Zeppelin had once appeared on stage at the Los Angeles Troubadour club in 1970 with Fairport Convention. Fairport were recording a live album there and the Zep men cheerfully joined in, playing under the pseudonym of the Birmingham Water Buffalo Society. Hence the call to Sandy Denny to sing on the track. In the story she was to act as the voice of a town crier, urging the people to throw down their weapons. Denny later said that Plant left her completely exhausted after their session together. As a reward, Denny was given her own special symbol of three pyramids on the album sleeve.

The marriage of rock and folk music had begun on the tour preceding the release of the album, when Zeppelin's acoustic set had been developed in the teeth of yelling fans. Unlike the other major acoustic number on the album, 'The Battle of Evermore' was rarely unleashed live, although it was played during the band's 1977 US tour. Page played mandolin, John Paul Jones played a triple-neck acoustic and also sang the lines originally delivered by Sandy Denny, with somewhat less flair.

STAIRWAY TO HEAVEN

Hailed as simply the finest rock ballad of all time, the track slipped almost unnoticed into the general public's consciousness as the band gradually introduced it into their live act. Their fans, of course, hearing it at such venues as the LA Forum, greeted it with tremendous applause. The first British fans heard of the rather good new Zeppelin number was when it was played at a particularly memorable gig at Belfast's Ulster Hall, on 5 March 1971.

The band had arrived in Northern Ireland at a time when the Troubles were at their height. In fact violent riots were going on just a few streets away during the concert, as an official later informed the fearful party of press and musicians. A petrol tanker was hijacked, a youth was shot dead and fire bombs were hurled the night Zeppelin came to town. Yet there was no hint of violence or trouble during the show. Quite the reverse. The band were showered with affection by a crowd almost hysterical in their appreciation and enthusiasm. Here was a rock band that actually had the courage to tour during a dangerous time. They kicked off with 'Immigrant Song' and previewed quite a bit of material from the fourth album that evening, including 'Black Dog'.

After a stunning version of 'Dazed and Confused' came the new unheralded song that at first intrigued and then swept away the audience. The magic and pathos of the piece seemed to be even more relevant in the warring atmosphere of the times. During the performance, Page played a double-necked guitar utilizing both 12 and six strings. The finger-picked contrapuntal guitar intro became one of rock's best-known phrases, beloved of all aspiring guitarists – and actually banned from being played in some musical instrument shops along with Deep Purple's 'Smoke on the Water'. Plant sang the romantic tale with all the passion at his command. If Plant announced it to the crowd, the title could barely be heard above the din. The set broke up with all the casual disorganization and lack of security of the times. "That's all, boys and girls, please go home now!" yelled the promoter, standing in the middle of the hall like a slightly distraught youth club organizer. Fans flocked unhindered into the band's tiny dressing room and an Irish Colleen looked at the visitors with some amazement. "They were really fantastic," she told me, "are they an English band? I thought they were from America. I always thought Robert Plant was fat and Jimmy Page was tall, from the picture I have at home. You get these funny notions."

I had a funny notion that the new song would be a hit and Plant was smiling when he talked about it on the flight back to London. It was a wonder that Plant was in a mood to smile – the night before, Bonham had aimed a punch at his head during an altercation in the hotel. I quaked in my hotel bedroom as I heard the row blazing and Bonham pounding on Peter Grant's door. "Peter, I've done something terrible. I've hit Robert!" "Shut up. And go to bed," growled Grant from the depths of his room. I never found out what caused the argument, but I had seen Plant earlier offering Bonham a banana after he'd completed his drum solo, as if rewarding a particularly clever chimp. They had a way of winding each other up.

On the flight home, Page, quiet, polite and friendly as ever, told me about the new songs on *Led Zeppelin IV*. He explained that the intro to 'Stairway' on the record also featured wooden recorders played by John

Paul Jones. "We can't reproduce them on stage, but the acoustic guitars come off well. The words are brilliant – they are the best Robert has ever written." The song had been assembled through a process of trial and experiment, but came together quite quickly. At the recording session they had put down a rehearsal version on tape first, which helped put the words into focus. Page later said: "I had 'Stairway' tucked away on my cassettes. Robert arrived at Headley Grange quite late in the day and I'd actually got all the musical part together from beginning to end. Robert came in with 60 per cent of the lyrics off the cuff, which was quite something. He was listening to the music, sitting on a stool by a log fire and jotting away, and suddenly he came out with all these lyrics. When we were recording it, there were little bits, little sections that I'd done. I was getting reference pieces down on cassette, and sometimes I referred back to them if I felt there was something right that could be included."

The crucial moment after the acoustic build-up, when John Bonham comes in with all drums blazing, was a brilliant touch. As Page remembers: "It was an idea I'd used before, to give it that extra kick. Then there's a fanfare towards the solo and Robert comes in with his tremendous vocal. 'Stairway to Heaven' crystallized the essence of the band. It had everything there and showed the band at its best. We were careful never to release it as a single. It was a milestone for us. Every musician wants to do something of lasting quality, something that will hold up for a long time, and I guess we did it with 'Stairway'."

The bulk of the eight-minute piece, including Page's fiery Fender Telecaster guitar solo over those familiar series of grandiose chords, was recorded at Island Studios in London. Page knew it was going to be a complex construction and he needed full studio facilities to complete the production work. One of the most difficult moments came when Bonham had to slot in the right beats when the 12-string section led into the main guitar solo. Engineer Andy Johns remembers that the song and its arrangement were done before the band came into the studio, then it was cut in straightforward fashion with Page on acoustic guitar, Jones at an upright Hohner electric piano and Bonham sat behind his kit. Once some bass had been put on, Page began adding guitar overdubs. "I knew it was going to be a monster," recalls the engineer. "I didn't know it would become a bloody anthem!"

The full impact of the song only really sank in when the album was finally released. Over the following years, as the song grew in stature, it became the most played track of all time on US radio. In London it became Number 1 in Capital Radio's *Top 500,* just one of many awards it picked up. As late as 1983 it was voted "All Time Greatest Track'" in the UK's *Kerrang!* magazine's readers' poll. In fact the buzz about the song grew to embarrassing proportions, which, in later years, led Plant to disown the blatant romanticism of the tale of the gilded lady. He almost refused to sing it when the band got together for their 1985 Live Aid appearance and dropped it from the Page-Plant tour of 1995, saying it was now irrelevant in a tougher age of rock. He felt there were many other Zeppelin songs that he could relate to with more confidence. He insisted that 'Kashmir' was the definitive Zeppelin song and not 'Stairway', which he called a "a nice, pleasant, well-meaning, naïve, very English little song". Yet Plant created genuine poetry with his selected use of words and imagery and there was no hint of cloying sweetness or banality in his opening line: "There's a lady who's sure all that glitters is gold and she's buying a stairway to heaven." The lyrics were tastefully reproduced on the LP's inner sleeve in special lettering that Page discovered in a back issue of an old arts magazine, *Studio*.

Plant recalls that work on the song began after Bonham and Jones left Headley Grange for the evening to visit London's Speakeasy Club, a popular musicians' watering hole. "Jimmy and I stayed and we got the themes and thread of it right there and then. The lyrics were a cynical thing about a woman getting everything she wanted all the time without giving anything back. It was all done very quickly. It was a very fluid, unnaturally easy track. There was something pushing it, saying 'You guys are okay but if you want to do something timeless, here's a wedding song for you.'"

Curiously, a phrase similar to Zeppelin's appears on 'Skip Softly My Moonbeams', a track on the 1968 Procol Harum album *Shine On Brightly*. Gary Brooker sings the Keith Reid lyric which goes: "The stairs to heaven lead straight down to hell." However, Reid does not believe there is any connection with the Led Zeppelin classic. "I've never even been aware of that. I shouldn't think Zeppelin ever noticed it, either. It's just one of those great coincidences," reflects Keith. Even stranger is the fact that Brooklyn-born songwriter Neil Sedaka had a Top Ten hit in America with a song called 'Stairway to Heaven', in 1960, but nobody remembered it during the Zeppelin era a decade later.

There was always a huge demand for the song to be released as a single, but the band and their management resisted the idea. Said Page: "They tried everything to convince us it should come out as a single, but we just said 'no'. It would have destroyed the whole feel of the album." As with previous Zep albums containing obvious hits, the LP topped the charts on both sides of the Atlantic. In fact 'Stairway' was briefly issued on a rare picture disc in the US with 'Hey Hey What Can I Do' on the B-side. In Australia an EP appeared called 'The Acoustic Side of Zeppelin', which featured 'Stairway to Heaven', 'Going to California' and 'Battle of Evermore'. In February 1992 a special limited edition promotional copy of the 'Stairway' was released to commemorate the song's 20th anniversary.

With its carefully constructed arrangement, tasteful use of dynamics and the grand climax that gradually fades to black, 'Stairway' has it all. The band were justly proud of their achievement and Page called it "a glittering thing". After the band had finished their March 1971 Ireland dates, they toured small venues in England, finishing with a show at the Marquee in London's Soho. In the packed and overheated club (which had first refused Zeppelin's booking on the grounds that they didn't believe the caller was serious, or indeed that he was Peter Grant), 'Stairway to Heaven' achieved a new kind of intimacy. Whatever the setting and whether played by symphony orchestras or cabaret singers, it reached out to people.

BELOW: Spotlight on Jimmy in 1972, as he sits down to play during those more subtle acoustic moments that always ran the gauntlet of noisy, yelling audiences.

"Every musician wants to do something which will hold up for a long time, and I guess we did it with 'Stairway to Heaven'."
JIMMY PAGE

MISTY MOUNTAIN HOP

Here was an early example of John Paul Jones using electric piano on a bright, fast-paced tune that Plant has often revived since its inception. Its dreamy lyrics have a "stoned hippie" feel, enlivened by a stomping bass drum beat. While it is an apparently simple theme, there is an odd feeling about the phrasing and rhythm. Plant sings rather menacingly: "Why don't you take a look at yourself and describe what you see?", which might possibly be a poke at record reviewers.

Plant has hinted the song was originally devised in honour of a love-in session that took place in London during the hippie era and was broken up by the police. Said Jimmy Page: "We were just playing around and suddenly I came up with the opening part of 'Misty Mountain Hop' and then we were off. Jonesy put the chords in for the chorus and that would shape it up. We used to work pretty fast."

FOUR STICKS

Heavy processing gives the vocals a strange electronic feel on this controversial piece, which has had both its detractors and supporters. Certainly it has taken on a new light in the wake of subsequent recording developments – what sounded strange and almost inhuman in 1971 now compares favourably with the electronic mixed-up music of the 90s. It has John Bonham playing with four sticks, while Plant offers his customary "Ooh yeahs". Some critics missed the point and called this track "messy and unrewarding". It is certainly insistent and hypnotic. As Page says: "It was supposed to be abstract." The song was originally recorded by Page and Plant during a visit to India, when they had set off around the world in search of ethnic musical influences beyond the blues.

"We tried different ways of approaching it," said Page, "because it wasn't four sticks to begin with, it was two. The idea was to get this abstract feel. We tried that on numerous occasions and it didn't come off until the day that Bonham had a Double Diamond beer, picked up two sets of four drum sticks and did it again. It was magic. One take and the whole thing had suddenly been made. It was probably because it was physically impossible for Bonham to do another take. But suddenly it happened and that was really great. It was actually done at Island Studios."

Andy Johns found the track very difficult to mix because of the amount of compression used on the drums, and was never happy with the final mix, even though he claimed it was "the best of five or six attempts". The track was later re-done with members of the Bombay Symphony Orchestra in 1972 in a version that has yet to see the light of day. 'Four Sticks' was only once played live by the band, at a gig in Copenhagen, during their 1970 European tour.

LEFT: "We might take things beyond what people are prepared to accept from us," Plant announced. The band pictured here, looking serious, to promote their February 1975 New York dates – Madison Square Garden and Nassau Coliseum.

One of Plant's most attractive melodies, this piece was somewhat influenced by Joni Mitchell, a much-favoured artist. Plant and Page both went to see her in concert. When Plant finally met her in the mid-70s he called it one of the great moments in his life. Mitchell had cut a song called 'California' on her album *Blue*.

Originally called 'A Guide to California', it was inspired by tales of earthquakes that constantly threaten the state. But in the song, Plant is apparently searching for a beautiful lady, rather than an earth tremor. He often sang it at concerts during the band's quieter acoustic moments and revived it for a reunion appearance at the 1990 Knebworth Festival.

It developed out of a late-night jam session at Headley Grange – as there were so few distractions at the house, there was nothing much else to do in the evening but get the acoustic guitars out. Jones and Page sat around the log fire and strummed their mandolins while Plant improvised the lyrics. Page, Andy Johns and Peter Grant later flew to California to mix the track at Sunset Sound and, as they landed, an earthquake struck the area, cracking a dam in nearby San Diego.

WHEN THE LEVEE BREAKS

"Boom-a-bom-bash!" In an age when drum kits were frequently padded with blankets, and even the cymbals were swathed in masking tape by anxious engineers, John Bonham achieved a miracle when he unleashed the vast and vibrant drum sound that permeates this stunning performance. The producer got the sound, but it was Bonham who played the sticks. The sheer metronomic intensity of this performance set a new standard for recorded drumming that was only fully appreciated years later, when the "Bonham sound" was sampled and used on many later records.

It seems that Bonham was invariably unhappy with the quality of sound he was getting on Zep sessions. After pondering the problem, Page and Andy Johns came up with some suggestions. Bonham and his roadies set up his brand-new kit in the hallway at Headley Grange while Johns hung a pair of M160 stereo microphones overhead, placing one on the first-floor landing. The sound was further enhanced by feeding it through a guitar echo unit and, says Johns, "compressing it like hell". Bonham kicked in with a walloping bass and a swaggering snare drum back beat of a kind only Bonham could deliver. The results were fantastic; nobody had ever heard anything like it.

Johns recalls it was the first time Bonham had got a drum sound he really liked. As Page remembers: "We worked on the ambience of the instruments all the way through our albums. I'd been on so many sessions where the drummer was stuck in a booth and he'd be hitting the drums for all he was worth and it would just sound as though he was hitting a cardboard box. I knew the drums had to breathe to get a proper sound. That drum sound is now captured digitally on machines, but we set a trend and it was more fun doing it our way. Once the drums were set up in the hall we got this phenomenal effect and that was going to be the drum sound for 'Levee'. The drum sound actually fired it. As soon as they were set up, that's when we went for it, and it worked. We'd had a couple of attempts before, when it just didn't feel right."

The walls of the building were lined with plaster and there was no furniture to act as a baffle, which also helped create the new effect. Said Johns: "That track marked the first time anyone consciously used just room microphones for drums."

Bonham's slow drag beat perfectly suited the bluesy feel of the piece, which was based on an old song by Memphis Minnie and Kansas Joe McCoy dug up by Plant from his collection. Although the lyrics were ostensibly about the dangers of man-made earthworks collapsing under a river's floodwaters, they could also be construed as a metaphor for sexual desires giving way to a sustained physical onslaught. At least that is the interpretation placed upon them by students of ethnic music and man's carnal appetites, which are not such strange bedfellows as they might seem.

Said Page: "I came up with the guitar riff and Robert sang the words, which were inspired by Memphis Minnie's original version, so we gave her a credit. If you heard the original Memphis Minnie version of this, you wouldn't recognize the two." This is a deliberately ramshackle performance, in which Plant howls like Howlin' Wolf, and the spluttering, shimmering bottleneck guitars and wailing harmonica suggest the humid heat of the Deep South. Their version ends with the still-crackling guitars being switched off for the night and returned to their velvet-lined cases. "I wanted to make his song sound as ominous as possible, and as each new verse comes, there's something new that happens." Page explained that the sound of the vocals changed on each new verse with slight phasing added. "The harp instrumentals were all done with backwards echo on them. At the end the whole effect starts to spiral, with the voice remaining constant in the middle. It only really comes out on headphones. This was very difficult to mix."

'When the Levee Breaks' was rarely played live, beyond a few dates on the 1975 US tour. It was, however, revived on the Page-Plant *Unledded* show in 1994.

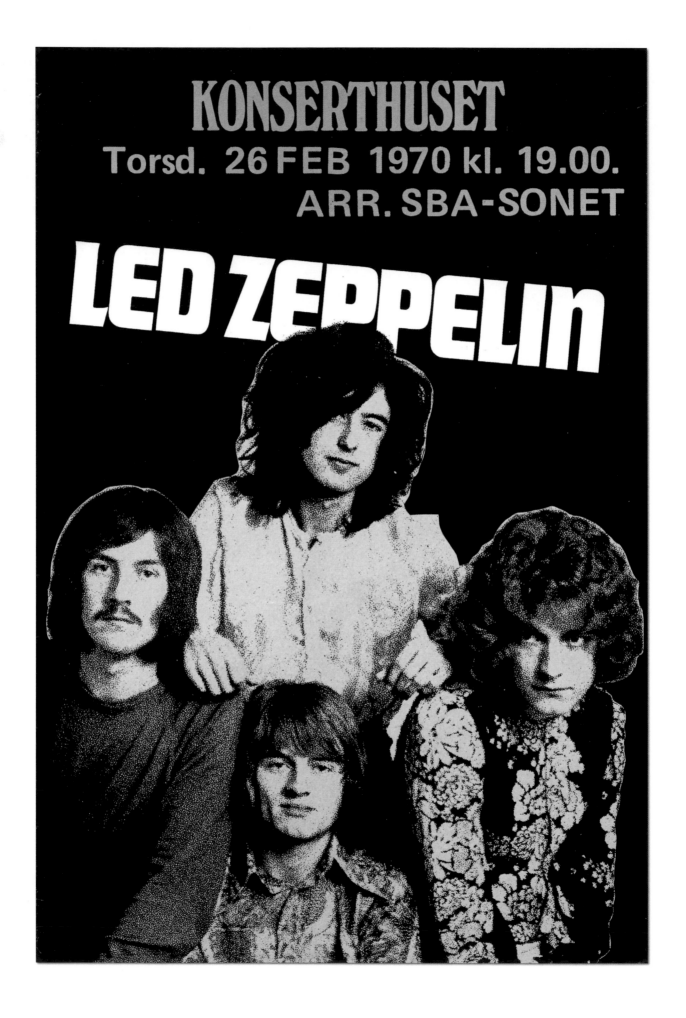

BALTIMORE CIVIC CENTER SAT. 5 APR. 8 P.M.

IN CONCERT!

A FULL 2 HOUR ★ SHOW ★

LED

"LIVIN' LOVIN' MAID"

"WHOLE LOTTA LOVE"

ZEPPELIN

#1 ALBUM IN THE COUNTRY "LED ZEPPELIN II"

TICKETS $7 - $6 - $5 - $4

GLOBE *Poster* CLASSIC © • BALTIMORE

OPPOSITE: A 1970 poster for Led Zeppelin's ten-set performance at Stockholm's famous Concert Hall. The band received a gold disc for Swedish sales of *Led Zeppelin II* while on tour there.

ABOVE: A Baltimore Civic Auditorium concert poster from 5 April 1970. The gig saw the band return to Baltimore once more to play an 18-song set to support the US Number 1 album, *Led Zeppelin II*.

ROBERT PLANT

The spirit of Led Zeppelin was encapsulated in the mischievous, romantic and powerful personality of the lyricist, balladeer and blues shouter supreme who inspired a generation of rock singers.

ROBERT PLANT

A mass of curly hair surmounting an exultant grin, bare-chested, in tight jeans, witty and blessed with boundless energy, Plant was the perfect figurehead. He was steeped in the blues and rock and roll, and his charisma, sensitivity and power also made him the perfect foil for Jimmy Page.

The moment Page and Grant set about devising the band that became Led Zeppelin they knew they wanted a blues singer, but one who could handle a range of material and contribute to the songwriting. At first they considered such fine singers as Steve Marriott, Steve Winwood and Terry Reid, but they all were with other bands or encumbered with contracts. Plant had no baggage and was relatively unknown outside the Midlands, although he had his own band and was already making records.

Robert Anthony Plant was born on 20 August 1948, in West Bromwich, Staffordshire. His father was a civil engineer and it was expected that he would enter the profession. However, inspired by the skiffle boom Robert was quick to pick up all and any available instruments including the kazoo, harmonica and washboard. He listened to all the latest British pop and rock and roll hits, and then a guitar-playing schoolfriend called Terry Foster turned him on to the blues …

"In the early 60s I was surrounded by English rock," he said. "Some of it was ballsy but a lot of it was half-baked. Then I'd discover the originals on the London American label and a lot more obscure labels coming out of New Orleans. I listened to Snooks Eaglin and then I heard Robert Johnson for the first time when I was 15. It was so sympathetic, almost as if the guitar was his vocal cords. There was tremendous emotional content in the guitar and the vocals. It was the most amazing thing I'd ever heard."

Robert began listening to Buddy Guy and Willie Dixon and absorbing a range of influences, but when he began singing aged 15 he rapidly developed his own kind of power. A tremendous range enabled him to swoop from the highest rock and roll scream to the most intimate interpretation of a ballad.

Like any normal teenager, Robert was as interested in girls and football as music, but he wasn't so enamoured of his lessons and kept on skipping school and joining groups. He began performing at the Seven Stars Blues Club in Stourbridge, playing harmonica with the Delta Blues Band. He'd work out on such favourites as 'Got My Mojo Working' with Chris Wood, who later joined Traffic, and guitarist Stan Webb, who would form Chicken Shack.

Plant tried folk clubs, too, but found the serious atmosphere too daunting. He needed an enthusiastic audience to perform properly. To placate his family he began studying to be a chartered accountant, but soon gave up. He dared not go home at night because his hair had grown so long; in the event he left home aged 16 as a roving musician.

One of his first gigs was as a "dep" with Andy Long and the Original Jurymen in Leicester, when their singer suffered a bout of laryngitis. He sang with the New Memphis Bluesbreakers, then Black Snake Moan, named after a song by Blind Lemon Jefferson, joined a jazzy outfit called the Banned and then the Crawling King Snakes, which featured a drummer called John Bonham. As Plant's reputation began to spread, he was asked to join the Tennessee Teens, a trio more influenced by Tamla Motown than Delta-style

blues. They changed their name to Listen and in 1966 Robert made his first record when they cut a single, 'You Better Run'. He also recorded two solo tracks, 'Long Time Coming' and 'Our Song', for CBS.

Listen went on the road, touring with Steampacket, featuring Rod Stewart and Long John Baldry. By now Plant was able to sing in a variety of styles, from Stax to Tamla to contemporary R&B. He was also writing material and formed his own group, the Band of Joy, but they had a falling-out when he complained the drummer was slowing down and their manager retorted that Robert couldn't sing.

Plant then formed a new Band of Joy, which reflected the trend towards psychedelia, with beads, bells and painted faces. Influenced by American groups Moby Grape and Love, they eschewed prevailing British bands such as Cream. Robert drove the wagon and brought in Bonham on drums. They travelled to London and played alongside Ten Years After and Fairport Convention, but there weren't enough gigs to support Robert and girlfriend Maureen and he had to get a job labouring, including laying asphalt on the roads of West Bromwich. The other "navvies" called Robert "the pop singer", but as he explained, the job "gave me an emergency tax code and big biceps".

The Band of Joy split up and Bonham joined American singer Tim Rose. Robert was dispirited and disillusioned. He sang with classic bluesman Alexis Korner and then a little-known outfit called Hobbstweedle. He was singing with them at a teacher-training college in Birmingham in July 1968 when he was seen by Page and Grant, on Terry Reid's recommendation.

When Jimmy first saw the "big guy" with long hair he thought he was a roadie, but, impressed, invited him to his home. "It was fantastic," Plant said. "I rummaged through his record collection and every album I pulled out was something I really dug. I knew we'd really click." Invited to join the New Yardbirds, Plant was genuinely thrilled. "The group really woke me up from inertia. Years with no success can keep you singing, but it can bring you down an awful lot."

The final verdict came from Page. "When I auditioned him and heard him sing I immediately thought there must be something wrong with him because I just couldn't understand why he hadn't become a big name yet. I thought Robert was fantastic."

Led Zeppelin had found a singer. Now what they needed was a drummer, and Plant had the solution: the mate he'd left behind, somewhere in the Midlands.

PREVIOUS PAGES: Bare-chested Plant in ecstasy on stage at Madison Square Garden, New York City, June 1977 when Zeppelin was at the peak of its fame and powers.
OPPOSITE: "The group really woke me up from inertia," Plant confessed. Pictured here alive and kicking at New York's Madison Square Garden, 3 February 1975.

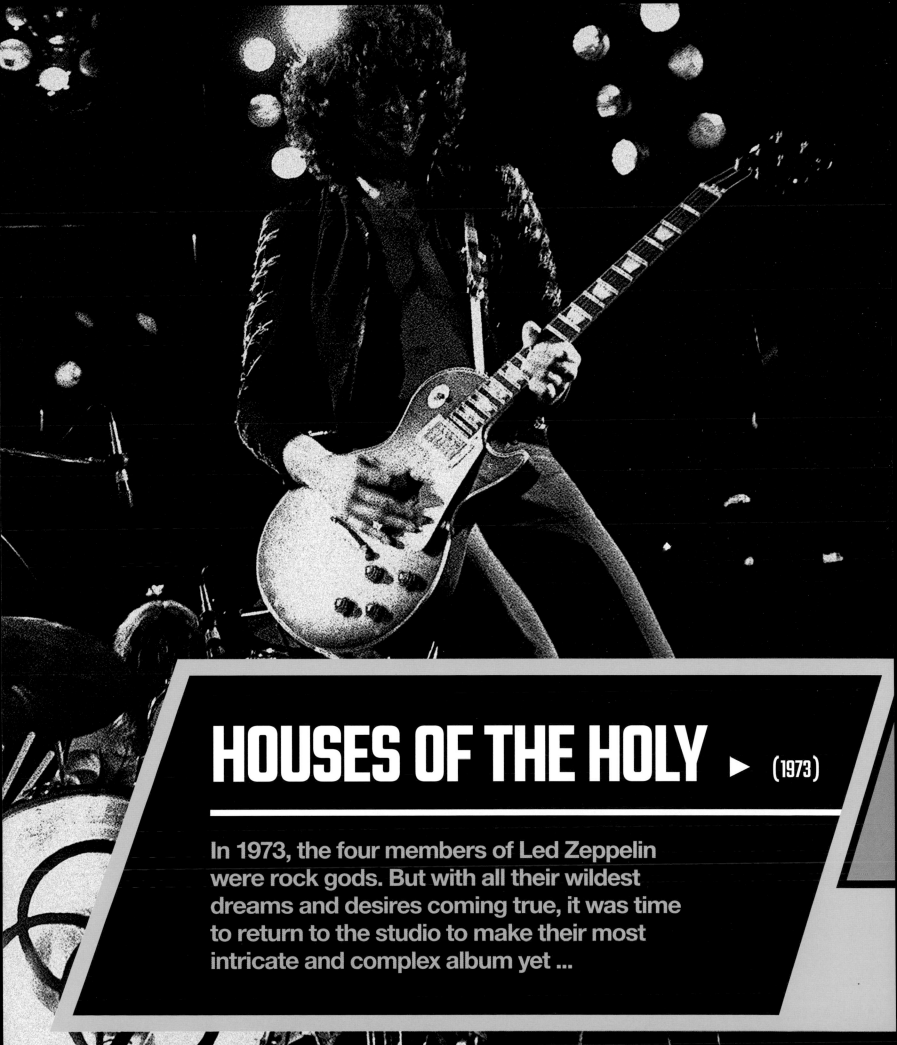

HOUSES OF THE HOLY ▶ (1973)

In 1973, the four members of Led Zeppelin were rock gods. But with all their wildest dreams and desires coming true, it was time to return to the studio to make their most intricate and complex album yet ...

HOUSES OF THE HOLY

The first track, 'The Song Remains the Same', is an outstanding performance that lights up the whole album. Its world-weary wisdom, conveyed in contemplative lyrics amid the grandeur of a commanding theme, represents Zeppelin at its best. More than 40 years later, the album still sounds as vital as it did in 1973.

Do what thou wilt . . .
But know by this summons
That on the night of the Full Moon
of 31st October, 1974

Led Zeppelin

request your presence
at a
Halloween Party
to celebrate
Swan Song Records'
first U.K. album release
'Silk Torpedo'
by

The Pretty Things

in
Chislehurst Caves,
Chislehurst, Kent.
Celebrations will commence
at 8.00 p.m. . . . .

Swan Song Records

Distributed by Atlantic Records

ouses of the Holy has some vintage material and splendid performances, notably by Jimmy Page, whose guitar work is inspired. Released on 28 March1973, it went straight to Number 1 in both the US and UK.

Again there was no title or name on the cover. The orange-hued gatefold LP sleeve was a tinted photograph of 11 naked young children (in reality, a montage of just two children, a brother and a sister) climbing over a rocky landscape, the Giant's Causeway in Northern Ireland. On the inner sleeve a man holds up one of the children in front of a ruined castle.

Despite the intriguing imagery, the cover didn't really relate to the music. It was, however, their first album to have a full title. *Houses of the Holy* was said to refer to the venues where Zeppelin played, as they communicated with their mass following. The song 'Houses of the Holy' didn't appear on the album but was featured later on *Physical Graffiti*.

When work began, the band had no set ideas and waited to see what would come out in the studio. Some tracks evolved from jam sessions that seemed like fun at the time, but there was no master plan or sustained system of songwriting. Although it looked like a concept album, it proved disjointed and the recorded sound didn't have quite the impact of *Four Symbols*.

'The Song Remains the Same' sets off at a blistering tempo, slowing down briefly to allow Robert's vocal extemporization as he muses on his travels from California to Calcutta and beyond. The speed rises again and Page unleashes a marvellous solo while the bass sustains the underlying theme. The vocals are processed to raise the pitch, so it sounds as if Plant is inhaling helium from a party balloon. The piece is so carefully structured it was originally entitled 'The Overture' and was to have featured as an instrumental until lyrics were added.

'The Rain Song' is gentle and slow, acoustic guitars supporting Robert's vocals. His voice glows with kindly warmth as he sings, "Speak to me only with your eyes, it is to you I give this tune." Jones adds a Mellotron to the backing, giving a suitably eerie and mournful effect. This unique keyboard instrument relied on a system of tapes to provide

PREVIOUS PAGES: Led Zeppelin in concert at the Forum, Los Angeles, 31 May 1973.

LEFT: Swan Song Records, the band's own label, was launched with a notoriously wild party in the depths of Chislehurst Caves with attendant fire-eaters and semi-naked wenches.

OPPOSITE: "I dare not drink before a gig because I'll get tired and blow it. So I have to sit drinking tea in a caravan, while everyone goes, 'Far out, man!'" John Bonham, pictured here in 1972.

sampled strings and was very popular with such groups as Genesis and the Moody Blues during the 1970s.

'Over the Hills and Far Away' sustains the low-key mood with a performance that wouldn't have been out of place in a folk club. Acoustic guitar chords chime as Robert intones sadly, "Many have I loved, many times been bitten …" Zeppelin sound like a different band, closer to the West Coast scene of the late Sixties, with elements of country rock surfacing amidst the choppy, accentuated beats. In true Zeppelin fashion, however, they move forward into different grooves before a tricky coda fades out, only to return. Released as a single in the US in May 1973, it peaked at Number 51 in the *Billboard* chart.

Next comes 'The Crunge', a spontaneous jam built over a funky beat Bonham began laying down as a studio warm-up. Jimmy uses his Fender Stratocaster's tremolo arm for a special effect every few bars. Robert's lyrics sound like a latter day rap as he refers obliquely to the early soul and blues singers that influenced him as an impressionable teenager.

'Dancing Days' is one of the album's better tracks, blending Eastern styles with rock influences. A grating, insistent guitar riff launches a melody Page and Plant picked up on a trip to Bombay, although they could have heard similar music in the curry-houses of Birmingham. Recorded at Stargroves and mixed at Electric Lady studio in New York, it has one of Plant's more unusual vocals.

'D'Yer Mak'er' (a pun on 'Jamaica') was a trip into reggae, a first for the band and the result of Robert's keen interest in different ethnic music forms. Bonham's drum sound is excellent, although his "heavy" approach doesn't necessarily suit the reggae rhythm. Surprisingly, it got to Number 20 in the *Billboard* singles chart in November 1973.

'No Quarter' is a much more interesting arrangement, built on Jones' piano and full of intriguing overtones. Robert sings about "The dogs of doom … howling" as Page locks into some jazzy improvisation pre-dating the sound of such latter outfits as the Cinematic Orchestra. It became a showcase number and was performed at the Earls Court shows in 1975.

Final track 'The Ocean' kicks off with Bonham chanting a gruff introduction before setting up a driving back beat. With Plant laughing and singing it's a gleeful performance enlivened by a sudden switch into a swing tempo that enables Page to solo with joyous freedom. 'The Ocean' in question was the vast audience the band performed to every night on tour. In his final lines Robert declaims, "I'm singing all my songs to the girl who won my heart … she's only three years old and it's a real fine way to start," a touching line dedicated to his daughter Carmen.

When some reviews were less than complimentary Plant responded: "So there's some buggers that don't like the album. Well, God bless 'em. I like it, and there's a few thousand other buggers that like it too."

OPPOSITE: Forever looking out for the next thrill, Jimmy, John and Robert give dirt bike riding a try while in Frenchs Forest, Sydney, Australia in February 1972.

BELOW: "I don't know how much more expressive you can get than being a rock and roll singer," Robert Plant said in 2010.

ALBUM TRACKS

Zeppelin's power and credibility was sustained by an album that was boldly experimental and highly popular as it topped the world's album charts, supported by enormous sold-out stadium shows. In the US, the album went platinum eleven times, and would go on to sell more than 10 milllion copies.

THE SONG REMAINS THE SAME

Led Zeppelin had the remarkable ability to surprise everyone with fresh ideas and arrangements that broke new ground and 'The Song Remains the Same' is a classic example.

With the sound of 'When the Levee Breaks' still rumbling in the distance, Zeppelin launched into a tune taken at such a tempo it seems to be played at 45 rpm – in fact, the vocal track was speeded up. Plant's lyrics describe his feelings about travelling the world from California to Calcutta and finding that music has much the same power everywhere.

The unexpectedly long introduction is like an overture to a rock opera. Guitar tracks pile on top of each other, until the tempo dramatically halves and Plant cries: "I had a dream – crazy dream". Bonham's drums place accents with all the accuracy of a precision bombing raid, then Jimmy Page rides again with a solo that is almost orthodox in its American-rock-style improvisation. Fans had grown used to Page flying off at tangents, but here he gets stuck into some of the most direct and fiery playing which Robert later described as the work of "genius". The chopped-up backing riff and dancing bass lines from John Paul Jones seem to be trying to check the progress of the song, like a speed governor in a high-performance car.

It was initially intended to be an instrumental, which explains the lengthy intro, and when first played its working title was 'The Overture'. When it was played on stage it became known as 'The Campaign', before eventually being bestowed with its more distinguished title.

ABOVE: The controversial cover art for *Houses of the Holy* involved a montage photograph of just two naked siblings climbing over Giant's Causeway in Ireland.

RIGHT: Surrounded by 50,000 fans, Zeppelin tear into songs from 'Rock and Roll' to 'The Ocean' as the sun shines over Kezar Stadium, San Francisco on 2 June 1973.

THE RAIN SONG

A tasteful, melodic performance, so low-key that it's almost the sort of thing you might expect to hear performed by a folksy lounge band at a Ramada Inn. Certainly Plant was in wistful, romantic mood when he penned the lyrics to this soliloquy on the changing moods of love. "This is the springtime of my loving," he intones breathlessly as Page renders a sensitive acoustic accompaniment using a Dan Electro guitar. The use of a Mellotron by John Paul Jones adds an orchestral flavour to the attractive backing. The Mellotron was an early attempt at creating a kind of semi-mechanical synthesizer, using tape loops triggered by a keyboard. While popular with Prog Rock bands, it was used only relatively rarely by Zeppelin. The piece ends with Plant's observation that "Upon us all a little rain must fall", the sort of motto usually found hand-stitched and placed upon a bedroom wall. It's said that the motivation for creating this ballad came from a chance conversation with future friend George Harrison, a big fan of Led Zeppelin. He was amazed when he discovered Zeppelin played three-hour sets on stage. He famously told John Bonham: "The problem with your band is that you don't do any ballads." This to the ensemble that had just created the decade's most famous ballad of all, 'Stairway to Heaven'. Nevertheless, 'The Rain Song' was retained for many of the band's shows between 1973 and 1975, and was performed as a solo piece towards the end of Zeppelin's career.

OVER THE HILLS AND FAR AWAY

A jerky, choppy rhythm breaks up this curious item, with its vaguely inconclusive coda. It only comes to life when Bonham's drums push Plant into singing, "Hey lady – you got the love I need". There is plenty of pleasant folk-style guitar work and the main theme is hypnotic, but it doesn't seem to want to go anywhere. According to Plant, the backing tracks were devised first then he came up with some appropriate lyrics. He found it difficult to sing to some of the increasingly complex melody lines, though they did give him a chance to indulge in his passion for ancient Celtic mythology.

Released as a single in the US in May 1973, 'Over the Hills and Far Away' failed to get into the Top 50. The song was played live before the album was released during their 1972 US tour and was performed at their 1979 Knebworth shows. It was also featured on Jimmy Page's 1988 *Outrider* tour.

> **"It's usually one of the roadies that rides along with us that gets us a bad reputation with his ... shenanigans."**
> ROBERT PLANT

THE CRUNGE

A song that happened by accident, it started with Bonham laying down a funky beat in the Stargroves studio – engineer George Chkiantz asks Bonham if he's "ready to rock". Then Jones joins in on bass and Page begins improvising an appropriate James Brown-style guitar rhythm. Plant adds vocals that encapsulate his feelings about favourite artists, from Otis Redding to Wilson Pickett. It was the sort of stuff they'd all be playing if they were in a "covers" band and not Led Zeppelin.

Being Led Zeppelin, they had to add their own slant to proceedings and came up with a dance groove that you couldn't dance to! Plant adopts a hipster voice and the swirling, interlocking riffs become ever more confusing. "Where's the bridge, where's the confounded bridge?" demands the singer, in best posh Long John Baldry tones.

The band were so enamoured of the idea of creating a new dance craze – The Crunge – that they considered putting some diagrammatic dance steps on the cover to explain how to cope with a beat that crossed over from "on" to "off" every few bars. But that would have been more difficult to produce than the seed catalogue design on *Led Zeppelin III*.

Page played a Fender Stratocaster guitar to get a suitable James Brown feel. You can hear him depressing a whammy bar at the end of each phrase. As Page said later: "Bonzo started the groove on 'The Crunge', then John Paul Jones started playing that descending bass line, and I just came in on the rhythm. You can hear the fun we were having." Plant's recollection was similar: "'The Crunge' was amazing because Bonzo and I were talking Black Country [a Midlands dialect] through the whole thing." The song was never included in the band's set as a full-blown piece, although Page occasionally threw in a few bars of 'The Crunge' riff and Plant linked it with a real James Brown number during shows at the Los Angeles Forum in 1975.

D'YER MAK'ER

Robert Plant was always interested and intrigued by ethnic music from around the world, particularly reggae, which was making a big impact on the UK music scene spearheaded by the internationally successful Bob Marley. This was Zeppelin's tribute to a genre that offered a whole new rhythmic impetus. John Bonham's heavy drumming lays down a decisive beat while Robert sings in sultry tones over cheerfully skipping guitar and bass.

Robert wanted it released as a single and backed with 'The Crunge' it went to Number 20 in the US *Billboard* chart in November 1973. While never performed "live", Plant would slip in a few lines during the medley section of their shows.

DANCING DAYS

One of the highlights of the album, 'Dancing Days' has a theme that successfully marries both Eastern and rock and roll influences. The tune was inspired by an Indian melody the band heard played on a strange instrument during a trip to Bombay. Plant was also influenced by the Indian music he often heard in the area of Birmingham where his girlfriend lived. The track also features one of Plant's most mystical and yet restrained vocals, held on to a single note for several of its hypnotic choruses. The curse of the squeaking bass drum pedal, noted on 'The Rain Song' and 'Over the Hills and Far Away', returned and managed to escape undetected on a tune that was played live some time before the album was recorded. But this is a minor problem on what is now seen by many Zeppelin fans as one of their most strangely affecting performances.

It was recorded at Stargroves and mixed at Electric Lady in New York, and engineer Eddie Kramer recalls seeing Page and Plant dancing in single file across the huge lawn outside the house, during the playback, to celebrate the completion of the song. Incidentally, Kramer had to put up with a series of practical jokes during the recording of this, including having various roadies bursting through his bedroom window all night while he was entertaining a new girlfriend. She left hurriedly in the morning.

The song was the first track from *Houses of the Holy* to be selected for radio promotion. This excellent, angular performance benefits by being heard on CD rather than vinyl; Robert's relaxed and untypical vocals flow through much more clearly.

OPPOSITE: Jimmy Page produces magical sounds as he delves into the mysterioso section of 'Dazed and Confused' before heading for a cataclysmic climax, Los Angeles 1973.

BELOW: *The Starship* was kitted out with TV, a bar, musical instruments and bedrooms. Led Zeppelin toured America aboard their leased Boeing jet in 1973 and 1975.

NO QUARTER

'No Quarter' was pinned together by John Paul Jones, who takes the reins and instils cohesion into the work. His eerie synth and piano sets up a mood that gives Plant a chance to put his vocal talents to good use. "Close the door, put out the light," he sings mysteriously, his voice processed through some sort of electronic cheese grater. "The dogs of doom are howling more," he warns us later, and reveals that when the winds of Thor are blowing cold, it's time to put on warm underwear, or at the very least "wear steel that's bright and true".

This interesting arrangement is full of pregnant pauses and, with his atmospheric keyboard playing, Jones adds extra depth to the song. A jazz-rock groove develops, but the lingering suspicion remains that this track is unlike anything the band had done before. Loose, not tight, 'No Quarter' had its origins in a piece tried out at Headley Grange, then slowed down in its final recorded version. It became Jones' major showcase number at live shows from 1973 onwards, including the brilliant Earls Court appearances in 1975, right up until Zeppelin's Knebworth dates in 1979. Robert Plant also featured the arrangement during his own Manic Nirvana tour in 1990.

And, in case you were wondering, "No quarter" was a pirate's phrase, much used by actor Robert Newton in his role as Long John Silver and beloved of the late Keith Moon.

THE OCEAN

Bonham counts in the beat in gruff tones: "We've done four already but now we're steady and then they went 1, 2, 3, 4," he intones, with a touch of menace. However, it seems likely he was referring to nothing more sinister than the four albums Zeppelin had already recorded.

'The Ocean' marked a return to form by a band playing purposefully together. The main riff dances around with a hip and a skip, and the elfin quality is heightened by a few bars of "la la" vocals that are imbued with a peculiar air of menace, perhaps because of the Birmingham cadences of the singers. There are a few choruses of really inspired playing, including a superbly jazzy guitar solo from Page, which is greeted by Plant crying out, "Oh, it's so good!" When the band break into a swing tempo, there is a palpable sense of joy all round. "Singing to an ocean, I can hear the oceans roar," sings Plant, using the phrase as an metaphor for the vast sea of living souls that comprised the nightly Zeppelin audience. "Singing songs until the night turns into day," warbles Plant on a number he dedicated to the audience whenever it was played on tour.

ABOVE: An explosive promo poster for *Houses of the Holy* showed Zeppelin hadn't lost the knack for using shock tactics to gain a response from their fans.

OPPOSITE: In 1977, at the Madison Square Garden show, 13 June, Jimmy becomes entangled in dry ice and lasers. The rock photographer Bob Gruen captured the moment.

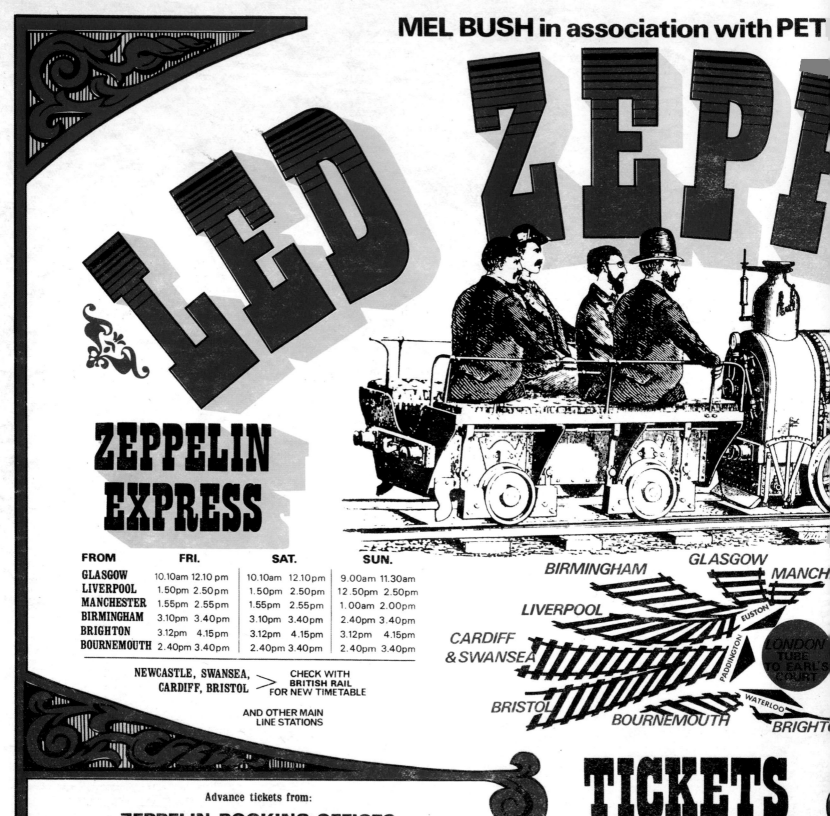

MEL BUSH in association with PET

LED ZEPP

ZEPPELIN EXPRESS

FROM	FRI.		SAT.		SUN.	
GLASGOW	10.10am	12.10 pm	10.10am	12.10pm	9.00am	11.30am
LIVERPOOL	1.50pm	2.50pm	1.50pm	2.50pm	12.50pm	2.50pm
MANCHESTER	1.55pm	2.55pm	1.55pm	2.55pm	1.00am	2.00pm
BIRMINGHAM	3.10pm	3.40pm	3.10pm	3.40pm	2.40pm	3.40pm
BRIGHTON	3.12pm	4.15pm	3.12pm	4.15pm	3.12pm	4.15pm
BOURNEMOUTH	2.40pm	3.40pm	2.40pm	3.40pm	2.40pm	3.40pm

NEWCASTLE, SWANSEA,
CARDIFF, BRISTOL > CHECK WITH
BRITISH RAIL
FOR NEW TIMETABLE

AND OTHER MAIN
LINE STATIONS

BIRMINGHAM   GLASGOW   MANCH

LIVERPOOL   EUSTON

CARDIFF
& SWANSEA   PADDINGTON   LONDON
TUBE
TO EARL'S
COURT

BRISTOL   WATERLOO

BOURNEMOUTH   BRIGHT

TICKETS
£2·50, £2·00
£1·50 & £1·00

Advance tickets from:

ZEPPELIN BOOKING OFFICES

EARL'S COURT EXHIBITION BUILDINGS, WARWICK ROAD
LONDON SW5   Telephone: 01- 401 6921/2

OPEN 11a.m - 6p.m. MON - SAT.

All cheques and P.O.'s made payable to " ZEPPELIN BOX OFFICE " Enclosing S.A.E.

EARL'S COURT

FRI   SAT   SUN
23rd **24**th **25**th

MAY at 8p.m.

Doors open
6 p.m.

Glasgow - Apollo Centre	041/332 6055	Cardiff - Buffalo Records	0222/27034
N'castle - Virgin Records	0632/24883	Bristol - Virgin Records	0272/297431
Liverpool - Cosmopolitan	051/709 3703	Brighton - Virgin Records	0273/28167
M'chester - Hime & Addison	061/834 8019	Bournem'th - Setchfields	0202/26925
B'gham - Virgin Records	021/236 9196	London Theatre Bookings	01/439 3371
Swansea - Virgin Records	0792/51499	& all branches Virgin Records	01/727 8070

ALL BOX OFFICES OPEN SAT. MARCH 15th, 10.00 a.m.

Designed by Peter Grainey Graphics Bournemouth

LEFT: Led Zeppelin played five legendary nights at London's Earl's Court in May 1975. The stylish poster played on the theme of arriving by train. Footage from the concerts was released on DVD 20 years later.

SHOW SOUVENIR

THIS BOOK IS DESIGNED FOR YOUR FURTHER ENJOYMENT OF THE SHOW

LED
ZEPPELIN

OPPOSITE: A rare flyer for a charity concert in Hiroshima, Japan, in 1971. Led Zeppelin toured Japan between 23-29 September 1971 and were one of the first English rock bands to perform in the country.

ABOVE AND NEXT SPREAD: A 1973 souvenir programme, featuring signatures of all band members. "Designed for your further enjoyment of the show", the spelling and grammar mistakes contained in the band biography within the programme made for interesting reading.

LED ZEPPELIN

Led Zeppelin began in a small, stuffy rehearsal hall, in London, late 1968. "Four of us got together in this two by two room and started playing. Then we knew - we started laughing at each other. Maybe it was from relief, or maybe from the kowledge that we knew we could groove together. But that was it. That was just how well it was going". Jimmy Page, master guitarist, former Yardbird, was watching his thoughts, his ambitions, his concealed desires as a musician, take shape in a new supergroup, Led Zeppelin.

"The statement of our first two weeks together is our album. We cut it in 15 hours, and between us wrote 8 of the tracks. Our main problem was knowing what channel to take it along musically. Everyone in the group had such a high musical content we thought each of us would be into our own thing. But it all fell together.

"We'll probably always be faced with the fact that individually, each member could cut his own album going in his own direction and it would be great. But all those ideas in one outfit, well , thats pretty fantastic too".

The formation of Led Zeppelin was on easy task. When it became generally known that Jimmy Page was putting a group together, he was indudated with calls from musicians all over the country. When Yardbirds finally split up in the summer of 1968, Jimmy was ready to take bass player Chris Dreja with him into Led Zeppelin.Chris eventually backed out of the arrangement, choosing instead to go into management.

"When I joined the Yardbirds, my main reason was to give myself the opportunity of playing my own music. Before that, my only interest was session work. I began to feel limited not being able to express myself. When I left, it was for almost exactly the same reasons. The group split because everyone began to feel the need to go in his own direction. The pity is, there would have still been great potential".

It was all down to Jimmy Page, alone, on a one man campaign to make himself heard. As a session guitarist he was, and still is, one of the finest in England, contributing his works to tracks by such stars as the Stones, Donovan, and latterly, Joe Cocker, who took the Beatles' "With A Little Help From My Freinds" to such a smash.

"I was working on the Dinovan album, "Hurdy Gurdy Man" with John Paul Jones who did some of the arrangements. He asked if I could Use a bass guitarist in Led Zeppelin. John is an incredible arranger and musician. He didn't need me for a job, but he felt the need to express himself and figured we could do that together.

"Sessions are great, but you can't get into your own thing. Both myself and John felt that in order to give what we had to offer we had to have a group. He wanted to be part of a group of musicians who could lay down some good things".

"I can't put a tag to our music . Every one of us has been influenced by the blues, but it's one's interpretation of it and how you utilize it. I wish someone would invent an expression, but "I want us to be raw and basic. That was the whole thing that made the Yardbirds happen. To go into your own thing is fine, but it has to be a form of experimentation that evolves from a basic sound that everyone else knows and can relate to."

It took two years for Led Zeppelin to emerge. The name was conceived by Jimmy Page when he was still with the Yardbirds and each member of the group took a shot at recording on his own. Jimmy penned "Beck's Bolero" for Jeff Beck. Today it's a Beck standard, then, it was a track on which the Who's Keith Moon played drums. "When we were kicking around group names, I suddenly remembered Led Zeppelin which I had come up with at that time."

That too would have been a supergroup. but every musician to his own bag, and for Jimmy Page, it's John Paul Jones, John Bonham and Robert Plant to make Led Zeppelin an example of great music. And this is a group that won two standing ovations and two encores on their first date in London, with only six hours of rehearsal behind them.

It's the greatest trip any selection of musicians can take their audience on, the greatest feeling of being into a scene, one which America is ready and waiting for. On this, their latest tour, every ticket at enery Theatre was sold within four hours of the announcement. Considering this a is thirty day package of the entire country it must give some idea of their popularity.

PHYSICAL GRAFFITI ▶ (1975)

With too much material available for a single album, *Physical Graffiti* became the band's first double set, a major work unleashing new Zeppelin classics 'Houses of the Holy', 'Trampled Underfoot' and 'Kashmir'.

PHYSICAL GRAFFITI

The band's sixth album was one of Led Zeppelin's most impressive works and a step towards achieving their ambition of creating the ultimate record. The mass of material on a double LP meant that not all of the tracks matched the much-admired 'Kashmir'. However, it was altogether Zeppelin's strongest showing in some years and restored the faith of fans and critics alike.

The bold confidence was reflected both in the music and the imaginative cover art. It was the first Zeppelin release on Swan Song and the band's name and album title were clearly displayed. Record buyers were intrigued by a cover that depicted the windows and blinds typically observed in a New York brownstone tenement building. Holes cut in the cardboard sleeve made it possible to slide the inner bags to reveal surreal images and activities going on inside the "apartments". Jimmy Page later described the effect as a "Peeping Tom's delight".

Physical Graffiti was released on 24 February 1975 with 15 tracks including eight that had been recorded at Headley Grange the previous year. There were also seven songs dating back to the days of *Led Zeppelin III*.

It was Zeppelin's longest studio album. Because they had enough new material for only one-and-a-half LPs, they decided to top it up with older recordings to complete the double set. When they met up to start work for the first time in six months it was after a period of uncertainty about their future. They had all been exhausted by lengthy American tours and needed time to recover and recharge their batteries.

Jimmy Page had spent some time at his home, working up ideas and themes. These were gradually pieced together and fleshed out during sessions that evolved out of studio warm-ups. Sometimes they'd simply play their old favourites to relax. Then a new piece would evolve and take on its own life.

The opening track, 'Custard Pie', immediately grabs the listener with its emphatic guitar riff and pounding back beat drums. Robert slips easily into his more raucous mode; a style that would inspire many a future heavy metal singer.

The strong pulse is maintained on 'The Rover', a seminal Seventies rock tune born out of an early acoustic version. It's a unified band performance with Robert's vocals dominating while Jimmy takes a relatively brief and melodic solo. The rock jam that develops in the final chorus harks back to the days of Eric Clapton's Cream.

The third track, 'In My Time of Dying', is an 11-minute marathon that commences with a slow-paced bluesy introduction from Jimmy setting the scene. His slide guitar licks are redolent of Southern swamps and cotton fields. Robert intones plaintively, "In my time of dying ..." as Bonzo interjects thunderous support from the depths of his drum kit. The whole piece picks up tempo and evolves into a spontaneous celebration as if the band are playing a "live" club gig. Page revealed later that the piece lacked a proper ending and they simply jammed their way towards a coda. In many ways this represented *le vrai* Zeppelin.

'Houses of the Holy' should perhaps have appeared on the 1973 album of the same name. The title refers to their "congregation" of fans and the supernatural atmosphere they generated at concerts. A sturdy rocker, Robert sings it lustily against a barrage of riffs. The number had its origins in the 1972 sessions held at the Olympic Studios in Barnes.

One of the biggest pleasures and surprises of *Physical Graffiti* is the launch into the realms of funk displayed on the irresistible and hypnotic 'Trampled Underfoot'. This gem is essentially a romp over a series of funky riffs with a stomping beat generated by Mr Bonham. It takes on a life of its own as John Paul Jones launches into a jazzy electric piano solo, complete with cliff-hanging breaks. When it jerks back into the beat again, the effect

PREVIOUS PAGES: Between 17 and 25 May 1975, Zeppelin play five shows at London's Earls Court. The band attracted 85,000 people and played for three-and-a-half hours each night.

LEFT AND OPPOSITE: Bonham's brother, Mick, was in the audience for these Earls Court shows, pictured: "Laser beams fired above the heads of the audience gave the effect of flaming arrows when they reflected off a mirror ball, filling the vast hall with snowflakes and stars," he said later.

is electrifying. It's one of those numbers that doesn't want to stop, a feeling echoed by the audience at Earls Court when they first heard it performed "live" in 1975.

As if this wasn't enough, the exciting 'Trampled Underfoot' is hotly pursued by the sensational 'Kashmir', a theme so dramatic it has been used in many a theatrical setting, including being frequently used on *The X Factor* talent show. Taken at a slow and ponderous tempo, the menacing aura that surrounds this Eastern-flavoured *magnum opus* is so unusual it aroused some puzzlement among the band's closest advisers. They referred to it as "the dirge" until its genuine majesty began to take effect.

Over the coming years, 'Kashmir' came to surpass even 'Stairway to Heaven' as the band's greatest set piece and all the band members proclaimed it a highlight of the band's career. The concept began life when Robert composed some lyrics during a long and bumpy holiday trip across the Sahara Desert. It was originally called 'Driving to Kashmir' – his dream destination. The mood it engendered revealed Plant and Page's increasing fascination with both Moorish and Indian music. The theme was worked up on demo recordings laid down by Page and Bonham and later arranged by John Paul Jones. The addition of an orchestra into the mix of guitars and drums worked perfectly.

'In the Light' that follows is another atmospheric piece that develops more slowly and is predicated on John Paul Jones use of a VCS synthesizer. It was recorded at Headley Grange and was never performed on stage due mainly to technical difficulties. But it remains an intriguing example of Zeppelin in cutting-edge experimental mode. Plant sings of self-revelation and the need for "the light" to exert a life balance.

'Bron-Yr-Aur' is different from the 'Bron-Y-Aur Stomp' that appeared on *Led Zeppelin III*. It features Jimmy Page playing solo Martin guitar on a two-minute acoustic instrumental that dates back to 1970.

On its 40th anniversary in February 2015, *Physical Graffiti* was re-released in a special Deluxe Edition. The package came in different formats, including the full original LP remastered on CD, a 3-CD set with extra tracks, versions on vinyl and a boxed set. *Daily Mail* critic Adrian Thrills gave it a five-star review and proclaimed, "The last great rock album just got better."

ABOVE: Robert Plant primal screaming in 1975.

OPPOSITE: As captured by Bob Gruen, Plant in 1974. "I think Led Zeppelin must have worn some of the most peculiar clothing that men had ever been seen to wear without cracking a smile," Robert said of the time.

ALBUM TRACKS

Hard rock, cool funk, boogie-woogie and Eastern influences all weave their way into the sonic textures of *Physical Graffiti*, a double whammy often hailed by critics as "an embarrassment of riches".

CUSTARD PIE

Physical is the word – a smack in the teeth for all those detractors who had begun to doubt Led Zeppelin's innate ability. Here was an ultra-tough riff with a raunchy beat that showed the band were back in business. They seemed a bolder, better band, playing together with a clearly defined sound and a firm sense of direction. No messy beats, no mangled vocals, just a mix of solid drums and guitar which combined to throw a custard pie in the face of a cynical world. John Paul Jones provided a sprightly electric clavinet riff in the background to a theme that has its roots in Blind Boy Fuller's 1939 recording 'I Want Some of Your Pie'. Sonny Terry and Brown McGhee had also recorded a song called 'Custard Pie Blues' in 1947. Bukka White's 'Shake 'em Down' is quoted in the lyrics. Big Joe Williams recorded yet another version, called 'Drop Down Mama', which may have

been the inspiration both for Zeppelin's 'Custard Pie' and for Plant's cry of "Drop down!" As Plant's harmonica wails, Page puts his solo through an ARP synthesizer. Strangely enough, this funky rebel-rouser was never played on tour by Zeppelin, but Plant sang a chorus or two during his solo tours in the 1980s and Page performed it during his *Outrider* tour.

TOP: Slide out the inner sleeves of the *Physical Graffiti* LP cover to reveal different scenes in the windows of a brownstone Manhattan tenement block.

BOTTOM: "We may not be brilliant every night, but we'll always be good," said Jimmy. The band knock out Newcastle City Hall on 1 December 1972.

OPPOSITE: Jimmy wore his famous white satin "poppy" suit while playing 'Dazed and Confused' at the Madison Square Garden show, 1977. It is now much admired by fashion designers.

THE ROVER

Hot on the heels of 'Custard Pie', this extremely raunchy number is pure mid-1970s rock. Once again the band can be heard truly playing together, rather than meeting as echoes on bits of salvaged demo tape. It was far removed from 1969-style Led Zeppelin blues, but then times, styles and recording techniques had moved on, and this was a different, more mature and cohesive beast. The kind of heavy rock-metal heard on 'The Rover' inspired many young metal bands to emulate their heroes – during the late 1980s in particular, it was almost impossible not to trip over Zep soundalike bands like White Lion and Kingdom Come.

Yet surprisingly the piece was first rehearsed as an acoustic blues piece. It was subsequently recorded as a full band number during the *Houses of the Holy* sessions at Stargroves. It was evidently remixed, with the powerful guitar solo added in 1974, in time for its addition to *Physical Graffiti*. Like many of the mid-period Zeppelin album tracks, it was not played live on stage, although a bootleg CD reveals it was played during rehearsals.

IN MY TIME OF DYING

A four-star classic, this 11-minute feat of Zeppelin engineering shows how imagination, wedded to organization, produces riveting results. A deeply blue guitar introduction ushers in Robert Plant's opening remarks. "In my time of dying ...," he sings with a gloomy foreboding, until the mood gives way to a more confident spirit. Violently powerful drums pick up the beat, then drums, bass and guitar simmer and boil as an obsessive riff builds to a shattering climax. Thus ended Side 1. Side 2, it should be said, contained the greatest sustained set of performances, not just in Zeppelin's own album history, but in the entire annals of rock recording.

The most extraordinary thing is that the best cuts on *Physical Graffiti* have grown in stature with the passing years. 'In My Time Of Dying' alone would be a highlight of any other band's output; the distinctly live feel shows that this is very much a spontaneous performance. "That's gotta be the one," says the voice of John Bonham at the end of the take.

The tune was based on a traditional song that Dylan played on his first album, *Bob Dylan*, released in 1962. It is said that the lyrics were from a 1927 Blind Willie Johnson record called 'Jesus Make Up My Dying Bed'. The number was played on the band's 1975 US tour and at Earls Court in London in May of that year when Plant dedicated the number to the Labour Party's Chancellor of the Exchequer, Dennis Healey.

Jimmy Page played it with his band on the 1988 *Outrider* tour. He recalls that the song was still being put together when they first recorded it. "It was jammed at the end and we didn't even have a proper way to stop the thing." Page liked this approach because it made the band sound like "a working group". On the other hand, Plant was apparently not too keen on singing 'In My Time of Dying' after suffering his serious car crash. As he said later: "Why the hell did I sing that song?"

HOUSES OF THE HOLY

The lost track from the album of the same name – if it had been included on the fifth album, it would have been a different story in terms of reviews and reaction. This is a highly acceptable piece of work. A clipped beat and an easy riff provided a platform for some of Page's most manic improvisation. A house of the holy is a church, temple or chapel, but in this case the plural term refers to the mysterious aura that Zeppelin felt was conjured at their concerts. Bonham's squeaking drum pedal can be heard again some three minutes into the song. 'Houses' was recorded and mixed at Olympic and Electric Lady studios, during a session that dates back to 1972. Oddly enough, it was never performed live.

> **"*Physical Graffiti* is a more personal album, and I think it allowed the listener to enter our world. You know, 'Here is the door. I am in.'"**
> JIMMY PAGE

TRAMPLED UNDERFOOT

Shock waves spread outwards when this thunderous track was first heard. Led Zeppelin had never played like this before. This was sheer honest-to-goodness funk, played with open-hearted spirit and relentless drive. It was all the more effective for being so completely unexpected. Not that 'Trampled Underfoot' was revolutionary – there was a touch of Stevie Wonder about the groove – but it was full of bounce. Zeppelin just threw caution to the wind and rocked out.

John Paul Jones proved his value, by providing the surging electric piano current that galvanized the rhythm section. John Bonham responded with a back beat so solid it threatened to punch holes through the floorboards. The staccato riff that went "beep, beep, deedle eedle eedle beep beep ..." was so tight it threatened to weld fingers to strings and keys. The band were delighted and hugely satisfied when they first developed the number out of a simple jam session. Robert Plant later revealed it was one of his all-time Zeppelin favourites.

Certainly it caused a sensation when the band played it live at their 1975 Earls Court shows. For years afterwards fans remembered the moment when the piece just took off with a life and momentum of its own. It seemed like the band wanted to go on playing it for ever.

Plant's lyrics were based on Robert Johnson's 1936 recording, 'Terraplane Blues' – at least in the sense that they are about using the vocabulary of motor cars as a sexual metaphor. Plant sings something along the lines of "Grease me down ... I could lay it on the road, mama, it ain't no sin. Talkin' about love ... Mama let me pump your gas... Baby I could rev all night .... come to me for service ... let me change your valves ..." and so on.

The song was released as a single in the US, where it got to Number 38 in the *Billboard* chart in May 1975. 'Trampled Underfoot' became a staple of all the band's shows after 1975 and Plant sang it on his 1988 *Now and Zen* tour.

KASHMIR

Rolling thunder and a sustained mood of ominous mystery pervade this, the mightiest of all Zeppelin master works. Like 'Trampled Underfoot', it seemed to come out of nowhere, defying all past precedents, but it was much more than a simple jam; it was the result of shared experiences and long hours of hard work. Here the band created a musical picture more effective than a thousand album covers. Once again John Bonham excelled. His contributions to 'Kashmir', 'In My Time of Dying' and 'Trampled Underfoot' served as a greater testament to his technique and style than any number of recorded drum solos. This powerful drama, which suggests a solemn, marching procession of hooded figures, also boasts one of Robert Plant's finest vocals. He sings with a new kind of humility and serious intent. Perhaps this reflected his own state of mind and a growing maturity.

The Eastern flavour and orchestral sound of 'Kashmir' seemed to launch Led Zeppelin into an entirely different direction. Most bands would be in a state of advanced decay by their sixth album. From the evidence of this song alone, here was a group undergoing a complete renaissance. The lyrics were composed by Plant during a holiday in southern Morocco, a desert kingdom in northwest Africa, which of course is nowhere near Kashmir, a disputed territory of south Asia noted for its rice-growing and beautiful mountain scenery. The song was originally called 'Driving to Kashmir', which meant he had a long way to go. However, the deeper meaning of the song was the strange link between the grandeur and mystical power of Arabian music and the communicative powers of rock.

Jimmy Page had two distinct riffs available on a home demo he'd made with Bonham. The main theme was based on a guitar tuning that he'd used on 'White Summer', 'Black Mountain Side' and the unheard 'Swan Song' theme. When the theme was eventually combined with a John Paul Jones arrangement, the piece burst into seething life. Page's use of strange Moorish-sounding chords, played on a Dan Electro guitar and backed by session string players, ensured that 'Kashmir' fulfilled its Eastern promise.

Plant explained: "The beat came from John. I wrote the lyrics after driving into the Sahara Desert." He had been heading from Goulimine to Tantan in what used to be called the Spanish Sahara. "I kept bumping down a desert track and there was nobody for miles, except a guy on a camel. The whole inspiration for the song came from the fact the road went on and on and on. It was a single-track road which cut neatly through the desert ... it looked like you were driving down a channel. I thought, this is great, but one day ... Kashmir. That's my Shangri-La."

Jones, Plant and Page all felt it was one of the greatest Zeppelin tracks ever and a highlight of the band's career. As Jones stated, "It's all there, all the elements that defined the band." Plant recalled: "'Kashmir' was tremendous for the mood. A lot of that was down to Bonzo." Page added: "The intensity of 'Kashmir' was such that when we'd done it, we knew that it was something so magnetic, you just couldn't describe what the quality was. It was just Bonzo and myself at Headley Grange at the start. He played the drums and I did the riff and the overdubs which get duplicated by an orchestra at the end, which brought it even more to life. It seemed so ominous. It's nice to go for a mood and know you've pulled it off." Incidentally, by one of those quirks of recording that beset even the most prudent engineers, a ghost of a previous orchestral track that was "'wiped" can be heard spilling faintly into the left stereo channel.

'Kashmir' was first played in Rotterdam, Holland in January 1975, and in every Zeppelin show thereafter. It was also played at the Atlantic Records birthday party show held at Madison Square Garden in the mid-1980s, and on the *Unledded* tour of 1995.

IN THE LIGHT

Recorded at Headley Grange using the late Ronnie Lane's mobile studio, 'In the Light' was largely the creation of John Paul Jones, who used a VCS synthesizer. The track was never performed live because Jones, in common with many synthesizer players in the 70s, found it impossible to keep the instrument in tune. The melody was based on another number called 'In the Morning' and was also called 'Take Me Home', which came complete with a different set of lyrics.

Page said: "We knew exactly what the construction of 'In the Light' would be, but nevertheless I had no idea at the time that John Paul was going to come up with such an amazing synthesizer intro. There were also bowed guitars at the beginning to give a drone effect." The vocals contain stock cries of "Ooh baby", but the Beatles-ish chord sequence works well.

TOP: The band end their triumphant Madison Square Garden show with 'Heartbreaker', New York, to rapturous applause from 20,000 fans, 12 February 1975.

BRON-YR-AUR

Quite different from 'Bron-Y-Aur Stomp', although this two-minute acoustic guitar instrumental was recorded during sessions for the *Led Zeppelin III* album way back in May 1970 at Island Studios. It's an exquisite piece played seriously, without affectation, and captures Page in a reflective and relaxed mood. The squeaking strings and occasional fluffed notes only add to the spontaneity of the performance. Here was the self-taught guitarist struggling against fate and the elements and producing musical magic.

The different spelling of 'Bron-Yr-Aur' has some significance. 'Bron-y-aur' with a small 'y' and 'a' means 'breast of gold' and refers to the beautiful countryside around the town of Machynlleth, near the river Dovey in Wales. 'Bron-Yr-Aur' is the name of the eighteenth-century cottage where Robert Plant spent his childhood holidays, and where Plant and Page stayed in 1970 to write the material that appeared on *Led Zeppelin III*. Welsh language experts have pointed out that place names shouldn't have hyphens.

The last acoustic piece recorded by Zeppelin, it was rarely performed live, but it can be heard on bootleg albums. It sounds much better on the Led Zeppelin boxed set CD version than on vinyl, with or without hyphens.

DOWN BY THE SEASIDE

Another item originally composed during the 'Bron-Yr-Aur' sessions of 1970 and intended to be an acoustic-type ditty, this was finally recorded as an electric version during the sessions that were scheduled for the fourth album. After much debate it was finally deemed "below standard" and held over. When it came to discussions about material for *Physical Graffiti*, Plant suggested they re-evaluate the tune and include it on the new album. "Everyone laughed when I suggested it," he recalls. Plant sings it with a bow and a curtsy to Neil Young while John Paul Jones' electric piano adds a pleasant country rock touch. The trembling guitar is a real tear-jerker and the waltzy feel is briefly interspersed by an unexpected twist rhythm.

TEN YEARS GONE

First love is the subject under discussion here. Plant cannot but allow himself a wry smile as he contemplates the destiny of an old girlfriend who had given him an ultimatum, some 10 years earlier. She wanted him to give up his music, his career and his fans, and settle down with her to a steady life of suburban contentment – rock and roll and Plant's fans won.

Jimmy Page used some 14 guitar tracks to overdub the harmony section on a piece that was first intended to be an instrumental number. Some fans suspect this is the long-lost 'Swan Song'. When it was played live during the band's 1977 dates, John Paul Jones employed a unique three-necked guitar to help re-create his wall of sound. The instrument was made for him by guitar technician Andy Manson and was used with special bass pedals, but it was too much for Jones to handle and the number was discarded.

NIGHT FLIGHT

Recorded at Headley Grange with the Rolling Stones' mobile, this 1971 composition was never played live, although it was performed during rehearsals for the 1973 US tour, notably at their gig on 5 July in Chicago. It has a brisk boogie-rock rhythm with a touch of the Who in the declamatory breaks. Pete Townshend and Keith Moon might have enjoyed putting this on one of their 70s albums. However, Jones' organ sound drops into a pub-rock mode that sounds curiously out of place. Another version of the tune was cut, with extra backing vocals.

THE WANTON SONG

This is a story about sex that Plant delivers with suitably thrusting energy. "Wanton" can mean maliciously cruel and destructive as well as dissolute, licentious or immoral; a wanton woman is therefore someone to be feared as much as admired.

Jimmy Page employs backwards echo during his solo here and the guitar is put through a Leslie speaker cabinet of the type used to create a Doppler effect with a Hammond organ. Page first began using backwards tape echo in the Yardbirds, and when he tried it on the earliest Zeppelin recordings he had to face considerable opposition from technicians who thought it wouldn't work.

'The Wanton Song' came about as the result of a jam session at rehearsals. It was played on some of the 1975 European and American dates before being dropped.

BOOGIE WITH STU

Stu was Ian Stewart, the Rolling Stones' road manager and sometime blues pianist, who died in 1985 from a heart attack. He was a much-loved character with a keen interest in jazz and blues, and had been a member of the Rolling Stones until image-conscious manager Andrew Oldham decided Stewart wasn't good-looking enough to be in the public eye.

This jam session was recorded at Headley Grange and the theme was based on Richie Valens' 1950s hit song, 'Ooh My Head'. The sleeve credits Mrs Valens among the co-composers to ensure the late singer's mother received some royalties. Plant cheerfully referred to the 'Head' arrangement as 'Sloppy Drunk' when it was first unveiled. He played guitar on the track, while Page played mandolin. However, some special effects were created by Page slapping a guitar synth. Stewart sounds as if he's playing a pub piano covered in beer bottles and filled with tin tacks. Laughter greets the final bars of a jolly hand-clapping, foot-stomping rhythm supplied by Bonham.

BLACK COUNTRY WOMAN

Originating from a session held in the back garden of Mick Jagger's country home, Stargroves, in April 1972, this was intended for *Houses of the Holy* and recorded at the same time as 'D'yer Mak'er'. Sub-titled 'Never Ending Doubting Woman Blues', this acoustic, country-style number originally had Plant adding those words as an extra tag line.

The outdoor location is revealed by the roar of an aeroplane flying overhead at the start of the sessions. It's possible to hear engineer Eddie Kramer muttering something like "I'm trying to get this airplane off", to which Plant replies, "No, leave it on." Recording outdoors was always more difficult than it seemed. Once when Plant tried to go outside to sing the song, he was attacked by a flock of angry geese.

Page used a special blues G-tuning on a number that was eventually performed by the band during their 1977 US tour. John Paul Jones was featured on the tune, playing an upright bass in true skiffle fashion.

OPPOSITE: Plant struts in San Francisco to the delight of 50,00 fans cramming the Kezar Stadium, at Zeppelin's concert on 2 June 1973. The band made $1,000 a minute. Not bad for a two-and-a-half-hour show.

SICK AGAIN

The Los Angeles groupie scene was the inspiration for this glam metal rocker, which refers to the heavy competition among girls for the band's favours. As at least two members of the band were married by this time, it was perhaps not the best subject for wide-ranging discussion.

The guitars have a sardonic ring and Plant's vocals are buried deep in the mix, but you can hear him in best Marc Bolan groove talking about "the teenage dream" and "the circus of LA queens". You could imagine the band jamming on this at some sleazy Hollywood bar, wearing feather boas

and costume jewellery – and strangely enough, the band did dress up in drag for one night of madness in New Orleans as one of the scenes from the album cover reveals. You can just about hear a suitably sickly cough at the end of the number, which emanates from the drummer, a man whose health was not always in the best condition after a night on the tiles.

The song was performed live on their 1975 and 1977 tour dates but, mourned Robert, who took his writing very seriously, "It was a pity you couldn't hear the lyrics."

ABOVE: Robert Plant armed with tambourine, Jimmy Page with twin-neck Gibson SG: Led Zeppelin were ready to rock.

OPPOSITE: A rare handbill announcing the "Internationally Famous" Led Zeppelin's appearance at the St Matthew's Baths Hall, Ipswich, 16 November 1971. The gig came just after the band had released their fourth album.

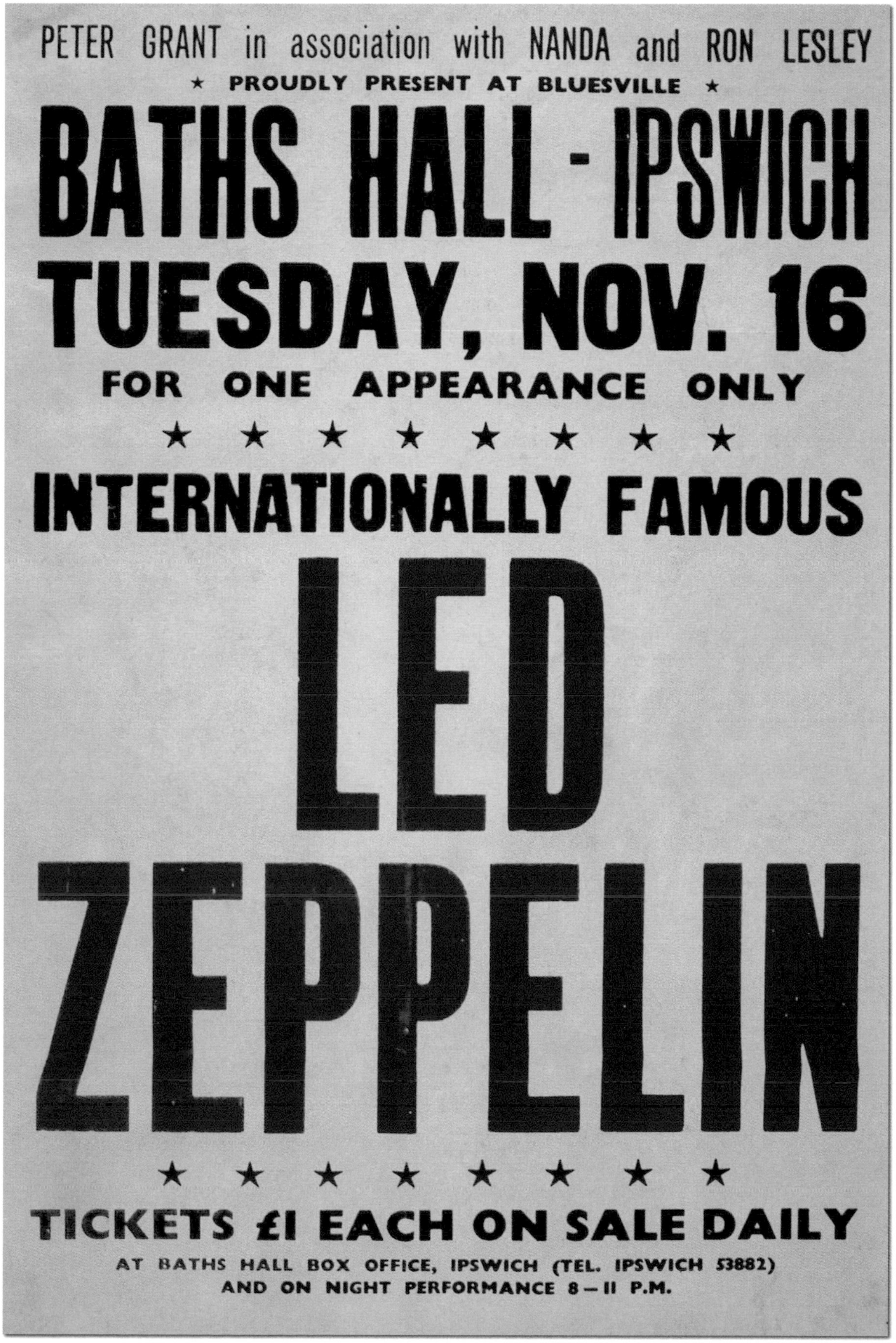
PETER GRANT in association with NANDA and RON LESLEY
★ PROUDLY PRESENT AT BLUESVILLE ★
BATHS HALL - IPSWICH
TUESDAY, NOV. 16
FOR ONE APPEARANCE ONLY
★ ★ ★ ★ ★ ★ ★ ★
INTERNATIONALLY FAMOUS
LED
ZEPPELIN
★ ★ ★ ★ ★ ★ ★ ★
TICKETS £1 EACH ON SALE DAILY
AT BATHS HALL BOX OFFICE, IPSWICH (TEL. IPSWICH 53882)
AND ON NIGHT PERFORMANCE 8 – 11 P.M.

JOHN BONHAM

A legend among drummers, a pillar of Led Zeppelin and one of rock's great characters, Bonham was a tower of strength and an innovative musician who inspired the band.

JOHN BONHAM

"Bonzo" was the heart and soul of Led Zeppelin. The Bonham sound, purposeful and commanding, was woven into their creative fabric. Many numbers were built around the drum and guitar riffs he and Page worked out together, such as 'Immigrant Song', Black Dog' and 'When the Levee Breaks'. His sense of swing came from his jazz and blues roots, and it was Bonham's clever use of cymbals and percussion that brought such drama to 'Dazed and Confused' and 'Whole Lotta Love'.

Page knew how to utilize Bonham's power to full effect in the studio. He would hold the drums back until they could make a grand entrance, most effectively on 'Stairway to Heaven'. All the key albums featured earth-shaking moments from Bonham, including his introduction to 'Rock and Roll', the thunder unleashed on 'Kashmir' and that most sampled of Zeppelin tracks, 'When the Levee Breaks'.

In an era when drummers became celebrities, Bonham stood out. His extended solos became a feature of concerts, as much part of the Zeppelin image as Page waving his violin bow or Plant's mighty screams.

John Henry Bonham was born in Redditch, Worcestershire, on 31 May 1948. Father Jack was a carpenter with his own building firm; mum Joan ran a newsagent's shop.

When John left school at 16 it was assumed he would go into the family business, and he often laboured on building sites, but as he said later, "Drumming was the only thing I was any good at and I stuck at it.'" At five, he'd begun hammering on pots and pans and used a handy bath salts container with wires across the bottom to give the effect of a snare drum. His father took him to see American drummer Sonny Payne with the Harry James Orchestra and he was mesmerized by Payne's soloing; Gene Krupa's drumming on 'Sing, Sing, Sing' in the film *The Benny Goodman Story* was another source of inspiration.

His father bought him a proper kit when he was 15: "It was almost prehistoric. Most of it was rust, but I was determined to be a drummer as soon as I left school."

His first semi-professional group, Terry Webb and the Spiders, dressed as Teddy Boys and played rock and roll. After a year, he joined A Way of Life and, aged 17, married girlfriend Pat. Although he occasionally had to return to building sites to earn a living, he carried on playing and worked with singer Nicky James. "I was so keen to play when I quit school I'd have played for nothing. I did for a long time but my parents stuck by me. I never had any lessons and just played the way I wanted. They used to say I was too loud and there was no future in playing that way." One exasperated recording engineer told Bonham he was "unrecordable" and ought to play quieter. It was the drummer's great delight some years later to send him a gold Led Zeppelin album with a note saying, "Thanks for the advice."

He had promised his wife he'd give up drumming, but couldn't resist getting behind a kit. He'd played with Steve Brett and the Mavericks before joining the Crawling King Snakes, where he met Plant. When Robert excitedly called him about a possible gig with the New Yardbirds, he wasn't interested.

Bonham had developed a reputation for his technique, which drew on influences from Sonny Payne to Buddy Rich and from Joe Morello to Carmine Appice of Vanilla Fudge; Appice's speed with a bass drum pedal particularly intrigued Bonham, who would develop his own powerful foot action.

Page had thought about recruiting BJ Wilson of Procol Harum and also contacted Aynsley Dunbar, who had worked with John Mayall's Bluesbreakers. When Aynsley joined Frank Zappa, Plant told Page about Bonham, explaining he was the loudest and heaviest drummer in the country and would be ideal.

Jimmy went to the Marquee to see Bonzo backing Tim Rose. He later called Grant in the States to report: "This guy plays so good and so loud we must get him. He plays so loud promoters won't rebook him!"

When Grant returned to London he discovered Bonham didn't have a working telephone. He sent a succession of telegrams which the drummer ignored, thinking the New Yardbirds sounded like a cabaret act.

Eventually John succumbed to pressure and came to London for the first rehearsal in Soho. He played well, but when Jimmy asked him to simplify the beat he carried on regardless. Page was visibly annoyed, and when Grant saw this he asked Bonham, "Do you like your job in the band? If so, do as this man says or f**k off. Behave yourself, Bonham, or you'll disappear, through different doors."

Once the ground rules were established, Bonham became a loyal and integral part of Led Zeppelin. His famed drum solo, dubbed 'Moby Dick', appeared on *Led Zeppelin II* and a live version on 1976's soundtrack album *The Song Remains The Same*. An unusual electronic drum solo, 'Bonzo's Montreux', appeared on the posthumous *Coda* album in 1982.

When Led Zeppelin became a mega-group John was happy to spend his pay on cars and property and become a gentleman farmer, but his greatest delight was being able to support his family and encourage son Jason, who would later became a top drummer in his own right, even playing with the revived Led Zeppelin.

The band embarked on a European tour in 1980. Although unwell, Bonham completed most of the dates, but died on 25 September 1980, after rehearsing at Page's house in Windsor prior to a planned US tour. Led Zeppelin died with him, but his drums roar on in the band's legacy.

PREVIOUS PAGES: John Bonham bangs the beat at the Forum, Los Angeles, 3 June 1973. After the show, he celebrates his 25th birthday, and throws George Harrison into the hotel's swimmng pool!
RIGHT: Captured in pensive mood, Bonham reveals the more serious side of a man often depicted as a free-spirited, wild man of rock.

PRESENCE ► (1976)

Robert Plant described *Presence*, the band's seventh album released in 1976, as "our stand against the Elements and Chance". Jimmy Page saw it as two fingers up against the forces of destruction.

PRESENCE

It was the album that nearly didn't happen. Injuries Robert Plant suffered in his 1975 car crash put him out of action. With a broken ankle and elbow, he was advised he wouldn't be able to walk for months, and recording and touring seemed out of the question, but by the end of the year Plant was well enough for the band to contemplate work on a new album. Led Zeppelin met at Musicland Studios in Germany. It was the first time they had chosen a European studio and the fresh location seemed to encourage them.

The stand-out track on *Presence* is undoubtedly 'Achilles' Last Stand', a magnificent performance by any band's standards. Taken at a galloping pace, the dramatic theme summons images of warriors on trusty steeds charging through forests and across the battlefields of myth and legend. It's hard to believe Robert Plant sang this song while on crutches; perhaps even in a wheelchair.

The glittering steely guitar overdubs unleashed during 'Achilles' Last Stand' clash like swords, except Page's weapon of choice was a Gibson Les Paul bonded to a trusty Marshall amplifier. An intensely powerful arrangement, it explored different movements in typical Zeppelin fashion. The song became a concert staple, taking its place alongside 'Kashmir' as a new classic.

After this, the rest of the album seemed an anti-climax to some, but there were plenty of nuggets meriting closer study, and just as rewarding in more subtle ways. 'For Your Life' examines aspects of the rock lifestyle they had all experienced and Robert found dissatisfying; he later described it as an admonition of those who fell into the trap of the LA drugs and groupie scene.

The next song, 'Royal Orleans', is another reflection on the strangeness of rock stars' lives, in particular, a tale of someone waking up in bed with a drag queen at a hotel in the French quarter of New Orleans. This "someone" was quite close to the band and it is further alleged the unlikely couple set the bed alight with a cigarette and the fire brigade had to be called.

'Nobody's Fault but Mine' is full of long pauses during the narrative and has strong harmonica playing from Plant, the blues aficionado. The number develops from hesitant beginnings and is said to have been inspired by a 1920s Blind Willie Johnson blues.

Rock and roller 'Candy Store Rock' harks back to the days when Teddy Boys ruled the UK youth scene. Bonham is in his element, driving the beat, while Robert improvises the lyrics from the dimly remembered Elvis records of his youth. It was released as a single in America in June 1976, backed with 'Royal Orleans'.

'Hots on for Nowhere' was devised in the studio and is a curious mixture of childlike innocence and seething bitterness, with its dancing beat and biting lyrics. Bonham plays with undiminished fire and Page offers a guitar break of dazzling dexterity. Its driving simplicity sets up the listener for the album's final track.

'Tea for One' is a beautiful song about pain and loneliness. Following an anguished guitar introduction, it becomes a ballad that's both tasteful and sombre, Page's extended guitar solo being described by Plant as "brilliant". The title came from a period during a US tour when Robert was feeling especially homesick and found himself sitting in a hotel room drinking "tea for one". Whatever moods the band members were enduring during difficult times, they hadn't lost their ability to lose themselves in the joy of making music for their own satisfaction.

The album was released in America on 31 March 1976, and in Britain on 6 April in a white sleeve designed by the Hipgnosis team, famed for Pink Floyd's *Dark Side of the Moon*. Unlike *Physical Graffiti* there was no band name or album title on the front, although they did appear along the spine. Some albums ended up being stickered! Aubrey Powell of Hipgnosis suggested the title, sensing a "presence" surrounding the band.

The cover photographs depict an all-American family contemplating a mysterious twisted piece of metal known as "The Object", partly inspired by the iconic "obelisk" featured in Stanley Kubrick's film *2001: A Space Odyssey*. As one point the album was to be called *Obelisk*, though Plant preferred *Thanksgiving* to express his relief at completing the task. However, *Presence* was Page's final choice.

Huge advance orders ensured it went gold immediately and it was Number 1 in the UK and US charts within weeks. Page later said he thought *Presence* was an underrated album and their best in terms of emotional content: yet it was all done in three weeks. Many bands could take as many months, years even, to finish an album.

Under deadline pressure, Page explained, they had cut all the frills, such as acoustic numbers and keyboard arrangements, and concentrated on the core of guitar riffs and vocals backed by bass and drums, spending up to 18 hours a day in the studio trying to get it all done. The best news for Plant after finishing the album was that he could walk unaided and make his true presence felt on stage again.

PREVIOUS PAGES: Armed and dangerous with his honeyburst Gibson Les Paul, Jimmy cuts yet another defining, and enduring, image for rock and roll, North American tour, 1975.

OPPOSITE: Jimmy's double-neck Gibson EDS 1275 enabled him to play songs like 'Stairway to Heaven' without switching guitars in the middle of a performance. Pictured here at the Forum, Los Angeles, 25 March 1975.

ALBUM TRACKS

Under the scrutiny of critics at a difficult time for the band, the innovative songs on *Presence* revealed a determination by Zeppelin to stay relevant, to experiment and keep the trust of fans. It's Jimmy Page's favourite album made by the group.

ACHILLES' LAST STAND

Achilles was the hero of Homer's *Iliad*, the son of Peleus and Thetis. It was Thetis who tried to make Achilles immortal by bathing him in the river Styx. Unfortunately she held him by the heel, which was not immersed and therefore his vulnerable point. When he went to the Trojan wars he was killed by Paris, who wounded him in the heel with an arrow.

Robert Plant sang in a wheelchair during the making of this Zeppelin blockbuster and so, perhaps, felt some empathy with Achilles after his own Greek experience with a broken ankle. He has said, however, that the song is concerned with the view from the top of the Atlas mountains in southern Morocco. Plant was so excited by the piece that he fell over during the session and nearly exacerbated his injury. "I was hobbling around in the middle of this great track when suddenly enthusiasm got the better of me. I was running to the vocal booth with this orthopaedic crutch when down I went, straight down on the bad foot. There was an almighty crack and a great flash of light and pain and I folded up in agony," he recalled. Page rushed out of the recording booth and held up his old friend. The band helped Plant into a chair while general factotum Richard Cole organized a swift trip to a nearby hospital, which almost certainly saved Plant from permanent damage. As it turned out, there were no fresh breaks, which would have been a disaster, as Plant realized: "If I had opened the fracture I would never have walked again." In the event, he was able to walk unaided by the end of December 1975.

The lyrics actually refer to the band's wanderings in Africa, rather than Greece, but this ten-minute piece trundles along with all the furious passage of a Trojan war chariot heading into battle. John Bonham's drums are like horses' hooves, while the guitars clash like flashing swords against clattering shields. The overdubbing facilities available at Musicland enabled Page to build up many layers of sound – Zeppelin had no need for orchestras or string sections when they could create a wall of sound like this. As the battering drums and rumbling bass fade away, we are left with strange, desultory guitar chords, chiming in empty space.

'Achilles' Last Stand' is a direct descendant of previous Eastern-influenced works, like 'The Song Remains the Same' and 'Kashmir', but has a much harder rock feel. It was achieved quickly, as Page remembers: "I built that track piece by piece and I got it in one night."

ABOVE, TOP: An enigmatic cover, typical of its designer Hipgnosis, in which the black "object" is the focus of a normal family's attention, yet also represents Zeppelin's alchemical power.

ABOVE, BOTTOM: Radiating a kaleidoscope of colours, Jimmy Page works magic with his famous bow, Madison Square Gardens, New York, 12 February 1975.

FOR YOUR LIFE

A song noted for its bitter, contemplative lyrics from Plant, still traumatized by recent events, but more relevantly, disillusioned with certain aspects of the rock lifestyle. After all, what did fame and fortune mean when you were in pain and separated from your home and family? The normal diversions found on the road suddenly seemed shallow; there had to be more to life.

A rattling tambourine fails to dissipate the doomy mood created by the singer, who seems to deliberately disguise his lyrics. Through the static interference of "Oh, ohs" and twisted enunciation, you can hear Plant sing, "She said – don't you want some cocaine and try a one-night stand?" He later said the song was "a sarcastic dig" at someone he knew and liked in Los Angeles who got sucked into the LA drugs scene. "'For Your Life' is sort of wagging the finger and saying 'watch it'," explained Plant.

The backing riff has the dramatic quality of a TV cop show theme tune. When guitar and bass play in unison, Page and Jones create a very funky groove that is almost rap style, a decade ahead of its time. Vocally, Plant seems to be struggling – a lemon squeezed dry, as one acerbic critic put it. Certainly lines like "Do it – if you wanna" suggest that a degree of mental and physical exhaustion had beset the once cheery, active youth of yesteryear. Jimmy Page used a blue 1962 Fender Stratocaster guitar for the first time on this piece, which he later used with the Firm. Despite his best efforts, 'For Your Life' doesn't want to take off, and although it got to rehearsal stage, it was never performed in a live setting. It was certainly a million miles from the Yardbirds and 'For Your Love'.

> "*Presence* was a reflection of the height of our emotions at the time. We did the whole thing in 18 days. There are no acoustic songs, no keyboards, no mellowness." JIMMY PAGE

ROYAL ORLEANS

Phil Carson, a long-term associate of Led Zeppelin, says: "Everyone should study the lyrics to 'Royal Orleans'. It's about a member of the band waking up in bed with a drag queen. Did it give him a shock? I don't think so." In fact it's very hard to decipher what Plant is singing about, or who he has in mind. The word "whiskers" pops up, so we can assume this is the physical characteristic that gives away the bedmate picked up on Bourbon Street.

'Royal Orleans' was a hotel in the French quarter of New Orleans at 621 St Louis Street, a place where the band relaxed and enjoyed life in their own inimitable fashion. They spent a lot of time in gay bars, where they found the drag queens more fun than boring "straights" and could drink without being hassled. Some authorities have suggested the lyrics refer to a session player known to both Page and Jones. Certainly Plant can be heard singing about "a man I know", so the party could have been someone closer to home.

In fact the band's indefatigable tour manager, Richard Cole, insists that it was one of the band who ended up with a drag queen in his room at the Royal Orleans, without realizing the true identity of his guest. Perhaps it was during the moment of discovery that they accidentally set the bed alight with a cigarette, which resulted in the fire brigade being called and all hell breaking loose.

RIGHT: A three-and-a-half-hour set at the Forum, Los Angeles, 25 March 1975. John Bonham said of the gig: "Our best gig where everything clicked was at the Forum. The people were so great that attended the show they made us play harder."

NOBODY'S FAULT BUT MINE

The guitar intro is very bluesy and features Plant singing wordless phrases in tight unison with the lead line. All clever stuff and especially effective when the band blasts into action. "It's nobody's fault but mine!" declares the singer, but adds later, "The devil he told me to roll." There are long, pregnant pauses in the musical narrative, and the way the vocals and Plant's excellent harmonica playing bounce off the drums recalls the work of Jack Bruce and Ginger Baker of Cream.

Plant really comes on in his "Wild Man of Blues" role. When he plays his old harmonica with such earthy power, you can imagine the mighty Led Zeppelin, kings of stadium rock, back in a small club playing for beer and peanuts. The number doesn't seem too promising at first, but picks up and develops a life of its own. Some crazed solo work from Page enlivens the final chorus or so. The tune was partly inspired by Blind Willie Johnson, who wrote similar lyrics way back in the 1920s. In the 1970s Led Zeppelin played it on their 1977 US tour and at Knebworth, England, in 1979. Plant also featured the number during his solo tours in the 1980s.

CANDY STORE ROCK

The spirits of Elvis, Gene Vincent and Eddie Cochran loom over this rock and roller, in which Bonham pushes the beat with commendable zeal. Heavy use of echo gives the guitars an authentic 1950s flavour as Plant sings from the depth of his plaster cast.

'Candy Store Rock' took little more than an hour to compose and was hailed as a great success. Page recorded most of the solos for these tracks during one 14-hour session, hoping to have everything done by the time they had to quit the studio, hence the spirit of urgency. Some have detected the influence of Gene Vincent's guitarist Cliff Gallup on the rockabilly guitar work.

This track was prepared for a live airing but in the event was never played on tour. It was, however, released as a single in the US in June 1976, backed with 'Royal Orleans', but failed to set the charts alight.

Plant described 'Candy Store Rock' as one of his personal favourites from the album: "This was me trying to be Ral Donner, and the rhythm section was inspired." Chicago-born singer Ral Donner had hits with 'Girl of My Best Friend' and the chart-topping 'Please Don't Go' way back in 1961. Narrator of the film *This is Elvis*, he died of cancer in 1984.

OPPOSITE: Stonehenge onstage: the band bring a bit of England to the Sunshine State, Oakland Coliseum, California, 23 July 1977.

HOTS ON FOR NOWHERE

Another studio creation and written in an hour, it has a dancing beat set to Plant's yelps of "la la la", which sound plain silly on first hearing but begin to make sense as the number grows on the listener with repeated plays. The lyrics were written during the band's rehearsals in Malibu and reflected a certain dissatisfaction "with friends who would give me fuck all", who are believed to be Messrs Grant and Page. This callously merry outing has lots of sharp stops for guitar breaks and the drumming is superb.

> "***Presence*** was a highly underrated record. It was our best in terms of uninterrupted emotion. We came in with nothing ... but everything just came pouring out."
>
> JIMMY PAGE

TEA FOR ONE

According to Robert Plant, this track and 'Candy Store Rock' share a common theme in that they explore the subject of loneliness, pain and hurt. Certainly the guitar intro sounds painful, until the tempo slows down for a more relaxed exploration of a slow, bluesy ballad. It develops into one of the band's most tasteful, low-key, sombre and reflective outpourings.

Page and Bonham exchange a wild outburst of passion before returning to *sotto voce* groove. The drummer keeps perfect time on his ride cymbal, while providing the occasional press roll to sustain Page's unusually long guitar solo. The languid mood is deceptive; while Plant sings with a rare show of restraint, the feeling is nonetheless passionate. The mood recalls their other great slow blues epic, 'Since I've Been Loving You', and reflects a yearning to return to the roots of their days of innocent and carefree youth. More directly, the lyrics came from Plant's increasing sense of homesickness while on the road in the States, exacerbated when he found himself alone in a New York hotel – drinking tea for one.

RIGHT: Spotlights shine their light on the gods of rock on what has become a legendary performance, the Forum, Los Angeles, 25 March 1975.

LEGACY

For British fans, 1975 was the year when Led Zeppelin dominated London's Earls Court for five sensational nights – 17, 18, 23, 24 and 25 May – regarded by many as their finest hours. They presented their full American production, unleashed new material and entranced another generation of fans. They also released one of their most important albums.

The year began with shows in Rotterdam (11 January) and Brussels (the 12th). Then Page, hurrying to a rehearsal, broke his left ring finger in a train door at London's Victoria Station. Grant feared the tenth US tour might be in jeopardy, and they'd sold 700,000 tickets. However, Page was back for the opening night at the Metro Sports Centre, Minneapolis, on 18 January, though he couldn't bend notes. 'Dazed and Confused' was replaced with 'How Many More Times' to protect Page's finger.

Although the tour was a success, fears were growing about the band's financial security. The UK tax rate on high earners was then 87 per cent. The group had to become "non-resident" and move abroad for a year; Bonham and Plant were particularly unhappy, but the band moved to France or Switzerland when they weren't in the States. Grant stayed in America, renting a house on Long Island.

The 1975 US tour exceeded all expectations. There were riots in Boston even before the band hit town. The show used a 70,000W PA system, laser-equipped lighting rig and a crew of 44 technicians.

Plant caught 'flu in Chicago and struggled through shows in Cleveland and Indianapolis. A date in St Louis on 26 January had to be cancelled. Robert holed up in a Chicago hotel while the others flew to LA for 24 hours' leave. As *The Starship* had its own bar and an electric piano, they were able to party on. The next day they flew to North Carolina for a show at Greensboro Coliseum (29 January), where 500 youths unable to get tickets tried to storm the venue and stoned their limos. When the drivers tried to abandon the band Grant commandeered a Cadillac, grabbed his charges and drove through the mob out of the arena, heading for the airport. After racing through red lights at 70mph (110kph) he completed several laps of honour around the waiting plane, then kicked the car, complaining it wasn't as fast as his Bentley.

During breaks in touring, the band got up to some of their more notorious hotel escapades, including stuffing Bonham's wardrobe with mudsharks, fished from the ocean, which fell out on an unsuspecting maid. Wild parties staged by promoter Bill Graham ended in food fights and mayhem. Bonham was even observed riding a motorbike along a corridor at the Hyatt "Riot" House in West Hollywood.

They could afford such mischief. In two months Led Zeppelin grossed $5 million. A highlight was playing six concerts to 120,000 fans in the New York area, including three nights at Madison Square Garden, with Mick

The premiere of the long-awaited Led Zeppelin film *The Song Remains the Same* was a highlight of a year when the group once more made their presence felt around the world. Even while *Physical Graffiti* was echoing across the airwaves, the band came up with a new album, but they avoided live appearances during 1976. Cinemas became the only venues where fans could get their musical thrills.

Jagger and David Bowie in the house. Rod Stewart went to one of three shows at Nassau Coliseum, which completed the first stage of the tour on 14 February. It ended with three shows at the Los Angeles Forum, concluding on 27 March.

During the trip Grant and the band went to see Elvis in Las Vegas. He stopped the show to announce that Led Zeppelin was in the audience and invited them back to his suite for a visit that lasted two and a half hours. An exhausted Grant dropped his 18 stone on to a sofa – and the legs of Elvis' father Vernon. Grant apologized to Mr Presley and then to Elvis. Elvis responded, "Stick around, kid; you might get a permanent job."

Physical Graffiti was released on 24 February, instantly going gold, then platinum, and topping the *Billboard* chart. Their entire back catalogue was revived and all their albums charted again.

In April Page, Plant and Grant flew to New York on Swan Song business and Jimmy began mixing the soundtrack for *The Song Remains the Same*. In May the five nights at Earls Court drew 85,000 people. Promoter Mel Bush could have sold twice as many. Reportedly, 51,000 tickets sold in two hours and the rest went over the weekend.

For the band's first UK appearances since 1973, Dallas-based Showco flew in the equipment and employed a 15-man crew. A video screen enabled the audience to see the band close up. They performed five numbers from the new album, notably the fast and funky 'Trampled Underfoot', while 'Dazed and Confused' went down a storm. Page, wreathed in smoke pierced by green laser beams, flailed his guitar with the bow to produce eerie howls around the cavernous venue. 'Moby Dick' and 'Whole Lotta Love' concluded shows presenting Zeppelin at the peak of their powers.

In Paris for New Year, Plant took his first steps since the crash five months earlier, joking: "One small step for man, one giant leap for six nights at Madison Square Garden."

While Page worked on mixing the film soundtrack, Plant was pressed into doing interviews to discuss their forthcoming album. In February Led Zeppelin won many of the categories in the *New Musical Express* annual

LEFT: John Paul, Robert, Jimmy and Bonzo pose in a field at Knebworth in 1979 for a photo used for an *In Through the Out Door* promo poster and for the festival programme.

Despite the traumas and tragedy, it seemed inconceivable that the world's greatest band should be allowed to fade away. Page was determined to keep Zeppelin airborne and with Grant - under orders to lose weight after stress-related heart trouble - made plans to restore the group to flying condition.

readers' poll. The following month Page returned to London from New York and did his share of interviews, and set up at the Swan Song offices in Fulham, London.

Although the group had cancelled all their tour dates following Robert's injury, he was able to put in an appearance on stage, jamming alongside Page at a Bad Company gig at the Los Angeles Forum on 23 May. Later that month rumours spread that the whole band might appear at London's Marquee Club, but in the event only Jones turned up to sit in with the Pretty Things.

In July anxious promoters hoped the band would put on a one-off show at Wembley Stadium. Whereas most artists would fall on their knees at such an offer, Zeppelin declined. They were too busy preparing their film, and in any case Plant wasn't ready for a strenuous stage performance. He did attend a rock festival in Cardiff, and shortly afterwards Dave Edmunds was signed to Swan Song.

During September Page produced a percussion track featuring Bonham that would eventually surface as 'Bonzo's Montreux' on the 1982 album *Coda*. In October TV viewers got a rare glimpse of the band on the small screen when BBC 2's *Old Grey Whistle Test* showed a clip from *The Song Remains the Same*.

On 20 October the film premiered at Cinema One in Manhattan, New York. A special quadraphonic sound system hired from Showco was installed in the theatre; powerful hi-fi sound was vital for the film's success. All the band members attended, with the $25,000 proceeds going to a children's charity. On 22 October the double soundtrack album was released simultaneously worldwide and the film was also given its West Coast premiere in Los Angeles.

The film director Peter Clifton finally managed to blend the famed fantasy sequences depicting the band members' personalities, backstage scenes and live footage shot at Madison Square Garden in 1973. Some scenes had been reshot at Shepperton Studios to help match the soundtrack and the footage.

Bonham's appearance driving a drag-racing car drew cheers from the crowd at the London premiere. The other sequences, such as Page climbing the mountain near Boleskin House and Jones as a night-rider, were greeted with some bemusement.

Some thought the star of the film was manager Grant, whose ferocity berating a concert promoter backstage in Baltimore in 1973 lit up the screen. In a towering rage, he was complaining about a pirate merchandiser being allowed to trade within the venue in order to profit from Zeppelin's show. The robbery at the Drake Hotel in New York also provided another dramatic episode when newsreel footage was acquired of Peter being arrested for assaulting a photographer at a press conference.

As a result of this candour, not all the reviews were complimentary. Dave Marsh in *Rolling Stone* said the film was "a tribute to their rapaciousness and inconsideration ... their sense of themselves merits only contempt". However, Chris Charlesworth in *Melody Maker* branded it a "classy, and surely enormously successful film". It grossed $200,000 in the first week of release and the soundtrack album went platinum and topped the charts. Page thought the film provided a good record of the band's past work and Grant later conceded: "Some of it was OK: but what did we know about making films? I did enjoy the premieres and meeting all the media folk. It was the most expensive home movie ever made."

On 30 October Led Zeppelin gave the news all their fans had been awaiting. With the film safely out of the way, the band would return to live gigs with a world tour due to start in America in February 1977.

Meanwhile a double European premiere was staged in two West End cinemas on 4 November, followed by a jolly party at the Floral Hall, Covent Garden, attended by Robert Plant. A couple of days later *The Song Remains the Same* was screened in Birmingham, Glasgow, Liverpool, Cambridge, Leeds, Reading and Southampton.

Led Zeppelin were harnessing the power of film and rock in a pioneering form, although the Woodstock documentary had already shown how mixed media could succeed. There was no doubt Led Zeppelin were happiest doing what they did best, and so they began rehearsing in London for their 1977 tour, kicking off with their hot new song 'Achilles' Last Stand'. They were ready for action but, once again, the fates would conspire against them.

The year began with the promise of a world tour, to begin in the US on 27 February. During January they began rehearsals at Manticore, a converted cinema in Fulham owned by rival supergroup Emerson, Lake and Palmer.

Punk rock was emerging; while many long-established groups felt threatened by aggressive new bands such as the Sex Pistols, who called them "dinosaurs", Led Zeppelin welcomed the trend towards anarchism. Plant and Page went to see the Damned at the Roxy in Covent Garden and announced they'd enjoyed the show, and Bonham and Plant saw Generation X, Eater and the Damned there. Maybe it was the foetid atmosphere at punk gigs, but Robert contracted tonsillitis and their 11th US tour had to be postponed. The dates were rescheduled and eventually they opened in Dallas on 1 April. Fifty-one concerts awaited, in 30 cities, and a million fans, cigarette lighters poised ready to hold aloft during 'Stairway to Heaven'. They would be playing for three hours a night, something which amazed recent convert George Harrison; the Beatles, he said, never played live for more than about 30 minutes. Video projector screens were set up at the biggest venues and Showco provided massive PA systems. Tickets sold at a rate of 72,000 a day.

Page seemed to take all the hard work in his stride, having recovered from the illness that had affected him on previous tours. It was reported he was taking a daily mixture of bananas and protein for strength. Said Plant:

"We've got a new Jimmy Page and he's the leader again. If he doesn't stay healthy, I'll kill him!"

Despite this nutritious diet, during one of four nights at the Chicago Stadium Page had to sit down while soloing on 'Ten Years Gone' and an hour in, the band was forced to stop. Page was taken back to his hotel, said to be suffering from food poisoning. "The pain was unbearable," he said later. "It was the first time we had to stop a gig like that. We always have a go because we're not a rip-off band." He insisted they were enjoying themselves on the road and rebutted rumours of an impending split: "It's a stag party that never ends, and it's great to be back on the road after all the trials and tribulations of the past year. It's great to see the smiles. This is no last tour. We're here and we'll always come back. It'd be a criminal act to break up this band."

Zeppelin broke the record set at Tampa in 1973 when they played to 76,229 fans at the Pontiac Silverdome on 30 April, earning them and the promoter $800,000. The hotel wrecking sprees continued, with Plant's room at the Ambassador East Hotel in Chicago a particular target. He paid for any damage, however, insisting it was not done out of boredom or "road fever" – but just for fun.

In May, about halfway through the tour they took a 17-day break; Page flew to Egypt to visit the pyramids. The others, plus Grant, went to London to receive an Ivor Novello Award on 12 May for their contribution to music. The tour resumed on 18 May in Birmingham, Alabama. At many shows there were riots and arrests as fans without tickets tried to get in. Some of the worst violence was at Tampa Stadium, Florida, on 3 June when 20 minutes in, during "The Song Remains the Same", lightning tore through the sky and the heavens opened. As rain was pouring on to the stage, the road crew feared the danger of electrocution. Robert told the crowd: "We have to stop or our equipment will blow up!" When there was crowd unrest, police in riot gear arrived and began bashing heads. More than 100 fans were injured and the Mayor announced Led Zeppelin would be forever banned from Tampa to protect its citizens. A replacement show the following day was cancelled.

They played six nights at Madison Square Garden, New York, between 7 and 14 June, and between 21 and 27 June slotted in another six at the Forum, Los Angeles. On 28 June they flew home for a rest, returning to the States on 17 July to play the Kingdome, Seattle. All seemed well; then on 23 July a violent scene developed backstage at a concert at the Coliseum in Oakland. Grant, tour manager Cole, Bonham and security man John Bindon were involved in a clash with promoter Bill Graham's own team, attacking a security man when he refused to let Grant's son Warren take a nameplate from a dressing-room door as a souvenir. The guard was hospitalized; Cole, Bonham, Bindon and Grant were arrested and charged with assault. A civil action followed, demanding $2 million in damages.

The following day the band flew to New Orleans for a date at the Superdome on 30 July. However, on the day they arrived, news came from England that Robert's son Karac had been taken ill with an infection. The next day he was worse, and was taken to hospital, but was dead on arrival. Robert immediately flew home and the rest of the tour was cancelled.

There was more talk of a split in September, but in London Page conducted several interviews to quash the rumours, angry at suggestions

RIGHT: A hard day's rockin' at the Oakland Coliseum on 23 July 1977. Robert Plant, the defining rock star of his generation, makes looking cool look easy.

they were under some sort of "curse". However, the future looked uncertain, and in the event Zeppelin would never return to the States in their original form. They left behind a lot of bad feeling, and *Rolling Stone* magazine's headline read: "The wrong goodbye: Led Zeppelin leaves America."

It was many months before Plant would recover from the shock of his son's death and he spent all his time at home with his family. Page spent his time writing songs and going through the vast mountain of tapes the band had accumulated over the years. He proposed using live material for an album that would put excerpts from concerts in chronological order. These would include shows at venues such as the Royal Albert Hall in 1969, Southampton University in 1971 and Earls Court in 1975. It would provide an official record of Zeppelin's growth as opposed to the many bootleg LPs

then circulating among record collectors: but it wasn't until the CD era that officially sanctioned Zeppelin compilations began to appear.

Meanwhile Bonham and Jones also spent their days at home with their families, perhaps coming to terms with what had happened in California and trying to escape from the rock and roll lifestyle.

Page was the only band member who felt able to conduct interviews during this crisis period and confirmed: "There's no question of splitting up. Robert wants to work again and he'll start working at his own pace."

On 16 February 1978, the criminal cases against Grant, Bonham, Cole and Bindon were heard in California and all received suspended prison sentences and fines. None of the men appeared in court.

It wasn't until May that the band reunited in somewhat chastened mood at Clearwell Castle in the Forest of Dean to rehearse and make plans. By the summer rumours began to spread that Led Zeppelin might perform in the UK, but these proved unfounded. Instead, Plant cheered himself up by singing with various bands of old mates in his former stamping-ground in the Black Country.

Having spent the early part of the year quietly with his family, Plant reappeared at Wolverley Memorial Hall in July, singing with an outfit entitled Melvin Giganticus and the Turd Burglars. His choice of songs included rousing versions of 'I Gotta Woman' and 'Blue Suede Shoes'. The following month he sang along with pub rockers Dr Feelgood at Club Amnesia in Ibiza. Atlantic executive Phil Carson sat in on bass guitar, reviving memories of his jams with Zeppelin in happier times. The club's manager Stu Lyons said later: "Robert looked in great shape and sounded fantastic."

On 15 September there was a Zeppelin "family" event when tour manager Cole got married, and the Fulham ceremony was attended by Page, Plant and Jones. The next day Plant joined Swan Song artist Dave Edmunds for his encore number at Birmingham Odeon. There was more music-making when Jones and Bonham were invited to participate in a recording session with Paul McCartney's Rockestra at Abbey Road Studios, to lay down tracks for the Wings album *Back to the Egg*.

In October Led Zeppelin got back to work and began rehearsals in London for a projected new album, but for tax reasons they had to get out of the country for a while and flew to Stockholm on 6 November to make the album which was to be called *In Through the Out Door* at ABBA's Polar Music studio.

Robert explained that ABBA had invited them to come to Sweden to try out the studios. Normally they would have gone to Los Angeles in order to soak up the vibes and get into heavy rock mode. "To trek to Sweden in the middle of winter, the studio had to be good and it was. It was sensational and had just the live sound that we like."

Once the recordings were completed, Jimmy Page began mixing the material at his home studio in Plumpton over the Christmas holiday. The year had flashed by, and for their fans around the world it seemed a deathly silence had fallen over the band. They feared they'd never hear 'Whole Lotta Love', 'Kashmir' and 'Stairway to Heaven' live again; but their patience was rewarded and anxiety allayed. Soon the announcements came in the music

LEFT: Rock God – Page and his Gibson take no prisoners, in front of 20,000 fans, at Madison Square Garden, New York, 7 June 1977.

"We've got a new Jimmy Page and he's the leader again. If he doesn't stay healthy this time ... I'll kill him!"

ROBERT PLANT

press. Led Zeppelin was staying together and did have plans for the future. 1979 would provide a reprieve for the band and they would be back on stage one more time with a show in the UK intended as a celebration: but in another twist of fate, it would prove to be their swansong.

The year began with good news: the birth of Robert and Maureen's son Logan on 21 January. Understandably, Plant wanted to spend time at home, but in February the band returned to Stockholm to continue mixing the album. There was even talk of a European tour, but instead, they spent time catching up on the simple pleasures they had missed during Zeppelin's early years; Jones and Plant went to Dave Edmunds' wedding reception on 8 May. Then on 22 May it was announced they would headline a show at Knebworth, Hertfordshire, promoted by Fred Bannister, creator of the Bath Festivals. It would coincide with the release of their eighth studio album, *In Through the Out Door*. They opted for a showcase rather than another tour because, as Grant explained: "We didn't want to start all over again. We're the biggest band in the world, so we'll go out there and show them we still are." Names being mentioned for the Knebworth bill included Dire Straits, Fairport Convention, Joni Mitchell, Little Feat, Bob Seger, Van Morrison, the Boomtown Rats, BB King, Aerosmith and the Marshall Tucker Band, though few of these were eventually booked. On 9 June Plant gave a BBC Radio 1 interview, his first in two years. Then on 4 July it was announced there would be another show at Knebworth, due to such huge demand. Zeppelin rehearsed at Bray Studios, and on 19 July it was confirmed that the New Barbarians, led by Rolling Stones Keith Richards and Ronnie Wood, would support them at the second event.

To warm up, Zeppelin went back to their roots with shows at the Falkoner Theatre, Copenhagen, on 23 and 24 July; they had first played in the city in September 1968. On 3 August they arrived at Knebworth to soundcheck and the following day took the stage supported by Fairport Convention, Commander Cody, Chas and Dave, Southside Johnny and the Asbury Jukes and Todd Rundgren's Utopia. Zeppelin played for three hours and did four encores. It was their first UK gig since 1975 and their first anywhere since July 1977. Showco installed a 100,000W PA, a 600,000W light show and a vast video screen.

At the second show on 11 August the line-up was almost identical, Keith Richards and the New Barbarians replacing Fairport. Both they and Zeppelin kept fans waiting, which didn't help the atmosphere. There was some debate about numbers, but Grant arranged a helicopter to photograph the crowd and sent the pictures to NASA, who reported there were 210,000 at the first show and 180,000 at the second.

Some reviews were brutal. As the decade ended, "new" sounds and fashions – punk, New Wave, New Romanticism, New Heavy Metal – were being touted to replace the supergroups. A new generation of critics saw Zeppelin as representing the "dinosaur" breed of despised stadium rockers, and were emboldened by the perceived loss of power and prestige they had

suffered in America. One review of *In Through the Out Door*, released on 20 August, called it "A Whole Lotta Bluff". *Rolling Stone* magazine at one point referred to "Sad Zep" and one Sunday newspaper described the band appearing at Knebworth as "the worst and noisiest group in the history of rock music". Another scribe said they had "squeezed their lemons dry a long time ago".

Not everyone hated them. *Musicians Only* stated: "In view of the excessive tripe written about Led Zeppelin at Knebworth it is a matter of urgency that fans who could not be present should be reassured. The band was excellent, their performance superb. The cacophony of orchestrated criticism which followed their appearance was laughable." Even so, the young Knebworth audience hadn't reacted as exuberantly as in the past, perhaps exhausted by the long wait for the New Barbarians and the lacklustre performance that followed; even Grant conceded they had been "rusty". It took Led Zeppelin at full blast to restore their enthusiasm, having been stuck in a field for long hours. At times it was possible to hear a pin drop as 100,000 stood in the darkness, craning to see the remote figures on stage or focus on the screens. Zeppelin performed 'Stairway to Heaven', 'No Quarter' and 'Trampled Underfoot', Jones showcased on piano as strongly as Page on guitar. Plant's voice had lost none of its spine-tingling vibrancy and was especially effective on slow blues. Bonham cut out his 'Moby Dick' solo but had all his old power; if anything, the band seemed even tighter and more cohesive. Despite some misgivings, Knebworth augured well for a creative future.

Though the press were taking swipes at what seemed like every possible opportunity, the group's fans remained loyal. Despite punk's supposed dominance, Zeppelin won most of the categories in the *Melody Maker* Annual Readers' Poll. Plant, Jones, Bonham and Grant attended the reception at the Waldorf Astoria on 28 November to collect seven awards. The much-derided *In Through the Out Door* rocketed up the charts and by the end of September had sold three million, remaining Number 1 in the US for seven weeks. Zeppelin's entire catalogue also appeared in *Billboard*'s Top 200 album chart, a feat no other artists had achieved up until that point.

In the run-up to Christmas the band allowed themselves the fun of attending other artists' gigs, including a trip to Wembley to see ABBA in action. Page went to see Paul McCartney and Wings in Brighton, and Paul and Linda McCartney, with Denny Laine, came to visit him at Plumpton. Zeppelin's comeback year ended when Plant, Jones and Bonham went to see Wings at the Hammersmith Odeon and joined McCartney on stage for a grand finale performed by his Rockestra ensemble.

Led Zeppelin had survived to fight another day. Now Page, Plant, Paul Jones and Bonham faced a new decade. With punk's young blood snapping at their "dinosaur" heels, they were determined to reclaim their crown as the world's greatest rock group.

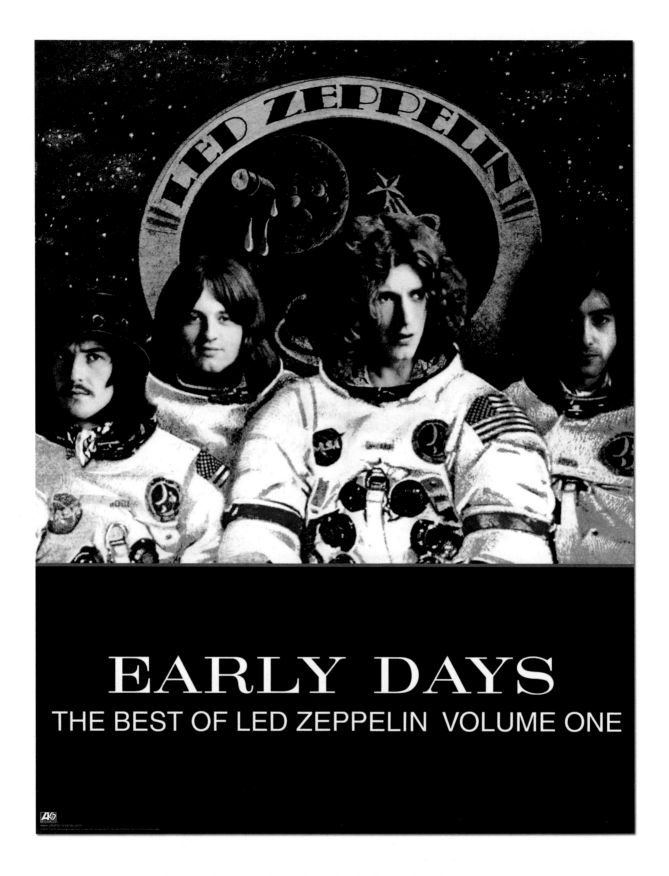

ABOVE: An advertising flyer for *Early Days*. Released in November 1999, the album was a 13-song greatest hits collection. Produced by Jimmy Page, the album artwork featured the band as astronauts.

ABOVE: The official poster for *The Song Remains The Same* film. Shot in tecnicolour, Jimmy Page has described the production as a "reasonably honest statement of where we were at that particular time."

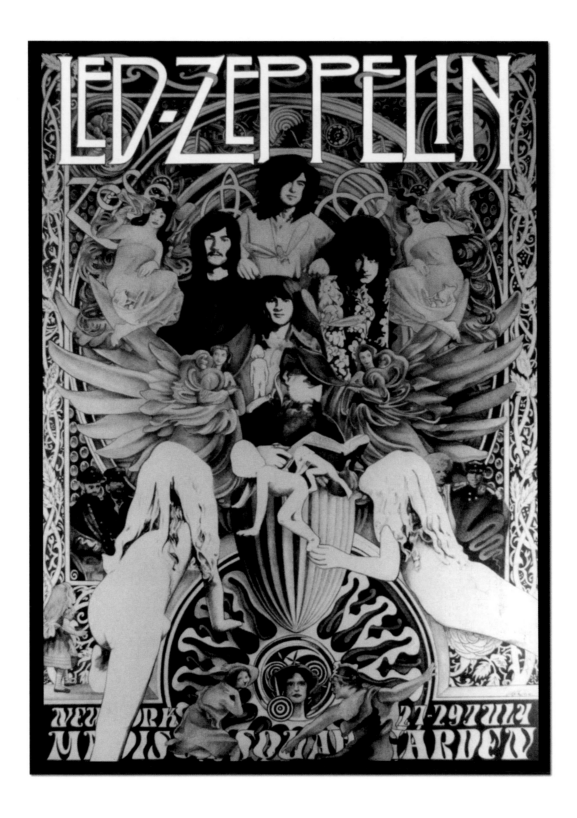

ABOVE: A poster for Led Zeppelin's concerts at Madison Square Garden, New York, 27-29 July 1973. All three of these shows were filmed for the band's concert film, *The Song Remains The Same*.

OPPOSITE:

1. The Object (as seen on the cover of Presence), 1976. Designed by Aubrey Powell and Storm Thorgerson at Hipgnosis, The Object is meant to represent the force and presence of the band.

2. A rare Japanese phonecard illustrated with back issues of *Record Collectors' Magazine*. The magazine issue from 1997 features an article with the band discussing their BBC Sessions live album.

3. An artists' pass for Led Zeppelin's Rock and Roll Hall of Fame induction. The band's highly ancipated induction in 1995 featured a rare live performance. Neil Young, Janis Joplin, Al Green, and Martha and the Vandellas were also inducted.

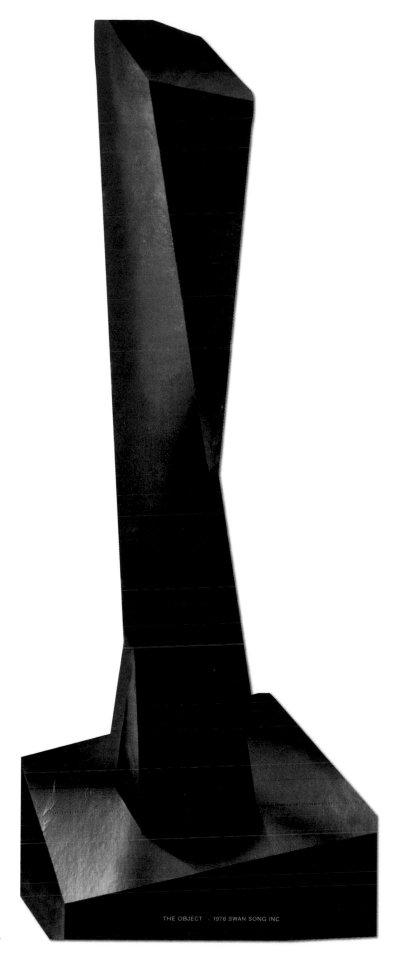

THE OBJECT · 1976 SWAN SONG INC

1.

1 9

9 8

2.

Rock and Roll
Hall of Fame and Museum
Grand Opening
Labor Day Weekend 1995

ARTIST

Cleveland, Ohio U.S.A.

3.

IN THROUGH THE OUT DOOR ▶ (1979)

In the wake of the band's last British appearances at Knebworth in August 1979 came what proved to be Led Zeppelin's final studio work, a poignant collection of performances that topped album charts around the world.

IN THROUGH THE OUT DOOR

Released shortly after the band's last British appearance at Knebworth in 1979, Led Zeppelin's eighth and final studio album was the group's last creative outing together before John Bonham's tragic death in September 1980. This album was to be their final encore and the last time fans would hear Bonham's beats ring out loud on new Led Zeppelin material.

They could have called it *The Last Chance Saloon*, if only because of the enigmatic album cover. It depicts a lonely man in a white hat and suit, sitting in a honky-tonk bar observed by various other characters including a pianist and bar-keeper. There were six different versions of the sleeve to entice collectors, but once again there was no mention of the band's name or album title. As with *Presence*, the relevant information could only be found printed in minute lettering on the spine.

In Through the Out Door opened up a turbulent stage in their career, when they faced the challenges of a new musical era. Disco, punk and electronic innovations were in the air. Zeppelin needed to bid farewell to the 1970s, but carried considerable baggage both musically and in terms of their history. On their eighth album they appeared determined to come up with interesting concepts worthy of their heritage. They seemed very keen to embrace new and different styles, while keeping faith with their rock and roll roots.

Two and a half years had elapsed since *Presence*. They convened at ABBA's Polar Studio in Stockholm at the invitation of the famed vocal group, who wanted them to experience the hi-tech facilities available. The British lads were assisted by Swedish engineers Leif Mases and Lennart Ostlund. The new album was eventually released in August 1979 and first impressions revealed a sharper, brighter, Nordic sound had been achieved. The band itself sounded different: tighter, less ramshackle and a tad more sophisticated.

Many of the songs evoked an introspective mood, but there were joyful moments and brash new rhythms that John Bonham in particular seemed to relish. 'In the Evening', the first of seven diverse tracks, begins with a cascade of guitar effects. An insistent theme performed with a stomping beat tends to swamp Robert Plant's vocals.

Only the cry of "I need your love" emerges from the clamour of hammered strings. Page uses a Gizmotron, the guitar effects device invented by Lol Creme and Kevin Godley of 10cc, to enhance distortion, and this complements the song's message about distorted values. As Plant points out: "It's lonely at the bottom and it's dizzy at the top."

'South Bound Saurez' has a choppy piano motif devised by John Paul Jones, and an angry, buzzing guitar solo peps up this old-time rock and roll revival with New Orleans roots.

The track 'Fool in the Rain' has some nifty and precise drumming from Bonham that shows how he was capable of playing so much more than just a heavy back beat. Robert sings in relaxed mode and is twice as effective than when screaming against the band. A samba rhythm pervades a song that would reach Number 21 in the *Billboard* singles chart in January 1980 but was never played live.

'Hot Dog' is close in spirit to Shakin' Stevens or even Bill Wyman's Rhythm Kings in its joyful celebration of 50s rockabilly. Robert is in his element, warbling through tricky lyrics about seeking a fetching Texan gal who takes off on a Greyhound bus. The band sound like they're whooping it up in the bar depicted on the album cover. The number was dedicated to Zeppelin's trusty Texan Showco road crew and was filmed for a promotional video.

'Carouselambra' is the biggest surprise. While not in quite the same league as 'Achilles' Last Stand' or 'Kashmir', this team effort still produces exhilarating results. Confident and thrusting, 'Carouselambra' is powered by storming drums and organ riffs that hark back to the Stax sound of the 60s.

During this ten-minute epic an unexpected change in mood sees the tempo dip as Page unleashes chiming, mysterious chords, casting a riveting, hypnotic spell. The lyrics are largely unfathomable but have a mystical origin and are aimed at a specific person for whom all will one day be revealed. As the song picks up the pace once more, cataclysmic drum fills round off one of Zeppelin's most underrated works.

'All My Love' is the penultimate number and is basically a pop song written by Plant and Jones, utilizing a synthesizer rather more than the guitar. It seems like the sort of material the senior members of the band might have played in their session days, and is far removed from the usual Zeppelin style.

'I'm Gonna Crawl' rounds off the album with a heartfelt performance. Delivered by Robert with all the passion of an Otis Redding or James Brown, it's complemented by a fine guitar solo from Jimmy. Given the sad mood that prevails as 'I'm Gonna Crawl' fades away into silence, Zeppelin's last stand is all the more poignant.

In Through the Out Door sold some four million copies in America and topped the US and UK charts, showing that the punk rock craze had no effect on Led Zeppelin's ability to generate massive sales. Jimmy Page had wanted the band to experiment during the making of this album. The music they produced pointed towards an intriguing but unknowable future ...

PREVIOUS PAGES: The group performing on stage during filming for *The Song Remains the Same*, Madison Square Garden, New York, 29 July 1973.

OPPOSITE: "How many people will be coming to the show?" Peter Grant chats with Robert and John Paul in the car park at Knebworth House, August 1979.

ALBUM TRACKS

Led Zeppelin found themselves in Stockholm in winter, when they recorded their final studio album. Unconcerned by the cold conditions, and closing the decade that unequivocally belonged to this band, *In Through the Out Door* is regarded as the (almost) fitting tribute to the group that redefined rock music in the 1970s.

IN THE EVENING

Strange, spooky sounds launch a piece that suddenly leaps from the speakers as we hear a band emerging from the audio fog of the 1970s. The new technology available at Polar Studios gave Zeppelin a real presence and depth they had only managed to get in the past by recording in stairwells and the depths of ancient manor houses. The guitar and keyboards have a very modern sound that foreshadows 80s techno-rock. Indeed the band were in advance of their contemporaries like Yes in updating and modernizing. So successful were they in their efforts to restructure, a few desultory passages of blues guitar heard here seem almost out of place in the environment of a sophisticated pop arrangement.

The main riff is a killer and there are all the unexpected twists and changes only Zeppelin would dare put into what is otherwise a basic hit single format. It's certainly half a league onwards from 'Bron-Yr-Aur'. Although John Paul Jones put his stamp on 'In the Evening', the introduction sees Jimmy Page using his old violin bow on the intro (crowds cheered this when he played the number at their Knebworth shows). He also utilizes his beloved Gizmotron, to produce and increase distortion. It's believed to be responsible for the peculiar slamming effect heard during the solo.

In the heartfelt lyrics, Plant muses about the pain and grief that people go through in life and the fact that all the success and riches in the world cannot alleviate it. "You can turn away from fortune because that's all that's left to you ... It's lonely at the bottom ... It's dizzy at the top."

SOUTH BOUND SAUREZ

A perky boogie-rocker set up by the itchy-fingered piano playing of John Paul Jones, which Plant gets stuck into with throaty gusto. A good-time New Orleans feeling permeates the piece, and while Page offers some nice background riffs, his solo is so erratic it practically stumbles through the out door. However, he often insisted that he preferred to leave in any mistakes in his guitar playing, rather than embark on an unrealistic search for perfection. Certainly the odd missed note and squeaky string adds to the drama or pathos of a piece. Bonham was on top form on this one and his bass drum pedal works overtime at what proves a demanding tempo.

A Jones-Plant composition, the title was incorrectly spelt on the label — it should have been *Suarez*, a Spanish word for party. Many thought it must refer to a bus trip to a little-known Mexican village, but it was in fact a celebration — of a celebration.

FOOL IN THE RAIN

John Bonham employs an unusually highly tuned snare drum sound on a lengthy number that shows the band becoming ever more adventurous. A kind of Tex Mex feel gives way to a samba rhythm launched by the effervescent piano of Jones. Who would have thought Zeppelin could play like this? It certainly has nothing to do with punk, so the theory of their being influenced by the Sex Pistols flies gracefully out of the window. Plant's voice is greatly improved over his performance on *Presence*.

The choice of samba rhythm was influenced by the Latin music heard on TV during the coverage of the 1978 World Cup football matches then being played in Argentina. Robert Plant, who pushed through his demands for greater musical flexibility, later observed that it was not intended to be an attempt to emulate Carlos Santana. The band cut several different versions of the song. Surprisingly, in view of this massive stylistic shift, 'Fool in the Rain' became a hit in the US, where it hit Number 21 in January 1980. Coming at the end of their career, this was their last chart hit... but was never played live.

HOT DOG

A count leads into the most cheerful good-time number Led Zeppelin ever cut, on which they seemed to throw all caution to the winds and indulge in a bit of fun. They needed it after all the bad luck and trouble they'd endured.

Page falters fractionally on his finger-pickin' intro, but the piano and drums join forces like a bar-room brawl ready to swig pitchers of beer and toss horse shoes all night long. If ever there was a full-scale hootenanny, this was it. Plant called the number a tribute to Texas and hillbilly, another of his great musical passions being the genre known as rockabilly. It is said that another passion was one of the female citizens of that fair state. Plant fantasizes about a girl who disappears after taking a Greyhound bus. "I searched the town ... she took my heart, she took my keys ... I'll never go to Texas any more." More prosaically, 'Hot Dog' is also dedicated to top American tour organizers Showco and their indefatigable road crew.

The tune began life at rehearsals in London. A rarely seen promo video was made of the song, making use of live footage shot at Knebworth. It was intended for showing at record stores across the States.

OPPOSITE: Jimmy and Robert peruse a pack of photographs at Stringfellow's nightclub, London, circa 1980.
RIGHT: Gimme Some Lovin: Plant makes eyes at fans in the front row, 1978.

CAROUSELAMBRA

A remarkable piece of cutting-edge-of-the-80s pop-rock, 'Carouselambra' showed how Zeppelin might have developed during the next decade. It has all the latest sounds, a majestic keyboard riff and some of Bonham's firmest, most authoritative drumming setting a rock-solid tempo – no need for click tracks or drum machines here. Shamefully overlooked at the time, it sounds fresh and exciting even now and could be a huge hit if revived by a currently popular band.

The ten-minute odyssey pauses unexpectedly halfway through for Page to play some haunting power chords using a Gibson double-neck guitar – and the Gizmotron was also rolled out. The sharp-tongued keyboards spark a return to the crisper tempo and this is a whole new Led Zeppelin in action. The lyrics are largely beyond comprehension and are left open to interpretation. Plant proclaimed that they deliberately hid a mystical intention aimed at a specific person who will one day discover their meaning.

John Paul Jones is in the driving seat of a piece that was originally assembled during rehearsals at Clearwell Castle in the spring of 1978. There are enough ideas and tones here to create an entire album of ambient music. Lambasted on release by sections of the rock press, it can be seen more than a decade later as one of Zeppelin's last classics. This was a new Led Zeppelin taking shape before the eyes of a populace blinded by over-familiarity. If the band had been able to continue along this path, they would have been able to create another eight great albums in the 80s.

I'M GONNA CRAWL

Page may have taken a back seat on the previous track, but here he reasserts his authority – and presence. Recorded at Polar Studios and mixed at Page's home studio in Plumpton, this is an immensely sad performance, in terms of its immediate impact and in the light of subsequent events. John Paul Jones is the foremost composer of a piece provisionally intended to re-create the mood of the 1960s soul-blues classics created by such singers as Otis Redding and Wilson Pickett.

Page's doleful guitar solo is an outstanding feature of a cocktail bar-type ballad. Plant also gives a wonderful performance bestriding an imaginary bar stool, mulling over a slow torch song in a style that owes as much to Mae West as it does to Wilson Pickett. He tells how a girl "drives me crazy ... she's the apple of my eye. I love that little lady. I got to be her fool." John Bonham later proclaimed that it was one of the best vocal performances that Plant had ever given. Plant, Page, Jones and Bonham sweep grandly through a piece that proved to be Led Zeppelin's swansong.

> **"I don't think we ever thought we were creating a legacy. We were just combining the influences of four good musicians and enjoying ourselves, keeping ourselves interested, alive and awake."**
> JOHN PAUL JONES

ABOVE: Robert and Jimmy having fun for a good cause, Live Aid concert, Philadelphia, 1985.
OPPOSITE: "I sometimes think I could quite easily get up and go, and leave everything, and end up in another part of the world as somebody else." Plant is pictured here in a different frame of mind, rocking the mic, in 1979.

ALL MY LOVE

Keyboards introduce a simple pop song, written by John Paul Jones and Robert Plant, which shows yet another facet of the band's ability. It's one of the few Zeppelin songs that does not have a Page composer credit and he plays with perfunctory professionalism, as if on somebody else's session. Jones' excellent synth solo has a classical pop feel. It's almost as if both musicians were unconsciously harking back to their roots, when they provided the backing for such artists as Herman and Donovan. The tune even changes key for the final chorus, in true pop ballad fashion.

Plant's vocals show a degree of maturity, with less reliance on "Ooh yeahs" – it is the kind of material he began to develop on his later solo albums.

'All My Love' may have been a tribute to Karac, Plant's son, as he sings "He is a feather in the wind". But on a strictly musical judgement Jimmy Page later professed disquiet at the direction of the track and commented: "It wasn't us."

CODA  (1982)

When John Bonham died on 25 September 1980, Led Zeppelin died with him. It was a sad end to the group, but *Coda* helped fans temper their loss by providing rare bonus items culled from extensive archives.

CODA

A poignant swansong emerged in the aftermath of Led Zeppelin's demise, but it took time for this "song'" – in the form of a final album – to be sung. In the turmoil of the early 1980s, as new musical fashions took hold, the very idea of the heavy rock group was deemed to be well past its sell-by date. But this ignored the sense of loss felt by fans worldwide, and the need for a line to be drawn under Zeppelin's recorded history. This came about with the release of their tenth and final album.

It was two years since Bonham's death. There had been no rush to pour out "tribute" albums, only a respectful silence and a long period of mourning. But feeling that Zeppelin deserved more than isolation and abandonment, Page set about compiling one last album as a tribute to John and to serve as as the group's memorial.

Zeppelin were contracted to produce another five albums for Atlantic on their Swan Song label. As it was impossible to produce new material, Page's solution was to go through the tapes stored at his home studio for unheard gems. He spent most of 1981 going through them all and making a final selection: eight tracks dating from 1969 to 1978. Plant and Jones were called in to help out with overdubs before they were ready for inclusion.

The appropriately named *Coda* was presented in a sombre grey and green gatefold sleeve that opened to reveal a montage of photographs showing Zeppelin on the road from the days of the 1970 Bath Festival to Knebworth in 1979.

The release was quite low-key, at least in the UK where pop groups such as Bucks Fizz gained more media attention: but the album again proved a huge seller, reaching Number 4 in the UK charts and Number 6 in America. Opener 'We're Gonna Groove' is a Ben E. King number played with all the zest of a confident young band making its way in a London studio in 1969. Plant's bluesy, echoing vocals are chased by Page's soulful guitar and while it's a somewhat chaotic production compared to later recordings, it sets a cheerful and optimistic mood for listeners delving into their own Zeppelin memories. Recorded at Morgan Studios on 25 June 1969, just before the Bath Festival and following a UK tour, it had been intended for *Led Zeppelin II*.

'Poor Tom' commences with a typically bluff and commanding drum rhythm, which Plant uses as a platform for his extemporizations. The feel is Delta blues and 'Poor Tom' sounds like a work song. Page's acoustic guitar chimes in the background of a recording made at Olympic Studios, Barnes, on 5 June 1970. The 'Poor Tom' of the story faces the noose, having shot his unfaithful wife. It might have been included on *Led Zeppelin III* but was supplanted by other Bron-Yr-Aur compositions.

'I Can't Quit You Baby' is Zeppelin's take on Willie Dixon's classic blues, recorded during a soundcheck at the Royal Albert Hall on 9 January 1970. As the concert was to be filmed, a Pye recording truck had been provided and the engineers fortuitously captured the band in their finest form – four musicians playing as if they were one. The result was even better than the version on their debut album. The empty hall gives great resonance to Plant's voice and Bonham's devastating drums; Zeppelin's dynamic range is fully explored as Jimmy's guitar alternately whispers and shouts and the mood leaps from frenzy to tantalizing delicacy. Jones' bass ensures the performance swings rather than rocks and Bonham's drumming is like Elvin Jones meeting the blues.

PREVIOUS PAGES: "I like the audience to go away feeling the same way you do at the end of a good chick, satisfied and exhausted." Robert Plant woos his fans.

LEFT: Jimmy relaxes in the Kings Road, London offices of Zeppelin's own Swan Song record label, listening to old-school vinyl in 1977. The label ceased operations in 1983.

OPPOSITE: Bonzo keeps a watchful eye on Jimmy, as he rips into a solo, 1977.

'Walter's Walk' is a strident rock and roll burn-up with layers of seemingly disconnected riffs stacking up over a pulsating heartbeat, Plant's near-hysterical delivery suiting the slightly manic tone. It was recorded using the Rolling Stones' mobile studio at Mick Jagger's home, Stargroves, in Berkshire on 15 May 1972, engineered by Eddie Kramer. Planned for *Houses of the Holy*, it made an exciting climax for Side 1 of *Coda*.

'Ozone Baby' is a rare pop performance, closer in spirit to Elvis Costello and Stiff Records than Willie Dixon. It's an interesting foray into new territory, although former session men Page and Jones could deliver this sort of performance at the tick of a studio clock. In fact, the studio where this was conceived was Polar in Stockholm during the sessions for *In Through the Out Door*.

'Darlene' is another gem from the Polar album session in November 1978. It is a rock and roll party track with Jones' boogie piano to the fore. There are pauses for piano and drum breaks and the jerky beat that launches the tune gives way to a swinging, saloon bar rave-up.

'Bonzo's Montreux' is a showcase for Bonham's skills, blending the bite of his acoustic drum kit with a special electronic treatment. Captured at Mountain Studios, Montreux, on 12 September 1976, it improved on the 'Moby Dick' solo featured on *Led Zeppelin II*. More creative and better

recorded, it sounds as if Bonham is using a double bass drum, such is the speed and dexterity of his pedal work and from his spot in the control room blended snare, tom toms, timpani and timbales build to form a wall of intense sound.

The album winds up with the raucous 'Wearing and Tearing', a breathless gallop that charges into the valley of rock with all cannons blazing. Sticking two fingers up to the punk rockers, it was to have been released as a single, under a different name, but unfortunately missed the deadline for the 1979 Knebworth show and didn't make it into *In Through the Out Door*.

Coda is a greater album than was thought at the time. Fans might have expected to find another 'Stairway to Heaven' or 'Kashmir' plucked from the archives: but it showed their music was always fresh, original and brilliantly performed, and that the band were always in competition with one very powerful rival – themselves.

BELOW: On 21 June Led Zeppelin performed a set that included 'Hot Dog' and 'Achilles' Last Stand' at Ahoy Halle, Rotterdam during their 1980 European tour.

OPPOSITE: Jimmy Page returned to the stage post-Zeppelin to play 'Stairway to Heaven' at the Ronnie Lane ARMS benefit concert at the Royal Albert Hall in September 1983.

ALBUM TRACKS

Coda helped sate Zeppelin fans' hunger for a tribute to the band so recently rent asunder. When Jimmy Page delved into their recorded heritage, he found plenty of material that would intrigue and delight, even as it left listeners wondering what other treasures lay hidden in the guitarist's archives.

ABOVE: Page pulls a classic guitarist's rock face while performing in 1979. "I think the quality of musicianship of the band has given it the longevity. I thought the music would endure, I didn't think I would ... I always thought I'd be dead by 30, then dead by 40 and on and on," said Jimmy in 2010.

OPPOSITE: Robert loves Kim Fowley, the producer behind the Runaways.

WE'RE GONNA GROOVE

Recorded at Morgan Studios, London, on 25 June 1969, at a time when the band had just finished a five-date British tour and were due to play at Bath Festival. Their schedule also included a recording session for BBC radio and appearances at London's Royal Albert Hall.

The tune is credited to soul giant Ben E King and James Bethea and is taken at a fast pace, with Plant in apparently angry, declaiming mood, although the lyrics suggest that when his baby returns from a recent trip on the railroad, he plans to raise a suitably groovy family. Some sub-octivider guitar effects were added later during mixing sessions at Page's Plumpton Sol studio in 1982. 'We're Gonna Groove' was intended to be used on *Led Zeppelin II* but didn't make it on to the album, instead serving as an opening number on their early 1970 tour dates.

I CAN'T QUIT YOU BABY

Worth the price of the album alone, this is a splendid performance by any standards. The band are captured during a soundcheck at the Royal Albert Hall, playing their tribute to composer Willie Dixon with fire and panache. The great thing is that here is a band, oblivious to the surroundings, playing for themselves. There's no audience, apart from a few blokes sweeping up cigarette butts and roadies humping gear. Up there on the stage are Robert Plant, Jimmy Page, John Paul Jones and John Bonham getting stuck into the blues.

The day this was recorded – 9 January 1970 – Zeppelin were due to be filmed for a proposed documentary, so a mobile truck was installed outside the Albert Hall, which accounts for the superb sound quality. This is a stronger version of 'I Can't Quit You Baby' than appears on the first album. Page's solo is cleaner and he cunningly drops down the volume, rudely interrupted by Bonham crashing in with a shattering drum break.

> **"The loss of our dear friend, and the deep respect we have for his family, together with the sense of undivided harmony felt by ourselves and our manager, have led us to decide that we could not continue as we were."**
>
> LED ZEPPELIN

POOR TOM

A heavy New Orleans-style shuffle rhythm forms the basis of this highly distinctive semi-acoustic cut that was recorded at Olympic Studios, Barnes, in June 1970. It is one of the tracks that didn't survive the selection process for *Led Zeppelin III* and was never performed live, although it had the credentials of having been written during the famous trip to Bron-y-Aur. Plant provides a traditional blues treatment, along with some fine harmonica playing.

'Poor Tom' is a heart-rending tale of old Tom, who had worked hard all his life and is apparently happily married, until he discovers that his wife, Ellie May, is running around and playing games while he's away at work. As a result, he gets hold of a gun and wreaks vengeance, resulting in more than a custodial sentence. Sings Plant: "Poor Tom ... you gotta die for what you've done".

WALTER'S WALK

Boogie-rock with added angst. Plant offers a brace of "Ooh yeahs" as he describes how he is trying hard to change his ways but "can't let go". A song of love, anguish and tears develops as he sings, "I'm walking the floor over you", while Page adds a violent, energetic guitar solo. There is too much echo on the vocals, but it adds to the sense of doomed love.

The piece was recorded in May 1972 during sessions at Mick Jagger's Stargroves studios in Berkshire. Eddie Kramer was in charge of engineering and the number was originally intended for *Houses of the Holy*. A strangely muddy sound pervades the piece, which lacks a strong melody. Some experts have suggested this was a backing track, updated later for inclusion in *Coda*. The tune was based on a riff that Page had worked up during performances of 'Dazed and Confused' when the band were on tour in the mid-1970s.

OZONE BABY

An interesting item from the Polar Studios sessions in Stockholm, recorded on 14 November 1978, this is very much a structured pop song, composed by Page and Plant and built over a strong bass guitar line. Plant tells how he hears his girl knocking at his door with a cry of "I've been saving this for ya honey". However, it is too late for her to be his honey, as he is tired of her doing "the things that you do". He adds "I don't want you ringing my bell" and threatens to go into "the darkness and sail away".

It's not too surprising that 'Ozone Baby' didn't make it on to *In Through the Out Door*. The hook line – "My own true love" – is somewhat trite, it has to be said. Even so, it might have made a hit if Zeppelin had disguised themselves as a Swedish pop group for the day.

DARLENE

An out-take from the Polar Studios sessions for *In Through the Out Door*, the track was recorded on 16 November 1978, and was a much better piece of work than was featured on the 1993 boxed CD set. The song grows in stature with repeated plays and has a strong rock and roll feel, enhanced by the busy piano work of Jones. Few rock bands of Zeppelin's ilk were so adaptable that they could try out so many different styles and play them with such consummate professionalism. Bonham plays some titanic breaks as the band gets stuck into a swing groove. The overall mood recalls Queen's 'Crazy Little Thing Called Love' and doubtless owes much to the same sources of inspiration.

Lyrically speaking, Plant is excited by the spectacle of one of his many mythical loves. She is wearing such a tight dress, he is inspired to call out, "Come on baby, give me some." Naturally enough, the dress also arouses the familiar passion of jealousy and he quite clearly explains that "When I see you walking with all those guys, it makes me feel so sick." This is just the sort of situation that leads to violence in many public bars and dance halls. The number eventually transmogrifies itself into an unexpected jam session with a long fade-out.

When it came to apportioning tracks on the original album, 'Darlene' would have been a much better bet than 'South Bound Saurez'.

BONZO'S MONTREUX

The Mighty Bonzo shows that the drums can be a musical instrument. Far removed from the tearaway stuff of 'Moby Dick', this is the drummer in thoughtful, constructive mode. He creates a tune on the drums, aided by electronically processed tymps, tom toms and that famous Ludwig snare drum that was usually at the heart of the matter. Dubbed the John Bonham Drum Orchestra, this was Bonham embarking on a percussion adventure that was devised with the aid of Page, who added electronic treatments, which included the use of a Harmonizer. It was recorded on 12 September 1976, at Mountain Studios, Montreux.

Divided into sections, the piece rumbles along at a leisurely pace, sounding not unlike a steel band about to fall down an escalator. Many found these rhythmic electronics harsh on the ears when first unveiled in 1982. 'Moby Dick' and 'Bonzo's Montreux' were slotted together on the remastered six-LP boxed set, *Led Zeppelin,* released in 1990.

Although Bonham was a master drummer, he had a realistic attitude to the role of the drummer in rock. "Not everybody likes or understands a drum solo, so I like to bring in effects and sounds to keep their interest," he explained. "I used to play a hand drum solo long before I joined Zeppelin. I played a solo on the Duke Ellington tune 'Caravan' when I was only 16. With Zeppelin I tried to play something different every night in my solos. I'd play for 20 minutes, but the longest ever was 30 minutes. It's a long time, but when I was playing it seemed to fly by. Sometimes you'd

come up against a brick wall and you'd think: 'How am I going to get out of this one?' Or sometimes you go into a fill and you'd know halfway through it was going to be disastrous. There were times when I blundered and got the dreaded look from the lads. But that was a good sign. It showed I'd attempted something I'd not tried before."

WEARING AND TEARING

"It starts out like a murmur then it grows like thunder," warns Plant. A fast jam from Polar Studios, cut on 21 November 1978, this is a splendid rave-up from a band who were already disappearing into the mists by the time *Coda* was released. It's a real headbanger, and a reminder that despite 'Ozone Baby' and 'All My Love', Led Zeppelin were still capable of rocking out – right to the end of their days. Plant's lyrics are mostly indecipherable, but you can hear him sing what sounds like: "I'm going to ask for medication ... who cares for medication when you're falling apart?" He later adds, "What's that creeping up behind you? It's just an old friend." The guitars blast back in response and suddenly the whole band shuts down, leaving a faint trace of echo, like the final shudder of an earthquake.

Page and Plant had said this was the number that would knock the young punk bands off their high horse, and was planned as a single for release in time for their 1979 Knebworth shows. However, it missed the deadline because of problems with the pressing. Robert Plant later said that they wanted to put the record out on a different label under the name of a phoney band to compete with the Damned and the Sex Pistols. "It was so vicious and so fresh," recalled Robert. It certainly would have been fun to confuse the critics and their perceived rivals and it would have shown that the members of Led Zeppelin were still young, fresh and just as virile as the opposition. It was presumably intended for inclusion on *In Through The Out Door*. In the event, it was never aired in public until Page and Plant performed it together at the Knebworth Festival in 1990.

OPPOSITE: Playing the acoustic numbers, and playing musical chairs, Chicago Stadium, 4 June 1977.

ABOVE: Stuff-strutting in front of 10,000 fans, Ahoy Halle, Rotterdam, the Netherlands, 21 June 1980.

JIMMY PAGE

A mature, experienced musician even before Led Zeppelin was conceived, Jimmy Page had a wealth of experience, combined with a cool intelligence and clear insight, that set him apart from his earliest days.

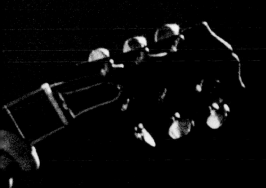

JIMMY PAGE

Jimmy Page strutting the stage amid a blaze of laser beams, raising a violin bow and attacking the strings of his guitar while performing 'Dazed and Confused', is one of rock's iconic images, but behind the virtuoso showman lies a master musician.

Born James Patrick Page (9 January 1944) in Heston, Middlesex, he grew up in a country house in Northampton belonging to a great-uncle. When he was eight, the family moved to Feltham, near London Airport. Jimmy had a happy childhood, took part in school sports and studied art. However, when his parents gave him a guitar for his 12th birthday his future was assured.

As airport noise grew worse the family moved again, to Epsom, Surrey, and Jimmy went to grammar school. The guitar had lain untouched for years, but one day he saw a boy singing skiffle and playing guitar on the playing-field and was impressed by the attention he was attracting. "I wondered how he did it and he showed me how to tune a guitar, and from then on I began going to guitar shops and watching other people play until people began watching me." What he really wanted to play was rock and roll. He had begun to emulate his favourite records, copying the solos note for note.

Among his earliest influences was American session guitarist James Burton, but Jimmy also developed a fondness for vocal harmony groups, appreciating the way guitars were integrated into the production. This was matched by his discovery of the hardcore blues that lay at the heart of rock and roll. Older friends would play him records by such artists as Sleepy John Estes and Arthur 'Big Boy' Crudup, esoteric names unknown to most teenagers on either side of the Atlantic.

Another good place to hear the blues, jazz and soul was AFN, the American Forces radio network. At the same time he discovered folk music, and in particular the guitar work of Bert Jansch. "He was a real dream weaver and incredibly original." Page never had formal lessons, but claims: "I just picked it up. When I was at school I had my guitar confiscated every day. They handed it back to me each afternoon at four o'clock."

On leaving school he plunged straight into the business, joining Neil Christian and the Crusaders aged 15. To pay for his guitars and amplifiers, he delivered morning newspapers, but soon found himself earning good money: £20 a week. He spent most of it on better guitars, including a Gretsch Country Gentleman. Said Jeff Beck: "It looked huge on him, because he was such a shrimp. All you saw was a big guitar being thrown around by a kid who was as thin as a pipe-cleaner." Page, Beck and another up-and-coming guitarist, Eric Clapton, became firm friends in the so-called Surrey blues belt.

The Crusaders played R&B, and the ever-improving guitarist began to make a name for himself. Said keyboard and bass player John Baldwin, later to become John Paul Jones: "I rated Jimmy Page for years. Even in 1962 I can remember people saying, "'You've got to listen to Neil Christian and the Crusaders. They've got an unbelievable young guitarist.'"

However, Jimmy grew tired of life on the road. He suffered from travel sickness and caught glandular fever. After collapsing from exhaustion, he left the Crusaders and played with blues harmonica man Cyril Davies at London's Marquee Club, but eventually left, not wishing to offend his former mentor Christian.

Aged 17, he decided to enrol at Sutton art college, but while jamming at the Marquee was spotted by producer Mike Leander, who asked him if he fancied some recording sessions. This meeting led to Page playing on hundreds of pop sessions in London between 1963 and 1966. Few session guys were capable of an authentic rock guitar sound, and Page found himself in demand. He played anonymously with big-name acts, notably the Kinks, Them and the Who, and worked alongside string and brass players, at the same time gaining an insight into studio technology. He was regarded as adaptable and reliable, and to his surprise found himself profiled in the *Sunday Times*' colour magazine.

Among the first groups Jimmy worked with was Carter-Lewis and the Southerners, later the Ivy League. He played on sessions with Lulu, Dave Berry, Donovan, PJ Proby, Cliff Richard, Burt Bacharach, Tom Jones, Val Doonican and the Bachelors, began songwriting with singer Jackie DeShannon and worked with drummer Bobbie Graham on solo tracks.

Jimmy even cut a 1965 single, 'She Just Satisfies' (Fontana), on which he sang as well as playing guitar. Page worked with producer Mickie Most and arranged and produced tracks for Andrew Oldham's Immediate Records. In the end, however, he began to feel session work was a dead end. "There was no individuality involved. The arranger said: 'This is what you play,' and that's what I played. I got fed up and it became a pain in the neck. When the Yardbirds came up, that was it."

In 1965 Page was invited to replace Clapton, who quit the Yardbirds in protest at their commerciality. Page didn't like the way the offer was presented and didn't fancy touring, so he recommended Beck. A year later, however, he saw them at an Oxford May Ball when singer Keith Relf freaked out on stage. Bassist Paul Samwell-Smith quit and Jimmy was asked to take over. He'd never played bass, and ultimately rhythm guitarist Chris Dreja took up this role while Page shared lead guitar duties with Beck. They began featuring "stereo sound" guitar duels, and the revitalized band went on a tour of America and also toured the UK supporting the Stones. However, after Beck's departure during a US tour in 1966, Page was left as sole lead guitarist. One number they began playing was 'Dazed and Confused', featuring Jimmy playing with a violin bow. The showman and leader was born.

PREVIOUS PAGES: Jimmy tears up the AHOY arena, Rotterdam, the Netherlands, 21 June 1980.
RIGHT: Following the death of John Bonham, Page didn't feel comfortable playing his guitars for ages.

Smoke, electrics and heavy rock and roll:
Led Zeppelin live in the mid-1970s.

REMASTERS & UNLEDDED

When the Masters of Rock remastered their legendary back catalogue, it was a fragile moment of truth for older fans and new converts. Could the band sound even better than before? Was that possible ... and how? The fans responded with a positive verdict – Led Zeppelin now sounded fresher and heavier than ever before.

I n 1990, Jimmy Page remastered the classic Led Zeppelin original recordings. The CDs released by Atlantic Records in the 1980s had been of dubious quality. Page remastered the material from the original tapes, for release in a special boxed set, and the results were brilliant. On 15 October 1990, a triple album and double CD/cassette called simply *Remasters* was released in the UK and Europe. This was the condensed version of the 54-track monster boxed set of six LPs called *Led Zeppelin* released in the US on 23 October 1990 and worldwide on 29 October 1990. Another compilation, *Led Zeppelin Boxed Set 2*, was released in 1993, comprising two CDs with all 31 tracks from the band's nine studio albums, not included on the 1990 boxed set, plus one previously unreleased track. The boxed sets sold more than several million units over a period of three years.

Spoilt for choice, fans were then presented with all the Led Zeppelin studio albums which were reissued, in re-mastered editions, in 1993's Atlantic boxed set *Led Zeppelin – The Complete Studio Recordings*.

> **"Live shows were what Led Zeppelin was all about for me. The records were kind of starting points for the live shows. That's what I look forward to the most, the tours and playing with Robert, John and Jimmy."**
>
> JOHN PAUL JONES

LEFT: Robert outside the Beverly Hilton Hotel, California, in 1978

OPPOSITE: "Without Jimmy it would have been no good." Plant and Page, the greatest partnership, rock and roll has – and will ever – see.

ALBUM TRACKS

"Some nights I just look out there and want to f**k the whole first row," said Plant of his ideal live show. It's no wonder that the band are often cited as the greatest, and loudest, live performers of all time. Their live recordings, and bootlegs, strike a powerful chord – even today, over four decades later.

TRAVELLING RIVERSIDE BLUES

A fairly routine blues number is transformed by some wonderful slide guitar work by Jimmy Page and cheeky, exuberant and muscular vocals from young Master Plant. "Squeeze my lemon until the juice runs down my leg," exhorts Plant, imbuing the time-honoured Robert Johnson phrase with new vigour. It's great to hear Zeppelin in the period when they were still an up-and-coming British blues band, long before they were elevated into the stadium rock-peerage. This track was originally recorded for DJ John Peel's *Top Gear* BBC radio show, on 24 June 1969, and has all the clean, efficient recording quality you'd expect from radio. No tricks or surprises, but the band is in tune, and you can hear all the instruments – it was a shame BBC engineers at the Maida Vale studios didn't work on producing rock albums in the 1960s. The track was recorded live in the studio without an audience, but there was no lack of atmosphere and Page was able to add some overdubs, including an excellent solo. He decided to add it to the boxed set because he had so many requests for information about the number during his US *Outrider* tour in 1988. The track itself had been released on a promo CD single and was played so frequently on US radio it became a *Billboard Rock Tracks* hit in November 1990. The song is credited to Plant, Page and Robert Johnson, who came up with the original lines back in 1937. Robert Plant was particularly enamoured of the free-wheeling, sexual spirit of the song, with its folk and blues roots. This performance, dubbed 'Travelling Riverside Blues 69', was produced by John Walters and broadcast on 28 June 1969. BBC Enterprises subsequently gave Page the go-ahead to include it on the boxed set.

RIGHT: Leaping from 'Moby Dick' into a guitar solo, Jimmy Page shoegazes at Madison Square Garden, New York, 8 June 1977.

HEY HEY WHAT CAN I DO

A relic of the *Led Zeppelin III* era, and written at Bron-y-Aur cottage, this was originally only available on a UK Atlantic Records sampler album called *The New Age of Atlantic*. Released in 1972, it sold for the princely sum of 99p. A jolly piece filled with strumming mandolins and acoustic guitars, it features Plant turning to the world for help as he announces: "Hey, hey, what can I do? I've got a little woman but she won't be true." A frequent problem but not one that causes the singer more than passing heartache. After all – he can always drink his sorrows away. Plant is nicely restrained on a pop-like song which requires him to sing in a lower key than usual with far less shouting. This group composition has a theme redolent of the West Coast and could be called a hippy's lament. It fades out in some chaos, which might suggest it was a trial run for a song weeded out of the final album-selection process. Yet according to Peter Grant the song was actually intended to be a single. Recorded at Island Studios in 1970, and engineered by Andy Johns, it was featured on the B-side of the US single 'Immigrant Song', released on 5 November 1970. The song was performed on the Plant/Page world tour of 1995.

MOBY DICK/BONZO'S MONTREUX

A clever blending of two John Bonham showcase numbers produces a fitting tribute. Both tracks ran at the same tempo, so Page used a metronome to check them out and a Synclavier at Atlantic's New York facilities to merge the two. 'Moby Dick' was originally recorded in 1969 at Mirror Sound, Los Angeles and at Mayfair Studios, New York and was released on *Led Zeppelin II* in 1969. 'Bonzo's Montreux' was recorded on 12 December 1976 at Mountain Studios, Montreux, Switzerland. The two cuts received the most internal votes from the band and Page didn't want to leave either one off the album; in fact, he discards Bonham's original 'Moby Dick' snare drum and tom tom work. After the familiar heavy guitar theme, the piece cuts straight to the more dynamic 'Bonzo's Montreux', with its electronic treatments. It all makes for a much more satisfying percussion outing. It's just a shame that nobody recorded Bonham's snare drum solo at Carnegie Hall in 1969, or any of his other more orthodox drum workouts.

> ## "I've never tried to consciously be one of the best drummers. I'm a simple, straight-ahead drummer and I don't pretend to be anything better than I am."
> JOHN BONHAM

WHITE SUMMER/BLACK MOUNTAIN SIDE

A superb demonstration of Page's acoustic guitar skills, this was recorded and broadcast live on 27 June 1969 at the Playhouse Theatre, London for a Radio One show produced by Jeff Griffin. The previously unreleased cut was included on the album by arrangement with the BBC. Intended as a pilot for Radio 1's *In Concert* series, it came about as a result of Page enjoying the previous BBC broadcast for *Top Gear* and asking if it was possible to expand the format to allow them to play more music. *In Concert* was a one-hour show and became a long-running institution. Jimmy Page has pointed out that although the track was cut live, the respectful audience sat in silent enjoyment. His extended performance here is worth the price of the boxed set alone – there is something rather touching about what is, in effect, a musical recital, stripped of screaming fans shouting, "Jimmy!" Everything else fades into the background, while the young guitar player becomes as one with his instrument – his subtle use of harmonics is remarkable. John Bonham carefully adds a little percussive support, but it's Jimmy Page playing acoustically, with greater fluidity and more space than he does on any studio albums, that remains the focal point. The guitar's constant changes of tempo, volume and tone create a hypnotic effect that clearly entrances the audience. Sheer music triumphs over all and says more than a thousand screams – or a thousand words.

LED ZEPPELIN BOXED SET 2
BABY COME ON HOME

What they used to call a slow rock-a-ballad in the heyday of 1960s soul, this is very much a tribute to the kind of music Plant loved and the sort of records Page and Jones might have played on during their session days in the 1960s. The only previously unreleased cut on the second boxed set, it shows a completely different side to Led Zeppelin. Apart from the cascading drum fills, which are unmistakably Bonham, this could be the genuine article from Detroit City. Plant gets down on his knees in supplication, while Jones and Page provide suitably sanctified gospel-style organ and guitar. Recorded at Olympic Studios, London, this curiosity was rescued from oblivion when a reel of tape was found marked "Yardbirds, October 10, 1968". The tape vanished for many years, but eventually turned up in a dustbin outside the studio in 1991. The piece was ironically marked by the engineer "Tribute to Bert Berns" who was the American composer of such hits as 'Hang On Sloopy', and producer of Van Morrison. It was later salvaged by Mike Fraser, who co-produced the Coverdale/Page album, and restored to its former glory.

NO QUARTER

As 1993 dawned Plant was busy with his *Fate of Nations* album and Page was shacked up with David Coverdale, but the Led Zeppelin reunion rumours just wouldn't go away. There had been so much speculation and so many repeated denials that it seemed that never the twain should meet. Yet when Plant arrived in Boston, Massachusetts, in November 1993, for one of his own shows, Page happened to be around and dropped by to see Plant's band, say hello and wish him luck. Plant had recently been invited by MTV to record an *Unplugged* show and suddenly it dawned on them that they could combine forces in a way that wouldn't just be a Zeppelin reunion. Plant was particularly excited about a CD he'd heard featuring Moroccan singer, Najat Aatabou; it was inspirational and it plugged into their affinities with the desert and the music of the Middle East.

The old mates went off to Marrakech to record some Moroccan-style material in a local market place, then they went on a nostalgic trip to Wales, near the scene of their 1970s trip to Bron-y-Aur cottage. Location filming went ahead for the proposed MTV special, then Plant and Page returned to London to begin rehearsing new numbers, with part of Plant's band, which consisted of his son-in-law Charlie Jones (bass) and exciting young drummer, Michael Lee. They brought in guitarist Porl Thompson, from the Cure, and put together an eight-piece Egyptian orchestra. The MTV show was recorded and, after transmission, was made available on a 90-minute Warner Music Vision video *No Quarter – Unledded* (1995). It wasn't Led Zeppelin, but it was a major step forward for two catalytic personalities.

One person was missing from this unexpected reunion – although John Paul Jones had appeared with Plant and Page on the occasional Led Zep reunion, he wasn't invited to take part in the new project, apparently to avoid too many comparisons with the old band. Jones had kept a low profile during the post-Zeppelin years and had spent much of his time in

his Devonshire home, keeping out of the public's eye. However, in 1984 he worked with film director Michael Winner on the music for Winner's film *Scream for Help*. On one of the tracks, 'When You Fall in Love,' Jones took the lead vocals. Jones also appeared in the Paul McCartney film *Give My Regards to Broad Street* and contributed three tracks to a Ben E King album called *Save the Last Dance for Me* (1987). More significantly, he encouraged Wayne Hussey's band the Mission, which was heavily influenced by Led Zeppelin. Jones had been sent the band's demo and then offered to become their producer on an album called *Children*, on which he played keyboards. He joined Page, Plant and Jason Bonham for the Atlantic Records Anniversary concert, and for more recent awards ceremonies, but remained the least visible of the Zeppelin line-up.

For all those who had waited to see them reunited so long, the next step for Page and Plant was even bolder. The duo were planning to set off on a complete world tour that would last an entire year. With the organizational help of Plant's manager Bill Curbishley, they could celebrate their past and create a real future. The tour began at the Pensacola Civic Centre, Florida, on 26 February 1995 and went on to criss-cross North America until the following May. During April they visited Boston, the city where Led Zeppelin first played in the US, way back in 1968, and where the new Plant-Page union was first conceived. They played to a crowd of 20,000, and this kind of attention was reminiscent of the old glory days. They played mostly Led Zeppelin material including such favourites as 'Thank You', 'Wanton Song', 'Bring It On Home' and a massive version of 'Kashmir'. However, one number was missing from the set list – 'Stairway to Heaven' was dismissed by Plant as redundant. It was a particularly auspicious home-coming when Page and Plant played at Madison Square Garden, New York on 26 and 27 October 1995. At the end of the evening Plant greeted the crowds with the oblique remark of "See you again when we have some new ideas."

While taking in dates in Mexico, South America and Japan, the tour also visited Europe in June and played Glastonbury Festival on 25 June. During the tour the band gradually played with less emphasis on the Egyptian effects and the songs returned to their more familiar rock setting. They went on to play several other major UK gigs and also managed to fit in a few low-key events at smaller venues. By the end of the tour, in March 1996 in Australia, Plant, Page and their entourage had played some 115 shows in 19 countries during 370 days of solid work.

Tracks on the Plant/Page *No Quarter* CD included a smaller selection of songs from the MTV show than were included on the video. 'Nobody's Fault But Mine', 'Thank You', 'No Quarter', 'Friends', 'Yallah', 'City Don't Cry', 'Since I've Been Loving You', The Battle Of Evermore', 'Wonderful One', 'Wah Wah', 'That's the Way', 'Gallows Pole', 'Four Sticks', and 'Kashmir' gave a fascinating taste of past triumphs mixed with contemporary world-music concepts. Certainly 'Gallows Pole' benefited from their updated treatment and 'Kashmir' took on a whole new and somewhat mystical light in their East-meets-West approach.

LEFT: Jones plays a triple-necked guitar, Alameda County Coliseum, Oakland, California, 24 July 1977.

YALLAH

Would this have been the way ahead if Led Zeppelin had survived after 1980, or were these desert songs just a riddle in the sands of time? On the *Unledded* video, 'Yallah' (also known as 'The Truth Explodes') featured Page and Plant performing to a backing tape of heavy Eastern drums in the crowded market place in Marrakech. Page uses the electronic Theramin during this hypnotic and strangely funky performance. As an electric guitar riff grinds behind him, Plant throws back his head to emit a cry of "Ah ah – oh oh", which seems to express the inner yearnings of the wandering nomad cut off from humanity; despite his loneliness, he is still assailed by the same temptations that face all mankind. Such simple vocal techniques can be heard among the inhabitants of central Asia, from the deserts to the mountains. These wailing tones have a timeless quality that stretches back to the days of the great caravans and, even, Biblical times. 'Yallah' was played live on the Plant-Page tour for the first time at Corestates Spectrum, Philadelphia on Tuesday, 4 April 1995, when it replaced 'Calling You', a song from Plant's *Fate of Nations* album, in the band's set list.

CITY DON'T CRY

"Oh City, don't cry!" implores Plant, "City don't weep." This is a call for peace, understanding and sympathy, set to a lilting melody. Situated in west-central Morocco, near the Atlas mountains, the city of Marrakech, with its population of 1,517,000, has extensive gardens and a fourteenth-century palace, while the minaret of the Koutoubya mosque dominates the skyline. The city was the historic setting for this attractive vignette on which Page plays understated acoustic guitar while Plant claps his hands and sings with quavering passion. This simple theme was filmed in a courtyard in Marrakech, with three Egyptian musicians playing traditional instruments, including hand drums and bongos which give a gentle rhythmic impetus.

WONDERFUL ONE

This track was recorded live in the London TV studios, with Page sitting on a large wooden chair, playing a double-neck guitar, while Plant sings a doleful melody and poetic lyrics with touching sincerity. The lyrics address women with rather more respect than is usual in blues-shouting circles. Plant seems to be addressing a desert maiden with her yashmak on, from a safe distance, "Who must lie beside the thief – whose golden tongue will she believe?" he asks. "Touch me with fire, my mind is undone – my freedom has come. I trip through desire my wonderful one." Here is a song that celebrates the joys of male and female bonding, Eastern style, and may have lessons for those engaged in the rather more debased courting habits prevalent in Western society. This was one of the tracks that intrigued Plant and Page sufficiently to go back into the studio and start performing new material together again.

WAH WAH

This was also recorded and filmed in the courtyard in Marrakech, and bongos and drums are to the fore as Plant sings, "Give me peace of mind and bury all my pain and years of being sad." The chorus of "Wah Wah" interrupts this reverie until Plant reiterates his plea to Allah to "bury all the pain beneath the sand". The piece begins to accelerate towards a dignified climax and, despite the apparent monotony of much Middle Eastern music, it is possible to identify the links with Western folk song and even Scottish bagpipes, which utilize the drone to such searing effect. Led Zeppelin began with the blues and spread out to embrace the music of the world, but their roots remain the same. After all, in the final analysis, "Wah Wah" is not so far removed in spirit from "Baby, baby".

ABOVE: Flash back to December 1968 when the fledglings gather in London for an early promo picture session. Top: Jimmy and Robert. Bottom: John Paul and John Bonham.

THE LONG FAREWELL

Led Zeppelin spanned just 12 years of frantic success, but after its demise the band members faced 35 years more of a life when cherished ambitions were fulfilled and past achievements celebrated.

THE LONG FAREWELL

Led Zeppelin may have gone in 1980, but their music continued to inspire new generations. Heavy Metal developed at a phenomenal pace during the 1980s, and most acknowledged a debt to the masters: US grunge bands in the early 1990s cited Zeppelin as the most important musical influence; copycats and tribute bands proliferated. Once dismissed as "old hat" and "dinosaurs", it seemed that everyone wanted them back.

Jimmy Page and Robert Plant were like nomads wandering in the desert, after the demise of Led Zeppelin. Exhausted and thirsty, they paused at the oasis of each new solo musical endeavour, hoping to find sustenance. Driven apart by the stresses and strains of the old group's latter days, they could not work together, but despite their best efforts, they could not work apart. There was no more poignant sight than Jimmy Page playing 'Stairway to Heaven' alone on stage at the Royal Albert Hall, in 1983. For his part, Robert Plant in solo mode could never command the huge audiences he had once enjoyed with Zeppelin. Pride kept the two apart, yet hell had no fury greater than Plant's when Page finally settled for working with other singers in the absence of his old partner.

For years they were assailed by an unending clamour for "a Led Zeppelin reunion", yet even their greatest fans feared the consequences if it were tried and went wrong. Nobody wanted to see such an event destroy the memory of the much-loved and respected band. Whenever they did give way to the pressure, the results seemed to bear out the fans' worst fears; two public attempts at a reunion produced plenty of nostalgia but nothing that resembled the power of the old band. Behind the scenes, rehearsals with a revamped Zeppelin came to nothing.

It was Plant who, understandably, seemed least keen on going back. While the public remembered a wildly successful and hugely influential rock band, he remembered all too well the negative aspects of Zeppelin's latter days. In 1980 he was still young and had the chance to create a working environment and take charge of his own destiny. At long last he could call the shots, and sing and play the music he wanted to do, perhaps in a more modern, contemporary style.

Plant described the end of Zeppelin in dramatic terms: "It was like staggering away from the vacuum caused by a great explosion, with your eardrums ringing. I found myself standing on a street corner, clutching 12 years of my life, with a lump in my throat and a tear in my eye, and not knowing which way to go. It was a most peculiar experience, because I knew that the dream was over and everything had gone. It was just a memory."

Plant and Page learned to deal with the situation in broadly similar ways. Plant had been cut off from the mainstream of musical activity by his 10-year commitment to Zeppelin. "With Zeppelin it was so comfortable that I never had a thought beyond our records and tours. Socially it might have been better for me to have met more people."

When Bonham died, Plant was convinced that Led Zeppelin was finished and there was no point in trying to carry on with a replacement drummer. In the immediate aftermath of the tragedy, he locked himself away and spent several months virtually in hiding. Eventually he began to come out to visit local clubs and watched bands play, met musicians and finally began to assemble his own group called the Honeydrippers. They even went out to play low-key gigs, without billing their celebrated singer. It was the same sort of tactics adopted by Paul McCartney when he was creating Wings in the aftermath of the Beatles. Plant found the exercise good therapy as he worked out his musical game plan. "The Honeydrippers got me at it again. It was great fun to be able to go out and play without any of the usual pressures," he recalled. The band's line-up included Robbie Blunt (guitar), Andy Sylvester (bass), Kevin O'Neil (drums) and a brace of sax players, and they made their debut in Stourbridge on 9 March 1981. There was hardly any publicity and few outside the area even knew the band existed. "It was an exercise for me to regain confidence and find out if I could still sing. I wanted to get back in front of people, face to face."

The band played mainly blues and R&B covers at their first few gigs. Problems arose when the band members began to wonder why they couldn't play bigger venues and earn some money. They wanted a shot at the big time; their lead singer was internationally famous and they should be able to command a serious fee. Plant wanted to keep to the small club circuit but was beginning to tire of playing the same old standards. Now he needed some new material and began writing songs in odd moments with the band's guitarist, Robbie Blunt.

Said Plant: "I had fun with the Honeydrippers and enjoyed myself tremendously, but felt it was high time to do some original material. We began to realize the limitations as things got repetitious, so between gigs we started sitting down at a four-track tape machine and writing." Blunt and Plant began working on Plant's long-awaited solo album, which was recorded at Rockfield Studios in Wales. Among those playing on the session were Cozy Powell (drums), Paul Martinez (bass) and Jess Woodroffe (keyboards);

PREVIOUS PAGES: Bathed in the spotlight for more than a decade, the band perform at Newcastle City Hall, 1 December 1972.

OPPOSITE: John Paul Jones, Robert Plant, Jason Bonham and Jimmy Page backstage at the 02 Arena ready for their historic reunion concert, 10 December 2007.

Phil Collins sat in on some sessions when Powell was busy elsewhere. Although Plant had known Blunt for years, he found it traumatic working with someone other than Jimmy Page. He and Page would work into the small hours, whereas his new partners got tired after a couple of hours in the studio. Furthermore, some of the older hands weren't afraid to give Plant advice – when the singer tried to be cool and laid-back in the studio, Cozy Powell shouted: "Go on, do all of that screaming!"

Plant went back to see his old mate for advice during this testing period. "When I was recording the album I kept taking tapes over to Jimmy to get his opinion. It was very emotional. Like there were times when I just wanted to cry and hold his hand. When I played Jimmy the complete album he knew then that I had gone, and I was forging ahead alone."

Pictures at Eleven, Plant's debut solo album and first studio work in three years, was released in June 1982. The critics were kind, new listeners were prepared to give it a hearing, and old fans gave it a qualified vote of approval. It wasn't quite what they'd been hoping for, but then Plant couldn't start afresh by singing 'Whole Lotta Love – Part II'. *Pictures* was the start of a series of sometimes rather serious, elliptical albums like *The Principle of Moments* (1983) and *Shaken'n'Stirred* (1985), lightened up by the inclusion of his bluesy ten-inch LP *The Honeydrippers Volume 1* (1984). During 1983 Plant broke up with his wife Maureen, and moved from the farm in the Midlands he'd bought in Zeppelin days, to live in London and be at the centre of the music business. He joked about life on his old ten-acre farm. "I had two dogs, six goats, several ducks and a beer belly."

BELOW: Robert Plant, Jimmy Page and John Paul Jones attend the premiere of *Led Zeppelin: Celebration Day* at Hammersmith Apollo, London, 12 October 2012.

His records sold well, and he had a hit with 'Big Log', a single from *The Principle of Moments*, but while the first album went gold, it didn't do as well as *Coda*, which sold a million copies worldwide. In 1988 he formed a new band and released *Now and Zen*, which yielded the singles 'Heaven Knows', the exciting 'Tall Cool One', and 'Ship of Fools.' It saw him return to his rock roots on an album that included several Zeppelin samples and even had Jimmy Page guesting on one track. In 1990 he released another album, *Manic Nirvana*, written and recorded during the previous year. In his tour programme that year Plant wrote: "Success is fleeting, obscurity's forever. Good luck, see you on the pile!"

After three solo albums and his 10-inch *Honeydrippers* set, which sold two million copies in the States (more than *The Principle of Moments*), Plant felt that his audience had become confused about his musical direction. "Some people lost the plot and the momentum changed and got distorted. I kept trucking along, pursuing this kind of aim to create an alternative brand of music that borrows from Led Zeppelin but is primarily me. People I was working with kept saying, 'Let's go back and do this,' and I'd say, 'No, you have to stop and take stock and write material that has more energy.'" Plant agreed that some of his post-Zeppelin work had become rather austere. "I was probably going up my own arse a bit in trying to be different, and trying to keep away from the mainstream. I thought I had better get back in there now 'cos I like the glory, y'know." Plant was angry that David Coverdale (with flowing blonde hair) was enjoying chart success with an act that seemed to be based on Plant's image as the sexy blonde blues man.

But if Whitesnake was hard to take, there was even more outrage to come when German singer Lenny Wolf created a complete Zeppelin-style band, called Kingdom Come, featuring guitarist Danny Stag, which played astoundingly accurate impersonations of the Zeppelin sound. Instead of

being rejected by outraged fans, it was actually welcomed by a younger audience, probably unfamiliar with the 20-year-old original albums that served as a role model. The technically perfect Kingdom Come album was a hit in America, only a month after the release of *Now and Zen*. The upstart band was short-lived and broke up in 1989. However, they had proved that there was a deep hunger for the kind of rock music that only Led Zeppelin could provide and if the originators wouldn't get back together, then the fans would get their music elsewhere.

Three years later *Fate of Nations*, Plant's 1993 offering, came hot on the heels of the *Coverdale/Page* album, the fruit of an unexpected collaboration between David Coverdale and the old master. Plant worked with producer Chris Hughes and was energized by Phonogram's A&R man, Dave Bates, who signed him to Fontana. His new music was mainly recorded live in the studio, using such musicians as Charlie Jones and Phil Johnstone, with Kevin Scott MacMichael on guitars. There were also guest appearances by artists like Richard Thompson and violinist Nigel Kennedy, who appeared on an Arabic-type track called 'Calling You'.

Plant said: "I made a conscious approach to get away from all the -isms and computer technology, all the self-conscious awareness of what's current and fashionable. I've always been neurotic about my voice. I remember getting all those awards in the early 1970s and being voted Top Male Vocalist in the polls. I look at the awards now and think – 'How did I ever do that!' At the time, with Led Zeppelin, I used to say 'Keep the voice down in the mix – keep it quiet.' With Zeppelin, part of the atmosphere was to get the voice woven into the instruments. The music on my *Fate of Nations* album was probably as near organically in construction and thought process as I will ever get to 'Ramble On' and stuff like that. Consciously and intentionally that's been my plan. Whether it's commercially viable or not I always have to be 100 per cent obsessed with what I'm doing. I have learnt to be more patient in the studio and learnt not to say, 'That's great, that'll do okay.' I did a lot of vocals over the years that probably could have been improved upon, although I've always had a reputation as being a distinctive vocalist and there have been a lot of people who have used my style as their style. I've always believed that what counts most of all is that the delivery is natural and impromptu. I couldn't imagine Howlin' Wolf dropping in line three on 'Smokestack Lightning', know what I mean?"

At this stage in his career, Plant found it quite an experience working with people who were ready to give their ideas and give him a firm sense of direction. "I had to learn a lot of restraint on my own personality. I'm quite a volatile character, y'know, and I've learnt that I'm not the only one who knows what's right, even though it's me singing and me writing the lyrics. It's been very interesting and I've enjoyed it. I like to try new things and see how they fit me. As a singer there's no point in keeping the same persona for ever and ever. You have to do things for yourself, not what everybody expects. I could not have kept the old line, like some 1960s singers who eke out a living by treading the same old path. I don't know whether they cry at night or roll over in bed scratching their fat bellies and say, 'Hey, that's another farewell tour we pulled off.' I've been to some of these reconstructions of youth and they don't really stick. I mean rock and roll was always supposed to be something that came from the mind, heart and loins. You can't work with the same people for ever and say: 'Hey, this is youth music!'"

In 1993, a year before the Plant/Page reunion, Plant was still resisting all attempts at re-creating Led Zeppelin as a commercial proposition. "Led Zeppelin came out of the underground scene. It was all a clannish thing. But people's vitality for music changes once they reach a certain age. It dulls off, so a lot of people who were into Zep have grown out of their denim jackets and they're listening to Chris Rea. Makes you weep to think about it! There are a lot of people jumping on to bandwagons. Some people just do it for the money. People say to me, 'You could really make a killing here.' And I say, 'Oh yeah, how would I do that?' Ha, ha! You see before Zep, Jimmy Page was in groups and I was in groups and after Zep, we went into different groups again. I love what we did together. Some of it was superb. I also remember some of the conditions it was created in, some of it not so good. But none of that matters now because Led Zeppelin is now a timepiece. You have to move on in every respect."

Jimmy Page had to move on too after the demise of Led Zeppelin, but for the man who had created the band, it was difficult to entirely shake off his roots. He was, after all, the personification of Zeppelin, a rock vision, burned into everyone's mind. Shattered mentally and physically by the stress and strain of the last five years, Page, like Plant, withdrew from the scene for the first years of the 1980s. John Paul Jones explained the background circumstances to their collective withdrawal from the scene: "When Bonzo died we had actually been rehearsing for the American tour and there was a lot of optimism. The band was in good form, but it just had to stop. The music needed those particular four people to make it work. We could have had another band with another drummer, but it wouldn't have been Zeppelin. That died with John."

Jimmy Page was so distraught by Bonham's death that it seemed he might never play the guitar again. Virtually overnight he had lost the part of his life that was devoted to touring, recording and making music with Led Zeppelin. Eventually, however, he plucked up courage and began to play at the odd jam session. He bought Sol Studios in Cookham, Berkshire, from producer Gus Dudgeon, and spent most of his time there working on various projects, with visitors like Elton John and George Harrison. But he remained a recluse as far as the outside world was concerned.

Then on 10 March 1981 he sat in with Jeff Beck at the Hammersmith Odeon and made a guest appearance that delighted the audience. Plant, Jones and Page also met up at a charity show at the Golden Lion pub in Fulham. Page finally returned to the studio to write and record the music for a new Michael Winner film *Death Wish II*, which yielded a soundtrack album. He took up cricket and snooker while working on remixing tracks for the *Coda* album. His first major appearances were in London on 20 and 21 September 1983, when he played alongside Eric Clapton and Jeff Beck at the ARMS charity show, watched by the Prince and Princess of Wales. He jammed with Clapton and Beck, and played some themes from *Death Wish II* as well as a moving instrumental version of 'Stairway to Heaven', backed by Simon Phillips on drums. A roar went up as soon as he ventured on stage clad in a grey-striped suit, clutching a Fender Telecaster, and with a cigarette drooping from his lower lip.

Page told me later: "Playing with Eric Clapton and Jeff Beck on the ARMS show was great ... brilliant. If only we'd had more time! It was very emotional when I played 'Stairway to Heaven'. I assumed Jeff Beck was going to come out and help me by playing the melody, but he didn't come on. I'd got the double-neck guitar on and everyone was assuming I was gonna play 'Stairway', so I was really in it, I just had to go for it. I saw the video afterwards and saw my face all screwed up. My God! But I was playing for my life!"

When the ARMS show went to America, Page found himself playing to big, enthusiastic audiences, which further helped restore his confidence. One of the guests on the tour was singer Paul Rodgers (ex-Free, and Bad Company). Rogers and Page began writing songs together, which led to the creation of a new band, the Firm. Page also worked with his old folk singer friend Roy Harper. They wrote some material together, recorded an album called *Whatever Happened to Jugula* (1985) and played 1984's Cambridge Folk Festival with a band that included future Firm member Tony Franklin on bass. Page and Harper also appeared on the BBC TV show *Old Grey Whistle Test*. It was a period when Page's guitar technique seemed to have slipped into reverse. Out of practice and sometimes nervous, he seemed to lack the fire that had once been his forte. But extensive rehearsals and touring with the Firm brought his guitar playing back up to scratch. Their first album *The Firm* was released on Atlantic in February 1985. The band debuted live in Stockholm in November 1984, followed by dates in Germany in December. They had a problem selling tickets in Copenhagen and Frankfurt because nobody knew anything about the Firm, as their album hadn't been released, and a lot of the audience were American servicemen.

Page felt that making the album and forming the band had given him his confidence back, and he certainly played with energy and fire on 'The Chase', an instrumental number on which he featured the violin bow. However, his

"I found myself standing on a street corner, clutching 12 years of my life, with a lump in my throat and a tear in my eye, and not knowing which way to go."

ROBERT PLANT

future plans were not limited to the Firm: "It started off as a one-off project, I've now got so many projects! The ARMS thing did me the world of good. You can't imagine. It gave me so much confidence. I realized people did want to see me play again. So I thought blow it, I'm not going to let things slip now. I wanted to get out there. The business aspect is a bore, but the music is fun. After Led Zeppelin I just felt really insecure. Absolutely. I was terrified. I guess that's why I played with Roy Harper whenever I could because I knew his stuff and knew him well. With the Firm it was rock and roll which I love. Whenever I feel miserable I put on some old rock and roll records and feel so much better. It makes the adrenaline rush. Roots music always has that effect on me. When I play a gig it's there for the moment, a thrill lost in time – unless it's bootlegged! The idea is to show people who had had a lot of faith in me that I'll go out and have a go. Believe me, a lot of fans touch your heart. After Zep I just didn't know what to do. I lived in a total vacuum. I didn't know what I was doing. In the end I went to Bali and just thought about things. And I wasn't sitting on the beach because it was the rainy season! I sat in my room thinking. Then I thought, 'Dammit I'm going to do the Firm and see if it works.' At this time in my life I should really just do what I enjoy. I used the violin bow in the Firm again because it's fun and I know everyone in the audience enjoys it. Showmanship is great. I've always gone to concerts to be entertained."

By the mid-1980s, Jimmy Page had recovered his nerve, was rebuilding his guitar technique and seemed very confident about his future plans. But would he work with Robert Plant again? "I see Robert a lot and we talk a lot and we're good mates still. Sure I'd love to work with Robert again, but God knows what sort of musical vehicle we'd be in. He's great. I know him inside out. That's the point. After all those years together you can't help but know each other inside, otherwise you'd have no sensitivity. When you see his big smile – at the end of the day, that's what it's all about." Like Plant, Page looked back on the Led Zeppelin legacy of albums with pride.

"I'm not ashamed of any of that. Led Zeppelin was magic for me. It was a privilege to play in that band. It would have been wrong for me to go out playing the same material and worse to get a singer in to sing all Robert's songs. It would have been morally wrong. I knew that Bonzo wanted that music to go on for ever. When I played long solos with Led Zeppelin, there was a lot of excitement and I got carried away. Now we keep everything to the point. I used to waffle sometimes in the past. Well, one thing the critics got wrong. If they didn't think we played with conviction they were damn wrong. They say everyone over 30 is finished – which will be fun when they get to 30, by the way. I feel sorry for people who only ever listen to one type of music. When I started playing guitar I got involved in all sorts of music and people; listened to everything from Ravi Shankar to Jimi Hendrix. I thought it was a brilliant time. I feel sorry about the way the scene has changed, but who am I to say? People put me down for what I've done in the past. So I'm waiting for them to be a bit adventurous. Led Zeppelin was the sort of band everyone dreams about. For me it was such an honour to be part of it. I always thought that John Bonham was the most underrated musician ever. He got such power out of his drums. As he got bigger and bigger kits, I had to get bigger amps! I used to play three-hour sets every night with Led Zeppelin, but I don't think I could get through that now. Once I came off the road after Zeppelin, it was such a major part of me missing. I had no vehicle to play in and I had such a reputation for playing live that I got frightened about doing it. If I did four bad gigs, nobody would want to know and I had a few more things I wanted to say in music. So now I'm past middle age. But what do you do when you get to middle age? The music press say you are fucked after you are 30. But I'm not and there's a lot more for me to do."

After playing British shows, the Firm went to America where they were warmly received. The tour climaxed at Madison Square Garden, New York in April 1985. The band returned to England to play some major venues including Birmingham's NEC and Wembley Arena. The shows weren't sell-outs, but at Wembley the fans cheered the return of their hero and a new generation got to see a living legend in action. Then, just as Plant and Page were about to make separate tours of the States, came the invitation to play as Led Zeppelin on Live Aid. It wasn't what they'd planned, but cajoled by an enthusiastic Bob Geldof, what else could they do? Page, Plant and John Paul Jones played 'Rock and Roll', 'Stairway to Heaven', and 'Whole Lotta Love', for old times' sake, and a huge wave of affection greeted the band. Phil Collins jetted across the Atlantic on Concorde to sit in on drums alongside Tony Thompson. As it turned out, it wasn't a particularly happy occasion for Collins, who had no chance to rehearse and came on stage cold, without any idea what they were going to play.

"I was on tour with my band in America while Live Aid was being set up," Collins commented. "Sting rang and asked me to do something with him vocally. But I wanted to play drums with somebody too. There was nobody

in England I could play drums with. My manager Tony Smith explained to me it was possible with Concorde to go to America and play there as well. I met Robert Plant in Dallas when he was rehearsing there. Robert said he'd like to do something on Live Aid and wouldn't it be great to get Jimmy involved and do a few Zeppelin songs? I said I'd love to play with him and Jimmy – it would be great. That's how it developed. So I did the English part of the show with Sting, which was over very quickly. I played some bum notes on the piano and he played some bum notes on the guitar and sang the wrong words. It seemed like magic on the day but when you watch it on video you think, 'Oh no!' I got a helicopter from Wembley to Heathrow, got on Concorde and flew to Kennedy. I took another helicopter to Philadelphia which took almost as long as Concorde, then I got a van to the gig, arrived just in time and checked my drums. I went to see Eric Clapton in his dressing room and he said he was playing 'White Room' and 'Layla' and then I went to Robert's dressing room and said 'What are you playing?' They said 'Stairway to Heaven', 'Whole Lotta Love', and 'Rock and Roll'. Well there was a blot on the copy book after that. First I went on stage and played with Eric and did my songs, then I played with Led Zeppelin, and at the end of it, I was like in a daze. Then I got the last helicopter back to New York and the Concorde home. The Zeppelin performance was a kind of funny experience. Tony Thompson was playing drums too and had rehearsed with Zeppelin. Obviously they hadn't played together for years and there was a lot on the line. It was the Zeppelin revival! I said I couldn't rehearse because I'd been out on tour and then did Live Aid. I had been on tour for five months.

"Anyway, I got together with them in the dressing room, with Jimmy, John Paul Jones, Robert and Tony Thompson and I had the funny feeling of being the new boy. Now Tony is a great drummer, but when you are playing with two drummers you have to have a certain attitude. You have to back off and not have so much ego and play as a unit. Tony didn't seem to want to do that and within five minutes of me being on stage I felt, 'Get me out of here.' It was just weird. If you are playing straight time one of the drummers can't start doing triplet fills 'cos it will start sounding real messy. It wasn't particularly enjoyable and because I hadn't rehearsed and because I'd flown across the Atlantic, Robert laid a lot of the blame at my door, whereas in fact I was trying to play as little as possible to get out of everybody's way. John Bonham was one of my favourite drummers. I grew up watching Zeppelin from their first gig at the Marquee. 'Whole Lotta Love' was a bit chaotic because they can rehearse until they are blue in the face but at the crucial moment they will do what they want to do. Jimmy was feeding back and getting his violin bow out – it was all a bit peculiar. Nice place to visit, but I wouldn't want to live there!" Said Jimmy Page later: "It was a bit of a kamikaze stunt. We only had an hour's rehearsal, but the spirit was there and it was the right time to have a get-together."

Robert Plant talked about the reunion a couple of years later, in 1988. "Oh no – it was bloody awful. I was hoarse and Pagey was out of tune. Phil Collins wasn't even at the rehearsal, which was painfully evident but not his fault. We came on as ramshackle as ever, and when I look at the video now I laugh my head off. One-and-a-half billion people and I'm hoarse and Pagey's out of tune and the whole thing is all over the place. So typical. And the roar of the crowd. They were all shouting for Zeppelin. I don't know if I'll ever get over the fact that I don't think I should ever have been a part of it, because it really just stirred the whole thing up again. I went back on my own solo tour a couple of nights later and my voice was perfect. Live Aid was a fine cause, but it was breaking my word to myself, to play there. I mean I'll play with Jimmy for ever at one-off occasions in the future, but people watching Live Aid thought they were seeing Led Zeppelin and they weren't. It was nowhere near Led Zeppelin. If Bonzo had been there, the whole thing would have gelled and it would have been stunningly good. It just goes to show even two drummers couldn't bring it home. It was such a big wire emotionally for me. I don't think I got over it for weeks. The expectations in the air and people weeping at the side of the stage. It showed how many people over the world had been touched by the Zeppelin experience, and I'm rather proud of that."

After the 1985 concert Led Zeppelin did attempt a permanent reunion although it was kept completely under wraps at the time. Tony Thompson came to England for some rehearsals with the three Zep men but got involved in a car crash in Bath and Plant decided he didn't want to pursue the idea any further. While Plant was touring with some success, Page's band, the Firm, released one more album, *The Firm Mean Business,* in April 1986, then rested for a while before being quietly disbanded after one more US tour. Paul Rodgers went off to form a new group with drummer Kenny Jones and Page eventually formed a better band with John Bonham's son Jason, now in his twenties and proving to be an excellent drummer in his own right. Jason Bonham had actually played with Led Zeppelin at Knebworth in 1979 during a soundcheck. Jimmy Page was out front listening to the sound balance and hadn't realized it was Jason and not his father behind the kit. Jason Bonham contributed to the next Zeppelin reunion held at the Atlantic Records 40th birthday celebrations in New York – there was no second drummer this time. It was his performance at this gig that led to his being invited to play with Page's new band. Page wasn't too happy with his own performance under the harsh glare of publicity at Madison Square Garden, scene of many past triumphs.

"That wasn't much fun at all. The rehearsals were fabulous. For the show itself we were supposed to play at a particular time and I usually pace myself towards doing something and we were taken from the hotel we were staying in to another hotel near Madison Square. We were ready, expecting to play within 30 minutes. Robert was already there because he had done his set and then we were kept waiting for two-and-a-half hours and I just got more and more nervous. Then the monitors weren't working properly and unfortunately it wasn't the best of performances. It was a shame really because one wanted to make amends for the frantic set that was done at Live Aid."

Page released his first solo album, *Outrider* (Geffen) in June 1988, but it proved a disappointment. His new band, with Jason Bonham, were much better live. They began a tour of the States on 6 September 1988. Page said later: "Jason is coming on very well indeed. It's funny, he knows the Led Zeppelin tracks better than I do! His father John was the greatest rock drummer ever as far as I'm concerned and Jason was obviously taught by his father and he has the same approach to the bass drum for example, and he has the same intensity. He's developing all the time and using sampling stuff with his kick drums. So he had the greatest teacher in the world and is growing with the music." After touring with Page, Jason Bonham later formed his own group simply called Bonham and in March 1989 released *The Disregard of Time Keeping,* followed by a US tour.

During the 1990s the legacy of Led Zeppelin still loomed large over the founding musicians. Page and Plant made a tantalizing appearance when they sang three Zeppelin numbers at Knebworth Silver Clef concert on 30 June 1990, among a host of other stars that included Eric Clapton. Asked if Led Zeppelin would ever re-form, Page simply replied: "You'll have to ask Robert. I love playing that stuff. It's part of me."

In 1993 Led Zeppelin fans were thrown into turmoil by the news that Jimmy Page was linking up – not with Robert Plant, but with his rival, David Coverdale. Many could not disguise their shock at this scheme, which appeared like a deliberate ploy to goad Plant into some sort of response. However, taken at face value, it was also a perfectly logical way to combine two talented performers who got on well. The result was the heavily promoted *Coverdale/Page* album. Was it a direct result of Plant turning down Page's 1990 request for a full Zeppelin reunion, with Jason Bonham on drums? It could have meant millions of dollars for Plant, but he stuck to his principles. Plant had collaborated with Page on one track on the latter's *Outrider* album, but this had failed to ignite the Zep-style excitement and *Coverdale/Page*, with tracks like 'Shake My Tree', 'Over Now', and 'Easy Does It', was much more dynamic.

Coverdale explained that the welcome offer to work with Page came at a difficult stage in his own career. "For us it was simply do or die. If it didn't work, it wouldn't be the end of the world. But of course we noticed that enormous expectations were being built up. It was fate that we met. I was in the depths of a personal and musical crisis at the end of 1990. I didn't know if I should continue at all. It was in the following year that I got a phone call from an agent, who asked me if I was interested in working with Jimmy Page. My first reaction was 'Yes, absolutely.'"

Page had also been faced with a crisis. He had been working on his second solo album and was auditioning singers and becoming increasingly frustrated at the lack of talent displayed. Yet the agent who brought them together was taking a gamble. Page and Coverdale only really knew each other by sight. Said David: "That's why our first meeting was so important. We had to find out if and how we would get on. We met in New York and after half-an-hour we left the officials and went for a walk in Manhattan. Suddenly we caused a little bit of traffic chaos. Cars stopped and drivers wound down their car windows and asked if we were working together. At that moment we both realized that this was what we owed our audience. We had to present them with a real killer album. That was our only task."

Following the 1992 New York meeting, Page went with Coverdale to his home in Lake Tahoe, then on to Barbados. Eventually 11 tracks were cut for the *Coverdale/Page* CD, which was released on 15 March 1993, and they played a few dates at the year's end in Japan. Meanwhile, Plant's US tour went so well it seemed to prove he had taken the right decision. Furthermore, the world had grown weary of speculation and now believed that a reunion would never happen. At which point Robert Plant and Jimmy Page finally decided to get together.

The 1994 release of the *No Quarter: Unledded* video and CD, followed by the subsequent hugely successful Page-Plant World Tour of 1995–96 showed that the stalwart rockers meant business. It was a welcome return after many worthy but less exciting projects. Together with young and enthusiastic backing musicians they created valid and intriguing new material, as well as revitalizing many of their greatest hits.

November 1997 saw the release of a double CD, *Led Zeppelin: BBC Sessions,* containing Zep performances recorded for radio in 1969 and 1971. Page selected and remastered all the tracks for the two CDs. It was the first official live release from the band since the 1976 soundtrack album from the concert film *The Song Remains the Same* and it debuted at Number 12 in the US charts.

In April 1998 a final Page and Plant studio album *Walking into Clarksdale*, recorded at London's Abbey Road studios, emerged. One of the tracks, 'Most High', was released as a single and received a Grammy Award for 'Best Hard Rock Performance' of 1999. The pair also made an appearance at a star-studded concert, for Amnesty International in Paris in December 1998, when they performed 'Gallows Pole', 'Rock and Roll' and 'Babe I'm Gonna Leave You'.

Over the next ten years, fascination for all things Zeppelin grew rather than receded as the pillars of the original group continued their quest for musical fulfilment. Then suddenly, speculation about a reunion came to an extraordinary climax. In 2007 the unthinkable became a reality. Led Zeppelin got back together and played a historic concert.

The road to the reunion had been long and winding. Jimmy Page was enjoying sitting in with such bands as the Black Crowes. In 2005 he hit the headlines when he was awarded an OBE (Order of the British Empire) by the Queen at Buckingham Palace in recognition of his charity work.

John Paul Jones had kept busy working as a producer. He had also released his own solo albums *Zooma* (1999) and *The Thunderthief* (2002) with Robert Fripp on guitar.

Robert Plant toured and recorded his own bands such as Priory of Brion and Strange Sensations, who released the *Mighty ReArranger* album in May 2005. In 2007, he enjoyed his greatest success outside the realms of Zeppelin with *Raising Sand,* a million-selling – and multi-Grammy Award-winning – album recorded with American bluegrass singer Alison Krauss.

However, the tragic catalyst for a historic gig that would see the three remaining members of Led Zeppelin re-form for the first time in the twenty-first century, was the death of a pivotal figure in Zeppelin history. On 14 December 2006 Ahmet Ertegun, the founder of Atlantic Records, had died aged 83. Ertegun had been in a coma since the previous October, after slipping backstage at a Rolling Stones concert and hitting his head. Ahmet had signed Zeppelin to the label in 1968 following negotiations with the band's manager Peter Grant, who had also died from a heart attack on 21 November 1995 aged 60.

It was announced that Led Zeppelin would reunite to perform the special concert, in memory of Ertegun. Some 25 million people from all over the world applied online for tickets, in a unique ballot organized by legendary promoter Harvey Goldsmith, who had staged many of their 1970s shows. And on Monday 10 December 2007 Led Zeppelin performed a stunning show at the 02 Arena in Greenwich, London.

It was the most eagerly anticipated rock reunion of all time. As Led Zeppelin blasted back on stage, they launched into 'Good Times Bad Times', the first song on their first album. It was clear the Zeppelin men were intent on performing as if their lives depended on it. An 18,000-strong crowd cheered Jimmy Page, Robert Plant, John Paul Jones and Jason Bonham as they tore into all the old Zeppelin favourites with astounding power and magical energy.

After a parade of guest artists including members of ELP, Maggie Bell and Paul Rodgers, Led Zeppelin came on at 9pm. There was no announcement, just a video clip on the giant projection screen showing the group in their 1970s heyday. Jimmy Page now resembled Hollywood movie star Stewart Granger, in his dark suit and mass of flowing white hair. He played brilliantly, his guitar work unhindered by a finger injury that made TV headline news. Robert Plant was on top form and had no trouble reaching his famous high notes. Drummer Jason and bassist John Paul Jones locked together as a powerful rhythm section and John Paul was back in keyboard action on the foot-tapping 'Trampled Under Foot'.

The 16-song set included 'Ramble On', 'Black Dog', 'In My Time of Dying', 'For Your Life', 'Nobody's Fault but Mine' and 'No Quarter' which featured Jimmy's Theremin with dry ice effects. 'Since I've been Loving You' was followed by 'Dazed and Confused.' Jimmy once again deployed his famed violin bow during a 20-minute workout.

They even climbed the 'Stairway to Heaven,' Robert having decided it was now time to pay tribute to American radio's most played song. Next came 'The Song Remains the Same', a brief snatch of 'I Can't Quit You Babe' and a few words from Jason Bonham before 'Misty Mountain Hop'. 'Kashmir' from *Physical Graffiti* was spellbinding and capped by two encores, 'Whole Lotta Love' and the ultimate version of 'Rock and Roll'.

Sir Paul McCartney, Jeff Beck and Oasis were among the VIP guests. By now the world's media had elevated Page and Plant to superstar status that rivalled the attention they had enjoyed as young men in the 1970s.

Page's iconic status in particular was reflected when he was asked to represent the London 2012 Olympic Games at the closing ceremony of the Beijing Games in August 2008. In one of the most singular live experiences of his extraordinary career, he unfurled the riff to 'Whole Lotta Love' on top of a London bus. *The X Factor* winner Leona Lewis was the somewhat unlikely choice to take the place of Robert Plant, and David Beckham joined them to kick a football into the waving athletes.

In the aftermath of the 02 concert, it was hoped that that show would lead to a full-scale tour by the band, to satisfying the worldwide demand for tickets. In September 2008 it was announced in the UK press that Led Zeppelin would be back and touring in 2009. Alas, this proved premature in some respects. Robert Plant was in the throes of a successful American *Raising Sand* tour with Alison Krauss and issued a denial on his website. A spokesman confirmed that after finishing his US tour in October: "Robert has no intention whatsoever of touring with anyone for at least the next two years. Contrary to recent reports Robert Plant will not be touring or recording with Led Zeppelin." Added Robert: "It's frustrating and ridiculous for this story to continue to rear its head when all the musicians that surround the story are keen to get on with their individual projects and move forward. I wish Jimmy Page, John Paul Jones and Jason Bonham nothing but success with any future projects." It appeared that Page and Jones had been auditioning with singers Steven Tyler (of Aerosmith) and Myles Kennedy, but that once Jones went back to touring and recording with his on-off side project, Them Crooked Vultures (with Dave Grohl and Josh Homme), the reunion was put off entirely. "That was a pretty definitive statement," Jimmy admitted.

In May 2014, the guitarist was interviewed for *Rolling Stone*, and made his position on a reunion very clear: "People ask me nearly every day about a possible reunion. The answer is no. It's been seven years since the 02. There's always a possibility that they can exhume me and put me onstage in a coffin and play a tape."

However, in one final twist of the Zeppelin tale, Robert Plant didn't entirely cancel the possibility of more shows. In 2014, he said: "All doors are open. All phone lines are open. I don't hear from anybody. Talk is cheap, but I just think everything has to be new. Do you know why the Eagles said they'd reunite when hell freezes over, but they did it anyway and keep touring? It's not because they were paid a fortune. It's not about the money. It's because they're bored. I'm not bored."

So, is Led Zeppelin's magnificent history complete, or are there more chapters yet to be written? The only way to find the answer you're looking for, it appears, is to stay tuned …

A 1969 publicity photograph of the newly formed Led Zeppelin. None of the four young men could have imagined the lasting success and influence they would have on popular music.

INDEX

CREDITS

The publishers would like to thank the following sources for their kind permission to reproduce the pictures in this book.

2. David Redfern/Redferns/Getty Images, 4. Michael Ochs Archives/Getty Images, 7. Globe Photos Inc/REX/Shutterstock, 9. Lester Cohen Archive/WireImage, 12-14. Jim Cummins/Michael Ochs Archives/Getty Images, 16-17. Gijsbert Hanekroot/Redferns/Getty Images, 19. Jorgen Angel/Redferns/Getty Images, 20. Michael Ochs Archives/Getty Images, 21. Michael Putland/Retna/Photoshot, 22. Ray Stevenson/REX/Shutterstock, 28-29. Frank White, 30. Chris Walter/WireImage/Getty Images, 31. Michael Putland/Retna/Photoshot, 32-33. Charles Bonnay/The LIFE Images Collection/Getty Images, 34. Jorgen Angel/Redferns/Getty Images, 35-37. Charles Bonnay/The LIFE Images Collection/Getty Images, 38. Jan Persson/Redferns/Getty Images, 39. Jim Cummins/Michael Ochs Archives/Getty Images, 40-41. Neal Preston/Retna/Photoshot, 42-44. Charles Bonnay/The LIFE Images Collection/Getty Images, 45. Laurance Ratner/WireImage/Getty Images, 46. Dick Barnatt/Redferns/Getty Images, 47. Express Newspapers/Getty Images, 48. Michael Ochs Archives/Getty Images, 49. James Fortune/REX/Shutterstock, 50-51. Michael Ochs Archives/Getty Images, 53. Charles Bonnay/The LIFE Images Collection/Getty Images, 54. Jorgen Angel/Redferns/Getty Images, 57. Ilp Musto/REX/Shutterstock, 60-61. Jorgen Angel/Redferns/Getty Images, 63. Michael Putland/Retna/Photoshot, 64-65. Charles Bonnay/The LIFE Images Collection/Getty Images, 66. David Gahr/Getty Images, 67. James Fortune/REX/Shutterstock, 68. Michael Ochs Archives/Getty Images, 69. Daily Express/Hulton Archive/Getty Images, 71. Robert Knight Archive/Redferns/Getty Images, 72. © Bob Gruen, 73. Walter Iooss Jr./Getty Images, 75. Michael Putland/Retna/Photoshot, 78-79. Ilpo Musto/REX/Shutterstock, 81. Fin Costello/Redferns/Getty Images, 82. Jorgen Angel/Redferns/Getty Images, 83. Gijsbert Hanekroot/Redferns/Getty Images, 85. Michael Ochs Archives/Getty Images, 86. Michael Ochs Archive/Getty Images, 90-91. Richard E. Aaron/Redfern/Getty Images, 93. © Bob Gruen, 94-95. James Fortune/REX/Shutterstock, 96. GAB Archive/Redferns/Getty Images, 97. Robert Knight Archive/Redferns/Getty Images, 98. News Ltd/Newspix/REX/Shutterstock, 99. Robert Knight Archive/Redferns/Getty Images, 100-101. James Fortune/

REX/Shutterstock, 102. James Fortune/REX/Shutterstock, 103. Hulton Archive/Getty Images, 104. GAB Archive/Redferns/Getty Images, 105. © Bob Gruen, 112-113. Ian Dickson/Redferns/Getty Images, 114. © Frank White, 115. Ian Dickson/Redferns/Getty Images, 116. J. Barry Peake/REX/Shutterstock, 117. © Bob Gruen, 118. Michael Putland/Getty Images, 119-121. © Bob Gruen, 123. James Fortune/REX/Shutterstock, 124. Jay Dickman/Corbis/Corbis via Getty Images, 126-127. Jeffrey Mayer/WireImage/Getty Images, 129. Michael Putland/Photoshot/Retna, 130-131. Robin Platzer/The LIFE Images Collection/Getty Images, 133. UrbanImage.tv/Adrian Boot, 134. © Bob Gruen, 135. UrbanImage.tv, 136. Ed Perlstein/Redferns/Getty Images, 137. Chris Walter/WireImage/Getty Images, 138-139. Michael Ochs Archives/Getty Images, 141. Ed Perlstein/Redferns/Getty Images, 142. © Bob Gruen, 148-149. David Redfern/Redferns/Getty Images, 151. Ian Cook/The LIFE Images Collection/Getty Images, 152. Dave Hogan/Hulton Archive/Getty Images, 153. Peter Still/Redferns/Getty Images, 154. Ebet Roberts/Redferns/Getty Images, 155. Peter Still/Redferns/Getty Images, 156-157. Janet Macoska/Retna Ltd/Photoshot, 158. Ray Stevenson/REX/Shutterstock, 159. Retna/Photoshot, 160. Rob Verhorst/Redferns/Getty Images, 161. Richard Young/REX/Shutterstock, 162. Terry O'Neill/Getty Images, 163. Retna/Photoshot, 164. Laurance Ratner/WireImage/Getty Images, 165. Rob Verhorst/Redferns/Getty Images, 166-167. Rob Verhorst/Redferns/Getty Images, 169. Ilpo Musto/REX/Shutterstock, 170-171. Neal Preston/Retna/Photoshot, 172. Fotos International/REX/Shutterstock, 173. UrbanImage.tv, 174. © Frank White, 176. Larry Hulst/Michael Ochs Archives/Getty Images, 177. Dick Barnatt/Redferns/Getty Images, 178-179. Michael Ochs Archives/Getty Images, 181. Ross Halfin/Exclusive by Getty Images, 182. Ferdaus Shamim/WireImage/Getty Images, 185. Alessandra Benedetti/Corbis via Getty Images, 188-189. Michael Ochs Archives/Getty Images, 192. Charles Bonnay/The LIFE Images Collection/Getty Images

Every effort has been made to acknowledge correctly and contact the source and/or copyright holder of each picture and Carlton Books Limited apologizes for any unintentional errors or omissions, which will be corrected in future editions of this book.